LIVING WITH
THE FLOWERS

LIVING WITH THE FLOWERS

by Denise Diamond
illustrations by Patricia Waters

A Guide
to Bringing Flowers
into Your Daily Life

Quill
New York   1982

Copyright © 1982 by Denise Diamond

Grateful acknowledgment is made for permission to reprint the following:

As the Epigraph, the poem, "A Flower Does Not Talk," taken from p. 205 of *A Flower Does Not Talk* by Abbot Zenkei Shibayama, copyright by Charles E. Tuttle Co., Inc. of Tokyo, Japan.

Library of Congress Cataloging in Publication Data

Diamond, Denise.
　　Living with the flowers.

　　　Bibliography: p.
　　　Includes index.
　　　1. Flowers. 2. Flower gardening. 3. Cookery (Flowers) 4. Flowers—Therapeutic use. 5. Herbal cosmetics. 6. Flowers—Folklore. 7. Flower arrangement.　I. Waters, Patricia.　　II. Title.
　　[SB404.9.D5]　　635.9　　81-18552
　　ISBN 0-688-00990-5　　　AACR2
　　ISBN 0-688-00991-3 (pbk.)

Printed in the United States of America

First Quill Edition

1 2 3 4 5 6 7 8 9 10

Designed by Sallie Baldwin, Antler & Baldwin

PUBLISHER'S WARNING

The information about flowers and herbs in this book includes historic tradition and folklore. Any plant, herb, or flower may be harmful to anyone who misuses it or is allergic to it. Any person utilizing any plant mentioned in this book in either internal or external applications does so at his own risk. The reader is therefore urged first to identify all plants accurately and then to consult his physician to obtain appropriate advice before using them.

To Martin Diamond,
my husband,
for his love, understanding,
and
invaluable assistance
in the creation of this book.

ACKNOWLEDGMENTS

Special thanks to my father and mother, Robert and Florie Fischgrund, for bringing flowers into my life; to Patricia Waters for her exquisite artwork; to Amy Louise Shapiro, my editor at Morrow, for her enthusiasm and helpful suggestions; to those who helped along the way—Robert Menzies, Elizabeth Rivers, Nan Koehler, Elia Haworth; to the rest of my family and friends for their support and to all of you who share my love of flowers.

CONTENTS

FLOWERING: AN INTRODUCTION   13

1. GETTING TO KNOW THE FLOWERS   17
2. GARDENING WITH FLOWERS   45
3. CREATIVE FLOWER CRAFT   87
4. NATURAL FLOWER FOODS   129
5. FLOWER ALCHEMY   181
6. AROMATHERAPY AND FLOWER ESSENCES   221
7. VISUALIZATIONS WITH FLOWERS   241
8. FLOWER FAIRIES AND NATURE SPIRITS   253

NOTES ON THE TEXT   269
APPENDIX OF SOURCES   271
BIBLIOGRAPHY   275
INDEX   279

LIST OF ILLUSTRATIONS

Petunia   Title page
Lily   Epigraph page
Narcissus   13
Jonquils   14
Hummingbird with fuchsia   17
Getting to know a flower: Foxglove   18
Parts of a flower: Mustard   21
Pollination: Bee and hollyhock   23
Inflorescence: *Spike,* sage; *Raceme,* monkey flower; *Panicle,* cam-
    panula; *Corymb,* yarrow; *Umbel,* fennel; *Cyme,* sweet William;
    Head, sunflower; *Catkin,* pussywillow; *Spadix,* Jack-in-the-
    pulpit   28
Wild rose   30
Sweet pea   31
Garden sage   32
Orchid   33
Daisy   35
Dogwood   36
Iris   37
Nasturtium   38
Petunia   40

Shirley poppy 41
Violet 42
Daffodil 45
Life Cycle of a rose 46
Preparing a raised bed 51
Zinnia 53
Transplanting: Snapdragon 56
Watering the garden: Hollyhock and hummingbirds 57
Weeding: Dandelion 59
Edible flowers: petunia, pansy, geranium 63
Flowers for Dyeing: Aster, dahlia, marigold, Canterbury bell, coreopsis 66
Flowers for cutting: Marigold, zinnia, gladiolus 68
Wild flowers: California poppy 70
Spring bulbs: Tulip 73
Flowering vines and climbing plants: Morning glory 76
Shade flowers: Impatiens, begonia, fuchsia 80
Flowers as companion plants: Marigold with cabbage 84
Strawflower and statice 87
Flower arrangement: Baby's breath, chrysanthemum, cosmos, larkspur, lily, marguerite, nicotiana, Oriental poppy, rosemary, rose, rudbeckia 88
Tuzzy-muzzy: White rosebuds (girlhood), lily-of-the-valley (return of happiness), and spring crocus (youthful gladness) 93
Dried bouquet: Rose 95
Drying flowers using a dessicant: Pansy 97
Flower press: Forget-me-not 101
Pressed flower picture: Clematis, fern, forget-me-not, hydrangea, rose leaves, wild rose 104
Daisy garland 107
Strawflower wreath 108
Steps in making a strawflower wreath 109
A rose gift basket: Rose jam, rose water, rose facial vinegar, rose honey facial, rose buds, rose sachet, rose hips, dried rose 111
Potpourris and sachets 114
Dyeing with flowers: Lupine 119
Dyeing with flowers: Acacia and yarn 123
Soothing sleep pillows: Chamomile, passionflower, rose geranium 126
Carnation 129
Petunia nectar 130
Flowering cornucopia: Chrysanthemum, day lily, apple blossom, pink, nasturtium, calendula, mallow, petunia, hibiscus, Johnny-jump-up, mustard flower, pansy, gladiolus, rose, violet 137
Spring blossom soup: Apple blossom 138
Stuffed nasturtiums: Nasturtium and Johnny-jump-up 142
Squash blossom feast: Squash blossom and chive flower 147

List of Illustrations

Chrysanthemum vegetables   148
Flowering circle salad: Calendula, Johnny-jump-up, pink,
        mustard, borage, nasturtium   150
Flowered fruit salad: Pansy, pink, calendula   154
Artichokes with lemon sauce and lemony flowers: Lemon
        blossom   155
Dill flower dressing   157
Carnation spice muffins   161
Flower herb tea: Borage and spearmint   167
Strawberry borage cooler   170
Mia's blueberry daylilies   172
Place setting: Rose geranium breakfast   180
Passionflower   181
Gathering flowers: Borage and calendula   182
Home distillation unit: Honeysuckle water   188
Bottling elder flower oil   191
Spring wild flower herb salve: Chickweed, cleavers, dock,
        mallow, miner's lettuce, plantain   196
Rose petal-rosemary-honey facial   203
Flower hair rinse: Clover   206
Lavender flower facial steam   208
Passionflower bath   211
Sweet scent flower sauna: Honeysuckle, jasmine, rose   214
The sensual flowers: Rose   219
Lilac   221
Sweet dreams: Hyacinth   222
Simple aromatherapy: Mock orange   225
Gathering flowers for fine French perfume: Rose   226
Damask rose   229
Jasmine   231
Lavender   232
Rosemary   233
Chamomile   234
Strewing flowers: Gardenia   236
The Bach flower remedies: Clematis, rock rose, mimulus, star
        of Bethlehem, impatiens   237
Making flower essences using the sun method: Star tulip   239
Gazania   241
Daisy mandala   242
Blossoming flower visualization: Hibiscus   245
Watch a flower grow: California poppy   247
Space journey with a flower guide: Bird of paradise   250
Relaxing flower journey: Water lily   251
Spider chrysanthemum fairy   253
Strawberry blossoms   254
Primrose fairies   257
Delphinium fairies   260
Pan: Scotch broom   263
Foxglove fairy   264
Titania, Queen of the Fairies, sleeping in a field of pansies   266

A FLOWER DOES NOT TALK

Silently a flower blooms,
In silence it falls away;
Yet here now, at this moment, at this place,
the whole of the flower, the whole of
the world is blooming.
This is the talk of the flower, the truth
of the blossom;
The glory of eternal life is fully shining here.

—ABBOT ZENKEI SHIBAYAMA,
A FLOWER DOES NOT TALK

FLOWERING:
AN
INTRODUCTION

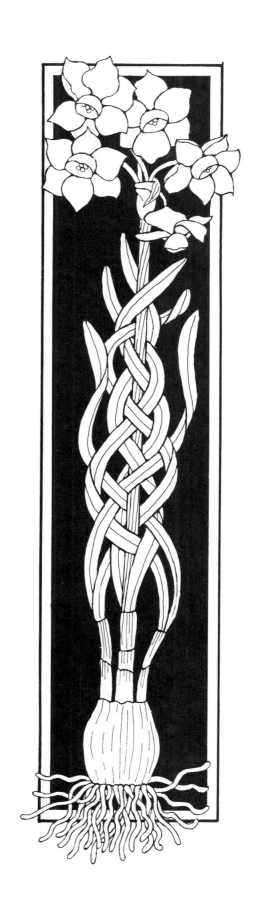

When I was a young girl I had a secret garden; it seemed very large and full. It was a special place for me, where I could enjoy a serene beauty and feel totally safe and hidden. Someone took very good care of the garden; the flowers were always vibrant, the lawn trimmed, and the weeds pulled. I tended it with my love and appreciation. Butterflies, ladybugs, birds, and bees were the only other visitors I saw there. I felt at peace, free to dream, and happy to be alive.

In the spring the narcissus, daffodils, and hyacinths poked their bright green leaves through the warmed earth and blossomed with an intoxicating fragrance. Leaves began to reappear on all the trees; forsythia was dressed in brilliant yellow; there were purple and white lilacs; tiny, scented violets; and robins dancing in the rhythm of so much life.

It was in this garden that my love for flowers was first born. I would sit for hours and watch them; their buds so eager to open and embrace the sun, the colors and designs of each petal, and the bees drinking nectar from flower to flower. I would sense the wonder of creation.

My favorite times were full-moon summer nights, when crickets chanted and the warm, soft air was perfumed with the sweetness of mock orange. Then I would silently slip away from home to visit my garden. Everything there was glowing silver, reflecting the moonlight, especially the white, night-blooming flowers. There was a luxuriousness in moon-bathing on the rich grass carpet and watching wisps of clouds fly across the moon, sometimes gently tinged in rainbow colors. I felt like a princess in her royal garden.

At that time I had a favorite book that had lovely paintings of fairies with prismed wings and gossamer gowns playing in enchanted gardens. I would let my fantasies transform my secret garden into the magical realm of my book. There, dainty fairies and gentle spirits danced with me among the flowers in midsummer joy.

I began to realize the powerful effect flowers had on me. I would run to the garden and feel comforted when I was upset; I would come there tired and leave with abundant energy. It was so nurturing that I would always look forward to returning. Each season brought its own mood. The fragrant rebirth of spring, the quiet heat of summer, the flush of autumn colors, the crystal clarity of winter. As I grew up, I stopped visiting my secret garden and went on to seemingly more important things. But the magic of it never left; a part of me had blossomed that still draws me to flowers and to something special in myself.

The flowers taught me many lessons that I only fully understood much later. In experiencing growing my own flower garden and the whole process of planting the seeds, watching them grow, flower, fade, and make seed, I learned about the cycles of life. I saw that it wasn't possible to hold onto that delicious fragrance, those perfect petals, the flitting butterfly or hummingbird. Everything in nature is constantly changing—moving toward completion as new life readies to take its place. I realized this as I watched the lovely tigridia flower open its exquisite petals and then close them again the same day. A fleeting instant, the purity of the present.

In recent years I've often experienced a sense of well-being and happiness in my Northern California garden when it is bursting with brilliant red, yellow, and soft pastel blossoms with their heady aromas. Quiet moments that I've spent enjoying the exquisite golden flowers and delicate perfume of my favorite rosebush have left me feeling calm and relaxed.

It's also very satisfying to gather blossoms that I've grown in my garden to bring into the house or give to friends. When my husband brings me a surprise gift of a bouquet I feel cared for and appreciated.

Over the years flowers have become an important part of my daily life in many ways. It is this rich experience that I want to share with you so that flowers can become much more than beautiful ornamentals in your life. I begin in Chapter 1 with Getting to Know the Flowers, which introduces you to basic flower botany; the wonder of the flowers' structures and functions. Chapter 2, Gardening with Flowers, describes the best ways to prepare soils and to plant flowers so that they will thrive in gardens and planter boxes. Because bringing flowers into my home has always been important to me, I present in Chapter 3 the many expressions of Creative Flower Craft, including flower arranging, drying, pressing, the making of potpourris and natural dyeing. In Chapter 4, Natural Flower Foods, I devise many new and delicious flower foods and expand on some of the traditional recipes that are a pleasure both visually and nutritionally. Chapter 5 discusses many forms of what I call Flower Alchemy: flower lotions, potions, salves, oils, and other preparations that are delightful to use. In Aromatherapy and Flower Essences, Chapter 6, you will discover how flowers can be used as a guide to health and well-being. Visualizations with Flowers, Chapter 7, provides ways of experiencing deep relaxation and learning to recognize the perfect flower within you waiting to bloom. I close with Chapter 8, Flower Fairies and Nature Spirits, traditionally ephemeral forces in garden lore. I want to share with each of you the world of flowers I have discovered; a vision that began with the flowering of a little girl's heart in her secret garden.

1
GETTING
TO KNOW
THE FLOWERS

I'd like to introduce you to some friends of mine—the flowers. Getting acquainted with them is the first step in learning about the many new ways of making them a part of your daily life. Find one growing near you and open all your senses to it. Smell it; is it sweet, spicy, or pungent? Touch it; is it soft, fuzzy, or rough? Look at its coloring, shape, and parts. What are they and why are they there? Notice the differences between flowers. Look inside them as though you were a bee looking for sweet nectar.

PLANT AND FLOWER PARTS

All flowers have the common function of continuing the life of the plant that bears them. The flowers contain the reproductive organs that produce the seeds to begin new life. In order to study them in detail, I have chosen as an example the mustard plant (*Brassica* spp.) that grows commonly throughout most of the United States. It has a simple and clear design that makes it a good example for identifying and studying the basic parts of a flower. There are many other members of the mustard family whose flowers are almost identical to the common mustard, including sweet alyssum, radish, watercress, wallflower, and stock. Any of these may also be examined using the parts of the mustard flower as a guide.

The mustard plant consists of the stem, leaves, roots, and flowers. The tall branching *stem* supports the whole plant and serves as an efficient method of carrying food to its other parts. Some plants have underground stems, such as the tulip *bulb,* iris *rhizome,* and potato *tuber.*

The *leaves* of the mustard grow in a rosette at the base of the plant and then continue up toward the flowers. Their broad, flat surfaces catch the sunlight to trigger the process of photosynthesis during which time chlorophyll is transformed by light into the sugars and starches that feed the plant.

Hidden from view are the *roots,* the strong base of the plant that anchors it in the ground. The roots receive and store nutrients for the leaves and reach deep into the earth to absorb water and minerals.

All these parts work together to help produce and nourish the *flowers,* those showy reproductive organs of the plant. Toward this end, flowers must first be pollinated, meaning that the male pollen must reach the female pistil that contains the egg cell in its ovary. Bees, wind, birds, moths, and other insects are the pollen-carrying lovers of flowers.

Pistils and Stamens

Pick a mustard flower and examine it; a magnifying glass is helpful. Compare it with the illustration of the mustard flower (see page 21). The center of the blossom is called the *pistil*, which grows out of the *receptacle*, or the enlarged end of the stem. The *pistil* is the female organ that bears the eggs and is made up of three easily identified sections: *ovary*, *stigma*, and *style*. The *ovary*, or egg case, is the lowest and largest part and holds the *ovules* that become the seeds after fertilization. This, then, becomes the *fruit*, or seed container. Throughout the plant world, the ovary appears in a variety of different forms, such as a pod, nut, grain, berry, or succulent fruit. The mustard ovary is divided into two compartments or chambers called *carpels*. The *stigma* is the roundish part at the top that receives the pollen. To facilitate this, it has a sticky surface. The *style* is the stalk that separates the *stigma* and *ovary*; it holds the *stigma* at the right height for pollination and serves as the pathway down which the pollen travels to reach the egg.

Surrounding the pistil are six *stamens*, the male organs that produce pollen. They are composed of the *anther* and *filament*. Notice the sac at the top of each one; it's the *anther* and contains the sweet pollen. The *filament* is the stalk that holds it upright. The pistil and stamens play the most essential parts in the flower's reproductive role.

Perianth, Corolla, and Calyx

Surrounding the pistil and stamens are two rows of leaf-like petals called the *perianth*. The inner group of four bright petals is the *corolla*, meaning "little crown." It serves to attract insects, supply them with a landing platform, and protect the pollen and nectar. In the mustard, the *corolla* is made up of separate petals, each one with a tapered base called a claw. In other kinds of flowers, such as the squash blossom, the petals are united with just their points visibly separate. Still others, like the petunia, have no separate petals, but a tube-like corolla.

The outer group of petals are green and known as the *calyx* or individually, as *sepals*. Really specialized leaves, they protect the young bud and the developing ovary. Sepals vary in size, shape, and number in different flowers. Often they are green, as in the mustard; but sometimes, as in the tulip, they are the same color as the petals.

Variations In Flower Parts

Flowers differ greatly in size, individual parts, and shape. Pistils vary to suit the kind of pollination available. Wind-pollinated flowers, such as those of the grasses and trees, have small green petals or none at all. Their pistils are fully exposed. Insect-pollinated plants usually have tall styles to lift the stigma above the petals, though in the buttercup the style is very short, and in the poppy it is absent and the stigma sits right

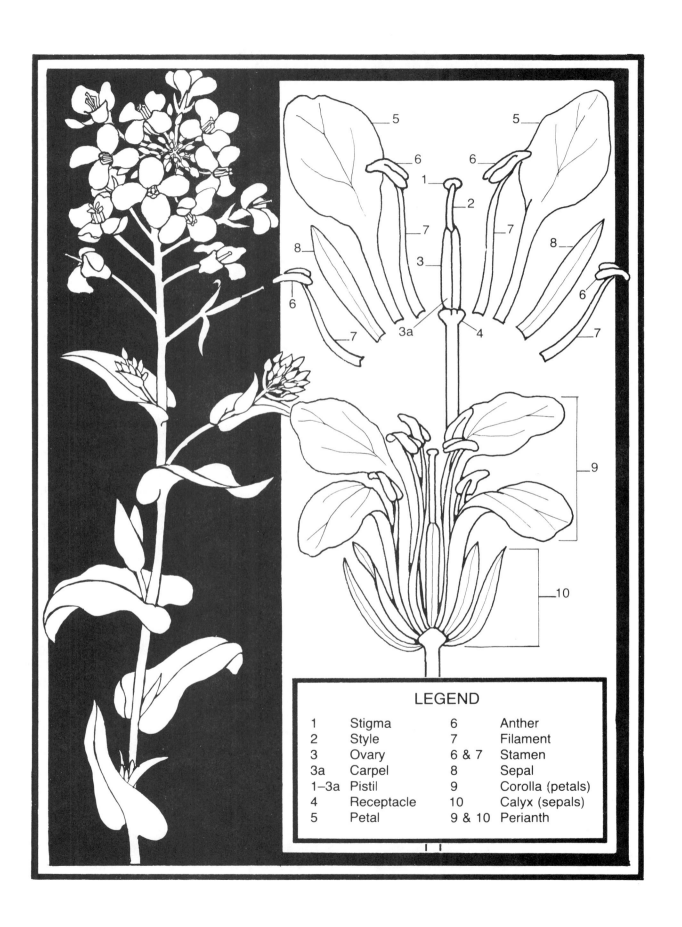

LEGEND

1	Stigma	6	Anther
2	Style	7	Filament
3	Ovary	6 & 7	Stamen
3a	Carpel	8	Sepal
1–3a	Pistil	9	Corolla (petals)
4	Receptacle	10	Calyx (sepals)
5	Petal	9 & 10	Perianth

on the ovary. Stigmas vary in shape and size from the petal-like iris stigma to those of the feathery grasses.

Since flowers first appeared on earth they have changed in form and structure to insure successful pollination. Some of the earliest and most primitive flowers had numerous pistils, stamens, and petals. The magnolia and buttercup blossoms have retained these characteristics. Very slowly, over the years plants developed more efficient flowers. A few stamens could work as effectively as hundreds. The many pistils were fused together with an ovary, one style, and the several open arms of the stigma. Fewer petals, which meant less expenditure of energy for the plant, were still attractive enough to interest pollinators. Some of the most efficiently pollinated flowers are in the mint and composite families, which I'll describe, along with some other flowers, later on in this chapter.

FERTILIZATION

The drama of the production of seed or *fertilization* is a lovely and simple one. The mustard flower can again serve as an example.

The sun is warm and the buds begin to swell on the mustard flowers. As the protecting calyx falls downward, bright yellow petals open and reflect the warmth. Their color and sweet fragrance attract the bees. Stamens ripen, their anthers fill with pollen and burst open making it available to visiting insects. Although there are exceptions, most flowers cross-fertilize to protect the purity and strength of the species. Their pistils and stamens mature at different times and thus insure that self-pollination will not take place. Flowers that pollinate themselves can weaken the species. After the stamens release their pollen they drop out of the way.

The stigma then grows a little longer and becomes sticky. It is ready to receive pollen from another plant as insects are drawn to it. When the pollen is on the stigma it grows into a tiny tube, or "root," which works its way down the style to reach an egg cell in the ovule. The germ material or nucleus of the male sperm cells in the pollen then combines with the nucleus in the female egg cell. This is fertilization.

After fertilization is complete, the stigma dies down and the sepals protect the ovary. The ovary, now fertilized, begins to stretch out and becomes the long, thin fruit or seed-bearing pod of the mustard called a *silique*. The seeds can remain viable and "alive" for weeks, months, or years. When the pod ripens it opens and scatters the seeds in the wind. They will rest on the ground where they land until the rains come and they germinate, growing into new mustard plants.

POLLINATION

Bright, sweet flowers have been colored, scented, shaped, and provided with nectar and pollen to attract the winged pollinators—bees, butterflies, moths, birds, and flies. I often sit in my garden on sunny mornings and watch the bees hum from flower to flower. They visit the glowing yellow mullein with its bright orange pollen, the star-like borage, the fragrant rose, and lavender. Nectar, manufactured in the nectaries and stored around the base of the pistil, as in the mint, or in special receptacles on the petals, as in the buttercup, is the reward a flower gives to insects for brushing against its waiting stigma or anther. Sometimes nectar is in unusual places where only certain pollinators can reach, as in the columbine's elongated petals, called spurs.

Flower petals often have markings known as *honey guides* that direct the insect to the nectar. As the insect drinks this sweet liquid it either picks up or deposits pollen. Johnny-jump-ups have strong lines, foxgloves have dots, pansies have faces, and the mints have shapes suited for particular insects.

Bees

Bees pollinate most flowers and gather pollen and nectar for storage in their hives. They are attracted to one species of a plant at a time so that cross-fertilization within that species takes place. From a bee's point of view, only the colors from yellow through blue and ultraviolet are visible; bees leave most red flowers to the hummingbirds and butterflies. Scientists believe that the nectar of the flower fluoresces as it absorbs ultraviolet light. This is only visible to the bee, so that as it flies through a garden it is seeing iridescent, glowing droplets of nectar in the center of the flowers.

Research has found that bees and other insects are also attracted by the aroma of flowers. Luther Burbank, who became famous for his skill as a plant breeder at his renowned Experimental Garden in California during the late nineteenth and early twentieth centuries, worked at creating a fragrant petunia. He developed many hybrid flowers, as well as fruits and vegetables, that contributed to the world's food supply. Burbank felt that he had succeeded in raising the petunia he wanted when he saw bees hovering over one of his experimental beds. These were indeed scented petunias.

The bee works most efficiently when it can land easily and be guided with marks to the nectary. On the way it brushes against the pollen-filled anthers or the receptive style. It sucks the nectar with its proboscis, which contains a long tongue that can reach into narrow tubes. Pollen sticks to many parts of the bee's body. It cleans itself periodically, moving the pollen to hairs on its back legs, called *pollen baskets*. When these are filled, the bee flies back to the hive before visiting other flowers.

Butterflies, Moths, and Other Pollinators

Butterflies have long proboscises and drink the nectar from the deep tubes of flowers such as milkweed, tithonia, or echium. Butterflies are drawn to red, orange, and purple colors that bees often ignore. They sit delicately on the flowers as they sip the nectar. Pollen sticks to the proboscis or to the butterfly's body and is transferred from flower to flower.

Moth-pollinated flowers are the silvery white or light yellow "moon" flowers that bloom and are fragrant at night—nicotiana, evening primrose, and honeysuckle. These flowers have long stamens and pistils extending out from the corolla and moths hover briefly at the flower without landing. When the moths dip their long proboscises into the nectaries their bodies brush against the stamens and pistils.

Flies also help pollinate and are often drawn by the decaying smell of a plant such as the skunk cabbage. *Hummingbirds* drink the nectar of bright red or orange fuchsia flowers, scarlet sage, and hibiscus. A hummingbird hovers like a moth; its long, graceful beak receives and delivers pollen.

Wind Pollination

Many plants are pollinated by the wind. These include the trees and grasses that bloom in the early spring when strong winds blow. At this time there are just a few young leaves on the trees to obstruct the pollen. It's these plants, as well as ragweed that flowers later in the summer, that cause hay-fever. Wind-pollinated plants often have stamens and pistils on different flowers: the male ones are called *staminate flowers;* the female ones, *pistillate flowers.* On the oak tree in the early spring the staminate- or pollen-producing flower looks like a hanging, knotted string; each knot is a flower. The pistillate flowers are directly attached to the branch and open to receive the pollen as the breeze blows over them. Some plants, ragweed, for example, have staminate and pistillate flowers on the same stalk. The pistils are at the bottom of the flowering stalk.

Wind-pollinated flowers differ from insect-pollinated flowers in several ways. They lack bright corollas; the petals, if any, are usually small and greenish. The calyx is also small, though strong enough to protect the blossom from the cold. The staminate flowers have long stems that easily swing in the wind to spread their pollen. Their anthers usually extend out beyond the sepals. Pistillate flowers often have furry or feathered stigmas to catch pollen as it floats over them.

Most plants are pollinated by insects, hummingbirds, or wind and only in an emergency will they pollinate themselves. There are, however, some flowers that have evolved as self-pollinators, such as those of the pea family and the violet. I'll discuss these later in this chapter.

CLASSIFICATION: What's In a Name?

The Doctrine of Signatures

The earliest peoples learned by trial and error which plants were harmful or helpful for human use. Taste, touch, and smell would all serve as indispensible guides. And as more and more healing plants were discovered, the first botanists, who were also healers, needed to classify them. The Doctrine of Signatures as described by Nicholas Culpeper, the seventeenth-century herbalist, stated:

> And by the icon or image of every herb, man first found out their virtues, ... Modern writers laugh at them for it, but I wonder in my heart how the virtues of the herbs first came to be known, if not by the signatures. The moderns have them from the writings of the ancients—the ancients had no writings to have them from.

Culpeper's classification of plants according to their appearance led, for example, to the use of eyebright to treat the eyes because the black spot on the flower looked like the pupil of an eye. The Canterbury bell flower resembled the throat and was good for throat problems. Plants with spotted leaves were used for skin eruptions; ones that gave off gum for wounds; ones with shedding bark for cleansing the body of impurities. This method of identification and application persisted until the eighteenth century.

The eighteenth-century Swedish botanist Carl von Linné, known as Linnaeus, classified plants according to the different characteristics of their sexual parts. Unfortunately this system did not always hold true, and plants began to be classified according to their ancestry or evolutionary development and their similarities or differences. From the simplest algae to pines to flowering plants, a classifying system was formed.

Most flowers are known by their common names, such as yarrow or carnation. This is fine for everyday communication and in most cases throughout the book I refer to flowers by their common names. But at times it is helpful to learn the Latin names of a plant in order to distinguish a particular species and to be certain that all concerned agree exactly on the identity of the plant in question. I have used Latin names in this chapter to illustrate how they are used, in Chapter 4 to identify precisely edible flowers, and wherever else I felt it was important to specify beyond any doubt the exact plant being discussed. All Latin names are given with the flower's common name in the Index.

The binomial system, originated by Linnaeus in its first organized form with the publication of his *Species Plantarum* in 1753, uses two Latin words to identify every species. A *species* is a simple unit of classification, and refers to plants that have common characteristics and which are descended from a common ancestor. A *genus* is a group of similar species. For example, yarrow is *Achillea millefolium;* Achillea refers to Achilles whose soldiers, in Roman times, supposedly carried bags of dried yarrow in battle to staunch their bleeding wounds. *Millefolium,* or thousand leaves, refers to the lacy foliage of the plant. The first word refers to the *genus,* and the second to the *species* (abbreviated as spp.). Sometimes there will be slight variations within a species; these are called *varieties.* This is indicated by "var." after the species name, such as *Achillea millefolium* var. *rubrum,* for red yarrow.

The carnation is *Dianthus,* a large genus that contains many species, such as *Dianthus barbatus* or *D. plumarius. Dianthus* comes from the Greek words *Di(ós)* meaning Zeus, and *ánthos,* meaning flower. It is the "divine flower." Pot marigold is *Calendula officinalis, officinalis* referring to its historical use in *pharmacopoeia* as a medicinal plant. *Calendula* is the genus. *Officinalis* narrows it down to a unique species within the genus. Pot marigold is an interesting example of how a plant becomes well known by its genus name; it is usually referred to as calendula.

The yarrow and calendula belong to the same family, *Compositae,* which has particular characteristics. A *family* is a group of *genera* (the plural of genus). (See the description of the daisy later on in this chapter for details about this family.) Classification continues on through increasingly broad categories: *order, subclass, subdivision, division,* and *kingdom.* Each of these classifications is used to identify a plant just as people are known by their first and last names, addresses, and countries.

Monocotyledons and Dicotyledons

All the flowering plants are in the Subdivision Angiosperm, which is characterized by protected enclosed seeds. These are then divided into two *subclasses: monocotyledons* (Monocots) and *dicotyledons* (Dicots). A *monocot* simply refers to a plant that has one leaf when the seed first sprouts. Lilies, orchids, and grasses are all monocots. They are characterized by:

One seed leaf
Parts numbered in threes or multiples of three
Petals and sepals that look alike
Leaves in one piece, not intricately edged
Parallel veined leaves
Underground stems
Low growth
Few branches

A *dicot* refers to a plant with two seed leaves and includes a large variety of flowering plants such as violets, dandelions, beans, and many trees. They are characterized by:

Two seed leaves
Parts numbered in groups of four or five
Distinct petals and sepals
Various shaped leaves
Network of veins
No underground stems
Variety of height
Branches in stems

You can examine these details in any flower. Of course, sometimes the common name or even a familiar scent is all you really need. But it's useful and interesting to know a plant's genus, species, and family. Discovering the distinctive characteristics of different flowers can lead you to appreciate wondrous details of structure, texture, or coloration that you might not otherwise have noticed.

INFLORESCENCE

The way in which a flower is arranged on its stem is called the *inflorescence*. In some flowers, such as the trillium or tulip, just one flower grows from a stem. This is called a *solitary flower*. Usually many blossoms grow on one stem to insure the success of reproduction. Bees are easily attracted to a mass of color and fragrance. Following are various types of inflorescences:

1. A *spike* is composed of many flowers without stalks on one simple stem, such as plantain, peppermint, and sage.
2. A *raceme* is a simple stem of flowers that have stalks, such as lily of the valley, hyacinth, foxglove, and monkey flower.
3. A *panicle* is a branching stem of flowers that have stalks, such as oats, goldenrod, and campanula.
4. A *corymb* is similar to a panicle in that it has a main branching stem. These branches are arranged so that it is a flat-topped cluster, such as yarrow and candytuft.
5. An *umbel* is a flat or convex topped flower cluster in which the stalks start from the same point, like a fan. A compound umbel has small flat-topped flower clusters at the end of each stalk, such as parsley, carrot, fennel, and Queen Anne's lace.
6. A *cyme* is a branching flower cluster often convex or flat-topped in which the central flower blooms first, such as sweet William, apple, and geranium. In all the other inflorescences, the flowers at the base or the outside bloom first and the tip or middle continues forming new flowers.
7. A *head* is a large number of small flowers growing together, such as daisy, clover, and sunflower.
8. A *catkin* is a dense spike of tiny flowers that hang freely, such as willow and birch.
9. A *spadix* is a fleshy spike with tiny flowers. This is surrounded by a *spathe* which is a one- or two-leaved bract. A *bract* is a modified leaf or leaf-like part. Jack-in-the-pulpit, anthurium, and calla are examples of spadix and spathe.

SPECIFIC FAMILIES AND FLOWERS

Now I would like to introduce you, in detail, to some flowers that are typical examples of five common plant families and also to six other flowers that happen to be among my favorites. I've given the common and Latin names of each family and flower. I have chosen these five families out of almost three hundred because they represent the flowers most frequently seen in cultivated gardens and in the wild. They are also families that are particularly efficient in reproduction. The families in order of their evolutionary development are: rose, pea, mint, orchid, and composite.

The other flowers I'll be describing illustrate interesting botanical characteristics: for example, the bracts of the dogwood, the petal-like sepals and style of the iris, the effective pollinating designs of the nasturtium and petunia, the poppy's unusual pistil, and the closed flowers of the violet.

ROSE FAMILY *Rosaceae*
Wild Rose (*Rosa* spp.)

There are thousands of varieties of roses, each with a different scent, number of petals, color, and name. They are prized for their beauty and aroma and raised with great care and love throughout the world. In the same family are the strawberry, blackberry, raspberry, apple, cherry, pear, plum, peach, and almond, among others.

The wild rose with its five single pink, white, or red petals can serve as a typical example of this family. It has many stamens, often as many as twenty, and sometimes multiple pistils. The fruit, known as the rose hip, is the receptacle and is cup-shaped with a small opening. Inside are the pistils; the stamens, petals, and calyx are attached to the rim. The seeds develop inside the receptacle. I pick these bright red or orange fruits every fall, string them, and hang the festive-looking strands from beams to dry. I use rose hips with their high vitamin C content to make tea.

Other members of this family have similar flowers, though not as showy and distinctively scented as the rose. They vary greatly in their fruits and how the flower parts relate to the receptacle. For example, the strawberry has a white cone-shaped receptacle from which the pistils grow. Sepals, petals, and stamens grow from its base. The sweet, juicy red part we eat is the enlarged receptacle with seeds on the outside. In the cherry, peach, and plum the receptacle is cup-like and wide open with the pistil coming from the bottom of the cup. Other parts grow from the rim of the cup. The fruit is actually the greatly enlarged ovary. In apples and pears the receptacle, the delicious fruit we eat, is totally closed, covering the ovary and seeds.

PEA FAMILY *Leguminosae*
Sweet Pea *(Lathyrus odoratus)*

This large family includes the pea, bean, clover, lupine, vetch, peanut, broom, licorice, and alfalfa, and it provides food, medicines, ornamentals, animal feed, and cover crops. As cover crops they are valuable because of the nodules along their roots that contain bacteria which help stabilize nitrogen in the soil. Planted in the fall, leguminous cover crops may be turned into the earth in the spring to enrich it.

Pea flowers, called papilionaceous, from the Latin word *pāpiliōn*, meaning butterfly, have a distinct form and position of petals that in fact resemble a butterfly. Look at the sweet pea flower. Notice the large top petal called the *standard*. It is upright and broad and serves as protection for the other petals before the flower fully opens. It also attracts insects with lines that guide them to the nectary. The two petals in front of the standard are the *wings*. Below these are the two remaining petals, slightly joined at their lower edges, forming the *keel*. Within the keel are ten stamens and one pistil. Nine of the stamens are almost totally united, forming a protective tube-like covering for the pistil or the future seed pod. The remaining stamen stands above the rest. The immature seed pod is a tapering, hairy part, which when ripe splits in half.

The sweet pea is ideally suited for insect pollination. The standard is brightly colored and the lower petals provide a landing platform. The weight of the insect can push the wings down, opening the keel so that the stamens come out leaving pollen on the underside of the insect's body while it searches for nectar. In some cases the keel is so tightly closed that only the weight of a heavy bumblebee or the perfect placement of its tongue will free the stamens and pistil. If the pea is not fertilized by an insect, it will pollinate itself within the keel. I've used a pen or pencil to open the keel to see how the stamens and pistil, once released, emerge from their home.

MINT FAMILY *Labiatae*
Garden Sage *(Salvia officinalis)*

Well-known members of this family include many aromatic herbs: sage, peppermint, spearmint, lavender, thyme, orange mint, catnip, rosemary, and lemon balm. Its name, *Labiatae,* comes from the Latin, *labium,* meaning lip, and refers to the flower petals, which are lip-like, the lower ones serving as a landing platform for insects.

Mint family plants have square stems and opposite leaves and a very efficient pollinating system that makes fertilization a certain and easy operation. Garden sage has gray green aromatic leaves and tall spikes of purplish blue flowers. Taking the blossom as an example, the first thing to notice is the large petal landing platform with markings or honey guides leading to the nectary. Nectar is secreted at the base of the ovary and nearly fills the corolla tube. When the bee lands on the flower, the stamens, which are attached by their filaments to the inside of the tubular corolla, are forced to move up and down. After the bee enters the flower, the lower end of the filaments rise causing the anther end to spring its pollen on the bee's body. When the pollen is dispersed, the pistil, which is against the top petal and out of the way, grows longer until it hangs in the mouth of the blossom. A bee flying in cannot help but leave some of the pollen from its back on the ripe stigma, insuring the plant's survival.

Sage has a long history in herbal tradition. Its genus name, *Salvia,* is derived from the Latin, *salvāre,* meaning to save. Sage was known to contribute to overall health and used specifically for respiratory problems, sore throat, and congestion. Sage tea will also help wean a baby from mother's milk. Because of its strong oil, sage should be used moderately. As a culinary herb, its flowers and leaves add flavor to many foods. Garden sage is easily cultivated and thrives with full sunlight in poor, well-drained soil.

ORCHID FAMILY *Orchidaceae*

Orchids are prized favorites. Their blooms have a spectacular yet subtle beauty that lasts for a long time. Once my husband and I visited an orchid jungle in Florida where hundreds of exquisite blossoms were thriving. In the middle of our tour there was a sudden cloudburst, followed by bright sunlight. My husband and I were able to sip the fresh raindrops out of the orchids whose flowers served as elegant, fragrant goblets.

The orchid is a monocot and has the typical parallel-veined leaves in one piece, underground stems, and few branches. Their startling diversity and attractiveness has to do with their need to interest pollinators in order to survive in the jungle, their natural home. Most orchids are epiphytes and grow on bushes or in sunny treetops, not in the soil. They survive on water and nutrients from the rain and air, not from the tree. Their stems are swollen pseudobulbs effective in holding water. There are some varieties of orchids—lady's slipper, ladies' tresses, calypso—that are terrestrial, growing in the ground in temperate climates. These are usually smaller and less ornate than their tropical relatives.

It is often difficult to identify the parts of an orchid flower. In the center of each is the *column,* composed of pistil and stamen united into one form. This varies in shape with different species. Anthers are attached to the side of the pistil. The pollen is called *pollina*—a waxy, sticky substance that forms small balls. There are three petals, one serving as a landing platform, such as the pouch in the lady's slipper. The three sepals are petal-like and often very colorful.

The orchid is constructed for efficient pollination. The pollina sticks to the insect's body, head, or tongue so that when the insect flies away the pollina is pulled from the anthers. The flowers produce enormous amounts of seeds in their fruit capsules. A single seed pod may contain three million seeds! Orchids differ greatly from one another and adapt to the particular situation in which they grow.

DAISY *(Bellis perennis)*
Composite *Compositae*

The composite family represents almost half of all flowering plants. Its members include: daisy, chamomile, dandelion, burdock, yarrow, sunflower, calendula, and thistle. They are all very efficient at reproduction, containing many flowers combined into one and therefore producing abundant seed. The persistent dandelion is proof of this. A gardener once told me as I watched lovely thistle "umbrellas" carrying seeds across my garden that one year's thistle seeds meant seven years' weeds—an indication of the reproductive power and vitality of the composite family. Its members will often fill entire fields with colorful flowers. Nectar is produced at the base of the style and fills the corolla tube, making it easy for insects to reach. Two other members of the composite family, wormwood and ragweed, are wind pollinated.

Look closely at a daisy as it grows on its three- to six-inch stalk. It appears to have a yellow button center surrounded by white, pink, or rose-colored petals. In reality, it consists of many smaller flowers collected into a compact head. The yellow center, or *disk floret,* is composed of a number of tubular-shaped flowers, called *tube florets,* that are composed of five stamens with their anthers grown together to form a tube. From the center of this tube, rising from the egg-shaped ovary below, is the pistil, which is crowned with small hairs. The petals, or *ray florets,* called *strap florets,* are long and narrow or strap-shaped. At the base of each one is the ovary from which the pistil rises; stamens are missing from these florets. Some species have just strap florets, such as dandelion and chickory; others have just tube florets, such as thistle and burdock. Sunflower and daisy have a combination of both tube and strap florets.

The daisy opens in the morning and was given the name day's eye in old English. Originally it was single petaled, but hybridization has created full, double varieties. The daisy's Latin name, *bellis perennis,* is thought to be derived from *bellus,* meaning beautiful, or *bellum,* meaning war. The latter refers to its historical use as a medicine for healing wounds on the battlefield. This also gave it the common name, bruisewort. When planting daisies, remember that they spread easily and can take over an entire area. The petals are edible and can be added to salads and the buds are delicious marinated as a vinegar pickle.

I remember fervently plucking the petals off a daisy, which has also been called a "measure of love," to find out if "he loves me" or if "he loves me not." The secret of obtaining a positive response is to begin with "he loves me." The flower usually has an odd number of petals and therefore will almost always confirm this love.

INTERESTING FLOWER SPECIES

DOGWOOD *(Cornus florida)*
Dogwood Family *Cornaceae*

This flower has brightly colored *bracts* that resemble petals, but which are small modified leaves that in many cases protect the flower before it opens. There are other plants that have bracts which are sometimes confused with flowers. Poinsettias have bright red, white, or variegated bracts that surround the true tiny, yellow flowers; bougainvillea have brilliant red, orange, or pink bracts; and the red and yellow Indian paintbrush is also made up of bracts. All of these bracts serve the flowers well by helping to attract pollinators. The dogwood has brownish bracts that shield the buds through the winter. They then open in the spring and become the familiar white and pink petal-like parts usually thought of as dogwood flowers. The actual flowers are the small yellow green clusters in the middle of these bracts.

This flowering dogwood is native to the eastern United States. I grew up in Indiana where the dogwoods put on a magnificent display each year, each one looking like a vibrant and tastefully arranged bouquet. In the fall the leaves turn gold and rust. Bright red fruits decorate it until early winter. The bark of this species was once used as a quinine substitute.

Another dogwood, the Cornelian cherry *(Cornus mas)*, has an edible fruit that can be made into preserves, desserts, and sauces. The yellow flowers and red fruits can both be used to make liqueur. This tree was originally grown as a fruit tree; later it became more popular in the ornamental garden.

IRIS *(Iris* spp.)
Iris Family *Iridaceae*

The iris is named after Iris, goddess of the rainbow in Greek and Roman mythology, and messenger of the gods. She used the multi-colored rainbow as her connection between gods and mortals.

At a glance this exquisite flower appears to have many petals. But when you look closer it becomes obvious that the sepals are colorful and look just like petals, a typical characteristic of monocots. The pistil is unusual because it is divided into three showy petal-like parts. These combine with the sepals to form a tunnel through which the bee moves, led by the guiding marks on the true petals. When the bee lands on the sepal, it heads toward the nectary, where it receives pollen from the anther, or brushes its pollen against the stigma.

Iris have been cultivated since earliest times and are found in illustrations at the ancient Temple of Karnak in Egypt. The Florentine iris *(I. florentine)*, a source of orrisroot used in the perfume industry, is a fixative for scents and has a distinct violet scent when dry. A bed of bearded iris adds a fragrant elegance to your garden and to flower arrangements. I look forward to the vivid purples and blues of wild iris every spring. There are about two hundred species of iris grown from bulb or rhizome, each with its unique characteristics.

NASTURTIUM *(Tropaeolum majus)*
Tropaeolum Family *Tropaeolaceae*

Look carefully at a bright flower of the nasturtium and notice the two upper petals. They are well marked with honey guides that lead to the nectar at the end of the sepal. The sepal is in the unusual form of a long tubular spur. Notice the lower petals, which make a convenient landing platform for insects. However, only large bees, butterflies, or an occasional hummingbird are welcome to the nasturtium. There is a narrow stalk on the lower petals that is covered with a protruding hairlike fringe which discourages unwanted insects, such as ants, that take nectar but are too small and have bodies that are too slippery to pollinate the plant.

When the anthers are filled with pollen, the stamens are directly in the way of flying pollinators whose bodies will be brushed with the rich pollen to carry to another flower. As soon as one anther has released its pollen it shrinks and another one stands up until all have discharged their supply. Then the pistil opens its stigma right in the path of the nectary. The insect's pollen-laden body can easily fertilize the ovary.

Nasturtium flowers were first found in South America in the sixteenth century. Their popularity reached a peak during Victorian times when the flowers and their bright green round leaves were grown in gardens and used for food and flower arrangements. In frost-free areas nasturtiums may be raised as perennials. They are grown easily as seasonal annuals in other areas and prefer average soil with little fertilizer and adequate water. They will trail along the ground, spill over the side of a container, or climb up a fence. The single or double flowers bloom profusely in shades of orange, red, or yellow. They grow best out of direct, hot sun in warmer climates or with full sun in cooler, coastal gardens. Too much shade or excess nitrogen in the soil will produce lush foliage with few flowers.

In herbal tradition nasturtiums have been known for their antiseptic qualities, their ability to help fight infection, as an expectorant, and as a source of vitamin C.

PETUNIA *(Petunia hybrida)*
Nightshade Family *Solanaceae*

Petunias are a favorite of mine; they grow easily and plentifully. Break one open carefully and notice the interesting arrangement nature has provided for pollination. The petals are joined together in one piece forming a tube. At the bottom of the tube is the stigma, the base of which holds the nectar. Two large anthers are in front of the pistil, two smaller ones behind it, and a fifth has a little extra pollen on a shorter stalk. Each stamen is attached for half its length to the tube of the flower. The rest of the stamen bends in toward the pistil. When an insect comes in search of the nectar at the pistil's base, its tongue presses against the stamens, the anthers bend down and leave pollen on the insect. When the anthers have shed their pollen, the stigma grows above the stamens and opens its receptive arms for the sweet pollen from subsequent visitors.

I enjoy petunias for their subtle fragrance and variety of color. Many hybrid petunias have been developed and they are available in a great

assortment of sizes. Some flowers are single and funnel-shaped; others are double, ruffled, and as full as carnations. They all have sticky foliage and are especially aromatic at night.

Petunias thrive in beds or planter boxes. The short-lived blossoms are quickly replaced with new flowers. They were originally grown as perennials in their native habitat of Central and South America. Though most petunias are grown as annuals, they often live for years in temperate climates. I have a planter box filled with deep purple petunias that have flourished for two years. Petunias require minimal care; watering, fertilizing, and occasional pruning are sufficient to keep them flourishing.

POPPY (*Papaver* spp.)
Poppy Family *Papaveraceae*

One year I grew five different types of poppies in my garden and delighted in their variety and delicate, rich coloring. I love watching the Oriental poppy buds swell in their protecting sepals, which are pushed off by their brilliant orange petals. Shirley poppies unfold from their "cocoons," like butterflies, in deep red, pink, orange, or white. Iceland poppies have soft petals that look like a ballerina's skirt in shades of pink, white, or yellow.

Poppies have a unique pistil that looks like a bowl with a fluted cover. Pollen is plentiful from the many anthers surrounding the pistil and bees dance eagerly among the blossoms. The mature ovary has inner seed compartments where hundreds of seeds develop. When the seeds are ripe, the top of the seed pod separates from the bottom creating small openings. I just shake the seeds out and reseed my garden for next year's flowers. The wind or any passing animal or person can also spread the tiny seeds.

Poppies have been known and cultivated since earliest times. They were sacred to the ancient Greek god of sleep and death, Morpheus. The opium poppy, whose Latin name, *P. somniferum*, refers to sleep, is a source for several pain-relieving drugs and narcotics including opium, heroin, morphine, and codeine. It's not legal to grow the opium poppy in the United States. It is chiefly cultivated in Thailand, India, and Turkey. Poppy seeds from the opium poppy and the Shirley poppy (*P. rhoeas*) are sold commercially for use in food preparations. As a child I remember my grandmother making delicious Hungarian baked goods bursting with little poppy seeds.

Poppies thrive in full sunlight with ordinary, fairly dry soil. One year, voracious little earwigs devoured almost all of my Shirley poppy seedlings. The only one that survived was growing in a neglected sandy crack in my brick pathway. It blossomed with layers of red silky petals.

VIOLET *(Viola odorata)*
Violet Family *Violaceae*

One of the sweetest spring flowers is the violet. My mother would pick tiny bouquets of the delicate, fragrant blossoms to bring inside which would assure us that spring had truly begun.

Violets produce two kinds of flowers on the same plant—some that are showy and designed to attract insects and some that are inconspicuous and closed that must fertilize themselves. Since violets bloom when cold weather or storms may harm the pistils and stamens or keep the bees from working, the closed flowers grow low, under the leaves, and near the ground. Violets are called cleistogamous, from the Greek words meaning "closed marriage." Nearly all species of violets have cleistogamous flowers. They contain within them the stamens and pistil in close proximity in order for self-pollination to take place. These flowers are very simple, with short stalks, no petals, dwarfed and closed calyx, and small amounts of pollen. There is a wise economy in their makeup; it takes a great expenditure of energy for the plant to advertise for insects with color, odor, large amounts of pollen, and long stems. Violets produce thousands of seeds, which insure their successful and plentiful propagation.

Violet flowers are usually deep purple, though I also grow white, yellow, and rose-colored varieties. Their leaves are heart-shaped, and the plants spread by runners that in a shady spot will quickly form a ground cover.

The plant is known in herbal tradition as a specific remedy for respiratory problems. The flowers can add their beneficial properties to cough syrup. Violets have also been used in teas to calm and soothe the nervous system and as a gentle laxative.

THE NEXT STEP—GROW YOUR OWN

You've now met some of the flowers and learned a bit about carefully observing and identifying them. One of the best ways of continuing your acquaintance with flowers is to plant a garden, a planter box, or just a pot of your favorite blossoms. Then you will be able to observe at close range nature's entire process, from seed to flower to seed. You can watch each flower grow, identify its parts, and notice which pollinators visit it. Gardening with Flowers will provide all the information you need to grow vibrant, healthy flowers.

2
GARDENING
WITH
FLOWERS

My first garden was a small area of flowers that I planted as a young girl. The seed packets with their bright pictures excited me. Could I really grow flowers that looked like that? It was a hot midwestern summer. I watered them regularly, weeded, and cared for the garden. I was proud of my colorful zinnias and bright orange marigolds.

I have learned much from gardening throughout my life. I've found that every aspect of it can be transformed from a routine chore into an opportunity to learn something about the nature of life and also about myself. A garden requires attention, care, and love. If there is a lack of these basic needs, a garden can't hide it.

Within the microcosm of a garden plants come and go in their own rhythms. Life and death can be witnessed daily. Such rapid changes prevent me from becoming too attached to a lovely rose that will wilt, a poppy plant that a gopher devours, or a hollyhock that becomes covered with rust.

I've also learned to be sensitive to the immediate needs of the garden, rather than bringing any preconceived ideas to it. For example, I may have recently watered, but the sweet peas are now looking slightly wilted and the soil is dry. I have developed an intuitive sense of my garden by being attuned to each plant's needs. They respond to loving attention by growing strong and healthy. Gardening has made me conscious of my relationship with the plants, myself, and the world.

EXERCISE IN THE GARDEN

Caring for the garden means keeping my body as well as my mind flexible. At times it seems like a dance with the plants as my partners. You can take advantage of gardening work to stretch your muscles and get in shape.

When pruning flowers, stand far enough away from them so that you have to reach your arms straight out. This helps condition the axial muscles running down the sides of the body, thus toning waist, arms, and hips. When weeding or planting, bend over from the waist with your feet apart and your legs straight. Stretch your arms and feel the gentle pull in the back of the thighs.

Lift heavy loads by bending down from the knees, with your back straight, until the object to be raised is level with your rib cage. Put your arms around it in an embrace and stand up. Keep it near your body as you move. Try carrying heavy baskets of fertilizer or weeds two at a time. Balance them equally in both arms to strengthen your arm muscles. Keep your shoulders relaxed and feel the lengthening of your neck muscles in response to the weight in your hands.

Preparing a planting bed can become a good aerobic exercise to help the heart and lungs. First weed, then dig the beds in a regular, rhythmic motion. Be aware of the muscles you are using and the rate of your pulse.

Even your hands and fingers will feel the effect of gardening— stretching, grasping, delicately planting, picking, and pruning. There are wheelbarrows to fill and push, compost heaps to turn, so many ways to tone the body and stay fit.

GARDENING FROM THE GROUND UP

Small-scale gardening is becoming increasingly popular with more and more people growing their own flowers, fruits, and vegetables. This can be done in pots on balconies or windowsills, in planter boxes on decks, or in small garden areas. It's not necessary to live in the country with acres of land to have a garden. Using the raised-bed method, you can grow lots of plants in a limited space.

Soil and Raised Beds

The soil is the foundation of the garden and contains the essential nutrients for the plant's growth. When I'm preparing a bed for flowers and vegetables I'm as conscientious about doing that as I am in preparing a meal for my family. I want my plants to receive all they will need to grow and live vibrant, full lives. I use organic materials such as manure and compost (soil prepared from decomposed plant materials) to enrich the soil, replacing whatever has been used up during the previous growing season. Organic gardening techniques help foster healthy plants and the garden becomes more fertile and prolific every year.

The gardening method I have been using over the years will guide you deep into the soil and introduce you to earthworms, manure, green matter, and compost. The raised beds are like a giant Earth Cake and they work![1] Soils prepared in this way can produce flowers and vegetables that are near perfection.

The beds look like gently sloping mounds of earth that are about one to one and a half feet above ground level. The outside perimeter of the mound may be surrounded by logs or stones, but this is not necessary. This method provides several advantages. The shape of the bed is ideal for planting many flowers and vegetables close together in a small space; much more than is possible in rows. It also prevents the trauma that plants can experience when the earth around their roots is stepped on. You don't walk on a mound after it is planted because the center can be easily reached from the sides. The raised bed also provides excellent drainage so the plants don't sit in water. The layered construction of plant materials and manure and compost helps to build the soil, eventually transforming it into a pleasant-smelling, rich texture. Because the plants are grown close together, they help form a natural mulch, keeping weeds from growing and the soil moist.

Tools, Materials, and the Method

To begin preparing a raised bed you will need some tools:

D-handled flat-bottomed spade
D-handled pitchfork
Wheelbarrow, basket, or bucket
Hand trowel
Sharp knife

You'll also need some well-aged cow or horse manure and/or compost, bone meal, and weeds. If you don't have easy access to compost (see the description of how to make compost later in this chapter) or manure, most plant nurseries carry them (as well as bone meal) in bags. Following is a recipe for making a six-foot by three-foot raised bed for average soil condition. Heavy clay, hard pan, and sand require special treatment.

6 cubic feet, or 2 to 3 wheelbarrows compost and/or aged manure
⅛ to ¼ pound bone meal
2 wheelbarrows weeds (optional)

1. Water a few days before digging so that the soil is barely moist. If it is too wet, it may clod together; if too dry, it may crumble.

2. Begin by clearing with your sharpened spade the area you wish to make into a garden. Try to "skim" the weeds from the surface of the soil, cutting them off just below ground level. Their roots can be left to decompose and become part of the soil. Use a sharp knife to remove any stubborn weeds. Make a weed pile. It will be used in the bed preparation.

3. For a 6 × 3-foot mound, start at one end and make a trench 3 feet across the width of the bed, about 1 foot wide and 10 to 12 inches deep. As you remove the soil, pile it near the opposite end of the bed.

4. Loosen the soil at the bottom of the empty trench with a pitchfork. Stand on it, if need be, and jostle it back and forth.

5. Put a layer of green matter, composed of weeds, a cover crop of beans, alfalfa, clover, comfrey, or green grasses, into the bottom of the trench. (If you don't have any green matter, this step may be omitted.)

6. Add a 2- to 3-inch layer of compost or manure. Sprinkle a handful of bone meal on top of it.

7. Make an identical trench next to the first one. As you dig out the soil, place it into the trench that you have just finished. Keep in mind the rounded shape of the raised mound with its gently sloping sides. Don't step on the newly dug area; this will compact the soil.

8. Continue digging, loosening the soil at the bottom, layering the weeds, adding manure, bone meal, and soil until you come to the last trench.

9. Fill in the last trench with the soil you set aside from the first trench.

10. Take your pitchfork and break up any large clumps of earth. I often abandon my tools at this point and use my hands. The soil should be as lump-free and fine as possible so that the roots of the plant will be able to grow freely and deeply.

11. Shape the mound. The top surface should be flat, flowing into rounded edges. If it's too steep, you can't plant on the sides and water will tend to run off. If too flat, the mound will not be raised enough off the ground. You may have to move the soil around for it to be even. Take your time, work slowly, and trust that it will turn out well. It's fine if your first bed isn't the perfect one, each year the soil will improve.

12. Add a 2- to 3-inch layer of uniformly textured compost or manure and a sprinkling of bone meal over the entire mound. Mix this gently with the topsoil, maintaining the shape you have created.

13. STAND BACK AND ADMIRE YOUR WORK!

14. If you are transplanting, the mound is now ready for plants. If you are sowing directly into the ground, scatter the seeds and cover them with a light layer of compost or manure, as described later in this chapter.

Once the beds have been dug for the first planting they will be easier to prepare the next time. Mulching or planting a cover crop in the winter protects and enriches the soil. Fava beans, clover, and alfalfa make good winter cover crops in temperate areas and add nitrogen and nutrients to the ground. In colder regions put layers of manure, seaweed, or other mulching materials over the garden. In warmer climates a winter garden can be planted. If the bed still seems to have rich soil and drains well after the spring/summer crops, simply add more manure or compost and bone meal to the top layer, turn it in lightly, and replant. It's important to replenish nutrients that are used during the growing season. The mounds should then be dug again for the next spring planting.

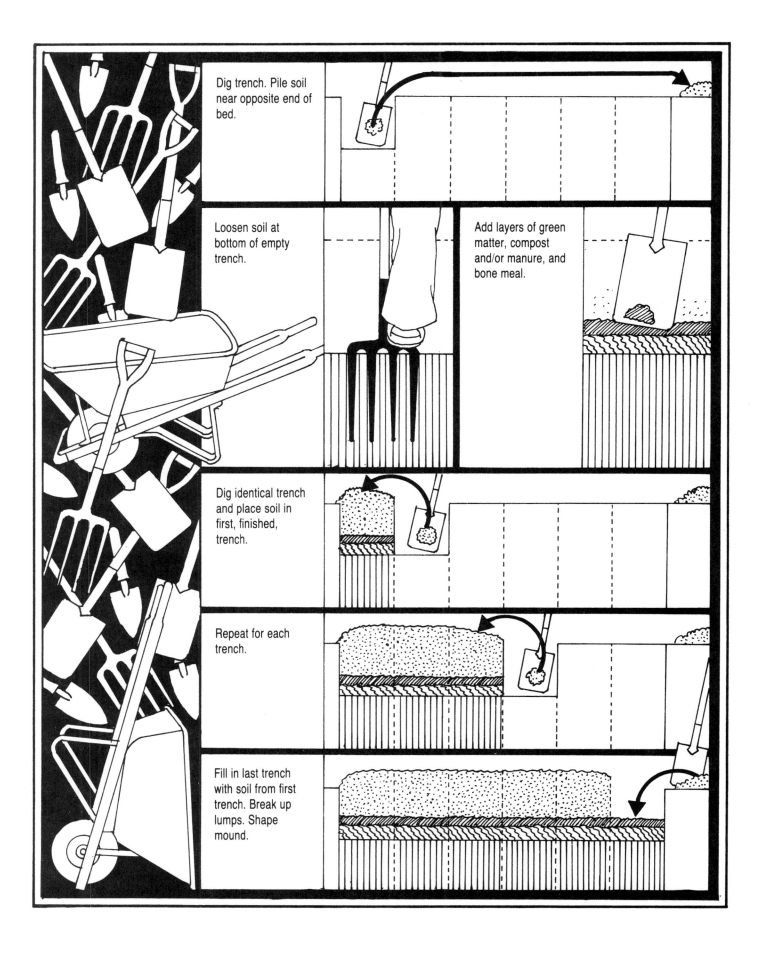

Dig trench. Pile soil near opposite end of bed.

Loosen soil at bottom of empty trench.

Add layers of green matter, compost and/or manure, and bone meal.

Dig identical trench and place soil in first, finished, trench.

Repeat for each trench.

Fill in last trench with soil from first trench. Break up lumps. Shape mound.

Planter Boxes, Pots, and Other Containers

Planter boxes or pots are simple to prepare for planting. First, make sure there is good drainage in the container, an unobstructed hole, no cracks or other openings. A piece of pottery over the hole and a layer of pebbles on the bottom of the pot will help insure that water flows through. Then prepare a mixture of:

Garden soil, ½ part
Compost or aged manure, ½ part
Bone meal, a dash

Combine these ingredients in a wheelbarrow, basket, or pail and fill the container a little over the top (the mixture will sink down when watered). An additional layer of manure or compost and bone meal can be added and mixed in lightly with the top layer of soil. If you are transplanting, the soil is now ready for use. If you are planting seeds, put them on top of the mixture and cover them with a thin layer (⅛- to ¼-inch) of the mixture. Potting soil may also be purchased at most nurseries if the individual ingredients aren't handy.

Flats

Another soil mixture you may want to prepare is for flats, in order to start your own seeds for transplants.

Oak leaf mold, optional
Sand, ⅓ part
Soil, ⅓ part
Compost, ⅓ part

Oak leaf mold (oak leaves that have partly decomposed into a crumbly blackish substance) can be gathered around deciduous oak trees or can be purchased. Line the bottom of the flat in a ½-inch layer to add warmth, drainage, and nutrients to the seedlings.

The best kind of sand to use is sharp mountain sand, usually found at nurseries. If unavailable, use any fine sand except salty sand from the seashore. If the soil and compost are heavy, sift them through a screen, made by nailing a ¼-inch medium weight screen onto a wooden frame measuring at least 2-feet-square. Combine the sifted mixture with the sand in a wheelbarrow and toss it in the air with a spade so that it becomes light and fluffy. Fill the wooden or plastic flat or other starting container to the top and press the soil down very gently. Sprinkle the seeds on top and cover them lightly with more of the mixture.

Seeds

I feel like the proverbial child in the candy store when I look through seed catalogs, especially ones with lovely pictures of flowers and vegetables. I wish I could plant them all, but good sense and the size of my garden keeps me from such extravagance. The planting of seeds, no matter the number, is always a special time for me. It is the giving of life. After planting, I often enjoy a moment of silence or the sweet music of a flute. It is a celebration.

The seed is an amazing kernel of life. It's sometimes difficult to comprehend fully how a colorful flower can grow from such a tiny bit of matter, but it does, persistently and beautifully. Each seed has within it a small plant called the *embryo* that will grow into another plant like its parent. The embryo contains one or two seed leaves called *cotyledons*; a *stalk* that becomes the roots and a *bud* that grows into the stem and leaves. Surrounding the embryo is the stored food needed to nourish the plant as it begins to grow, the *endosperm*.

Most seeds have one or two protecting coats. Some of these outer coverings are so tough they have allowed some seeds to survive over a thousand years and still germinate. When there is adequate water, air, and warmth, the seed swells and its covering breaks. The embryo emerges as roots, which grow toward the moist ground, and stem and leaves which grow toward the light. A flowering plant is born.

Most flowers transplant well and therefore can be started from seed in flats, peat pots, plastic pots, seedling trays, or other containers. Starting flowers in this way enables you to control the number of plants and gives the seedlings a chance to develop strong root systems in a protected and controlled environment.

However some seeds, such as poppies, nasturtiums, and most wild flowers, don't transplant well. These should be planted where they are to grow. Hardy annuals can also be planted directly in beds outdoors when danger of frost is past. Check with your local nursery and planting guides to find out the optimum conditions.

Sow a few more seeds than the number of flowers you'll want, to insure against incomplete germination. Extra plants can be thinned out later. Space the seeds one to two inches apart; the leaves of the seedlings will almost touch when they are ready to be transplanted. Cover the seeds with a light layer of soil that is just moist, not too soggy. Then water the seeds whenever the soil looks dry; this may be frequently if the weather is hot. Alternating wet and dry periods helps accelerate the sprouting process.

Keep flats inside if you're starting seeds when it is still cold outside. Put the flats in a place where they will receive strong light. If the planting bed is too shady, the seedlings will become leggy, reaching for the light. After danger of frost is past "harden" the plants by putting the flats outside for a week before planting. It may be too much of a shock for them to go from the protection and warmth of indoors directly to the garden. In more temperate zones the plants can be started in flats outdoors.

I usually sow seeds just before the new moon. Planting by the moon cycles is an ancient custom that has been reinterpreted in modern times and is based upon the belief that the moon affects the waters of the land as well as the ocean tides. Following this principle, the time for most accelerated growth is just before or at the new moon when the moon's "force" helps activate a seed's growth. The moon almost seems to draw the sprout into life, with the plant responding to the increasing light and gravitational pull. After the full moon, as its force decreases, activity above the ground slows down and the roots can then match their growth to that of the plant. This is the best time to plant seedlings so that their roots have time to become accustomed to their environment. I have experimented and found that seeds planted at the new moon definitely germinate faster and seem hardier than those planted at the full moon.

It's possible to gather seeds by allowing the flowers of strong, healthy plants to "go to seed." Allow the flowers to mature fully on the plant; they will then develop seed pods. When these appear to be dry, the seeds are usually ready. Remove the seed capsule from the plant and crumble it into a bowl to sort out any plant material. Then put the seeds in labeled and dated bags. Store them in tightly closed jars in a cool, dry place out of direct light.

In order to grow plants from seed that will be true to their parents you must gather seeds from flowers that are not hybrids. Most plants when purchased from a nursery are clearly marked as hybrids. Plant breeders create hybrid varieties by taking the pollen from a chosen plant and carefully placing it on another desirable plant. The result is seed that contains the favorable traits of both parent flowers. Seeds *grown* from hybrids will result in plants that revert back to the characteristics of one parent or the other. You can't predict what the offspring plant or flowers will look like. Some hybrid plants have seeds that are sterile and can only be propagated by making cuttings. Before you gather your own seeds investigate the parent plant to be sure it is not a hybrid.

Transplanting and Spacing

Seeds sown at the new moon will be grown into plants ready to transplant at the full moon, six weeks later. Transplant late in the day or on cloudy, foggy days as sun and wind can damage seedlings. If the beds have been well prepared, the plants will usually not experience much shock because they go into soil that is nourishing.

Use a knife to separate each individual seedling with its root ball and carefully remove it from the flat with a hand trowel or large spoon, leaving the soil intact around the roots of each plant. Decide where the new plants are to go and mark the spots. Spacing is important. Determine how large the plant will be when mature and leave enough room so that when it is full sized its leaves barely touch the leaves of its neighbor. In this way the leaves create a natural mulch for the soil, helping to keep it moist and weed-free. For example, calendulas will need to be about eight to ten inches apart when grown; Johnny-jump-ups six to eight inches; lavender ten to twelve inches; and sweet alyssum three to four inches. Plant a little bit more closely than is usually indicated on seed packets.

Arrange the plants so that they are staggered. Plant one row of snapdragons across the mound, then plant another row centered between the first plants, but about eight inches away from them. The third row is positioned like the first; the fourth like the second, as shown in the illustration (see page 56). Use a similar staggered spacing in planter boxes and other containers. They may be planted closer to each other than when grown in a garden bed.

Transplant the seedlings by first digging holes to accommodate their root balls, then put them in and firm the soil by pushing it down with your hands. When the plants are happily in the ground, water them carefully around their bases. Try to avoid watering the leaves. A plant with wet foliage is more vulnerable to shock and has a harder time directing its growth toward the roots. Water the plant in this way two or three times over a fifteen- to thirty-minute period. Make sure that all the surrounding soil is wet. A long-spouted watering can or a bent tin can works well. When all the little transplants have had a good drink, bless them and leave them to enjoy their new home.

Watering

Two days later the plants can be watered again. This break gives the plants time to adjust to their new surroundings. Watering provides an important part of plant nourishment; it is a life-sustaining ritual that can create a communion between you and your plants. They will respond by looking vital and giving off their delicious aroma; a plant's way of smiling.

It's usually best to water in the late afternoon when the moisture will have time to soak into the ground overnight. This prohibits evaporation by the sun. If your garden has an abundance of snails or slugs or if it happens that there is very damp and foggy weather, it may be best to water early in the morning so the heat of the day can dry off the plants. Snails and slugs thrive on wet foliage and will devour your plants during the night. Foggy, damp weather can lead to rot, mildew, and mold.

In my garden I almost always use an overhead, oscillator-type of watering device and water deeply, about once a week, for one and a half to two hours. This is better than shallow watering, which keeps the roots close to the surface. To water my roses and other plants that are susceptible to becoming diseased from wet leaves I use a soaker hose on the ground. For containers, flats, and other areas that can't be reached by the oscillator, I use a fan or wand-type device for a light flow of water that falls on the plants like soft rain. I like watering this way because I can see small rainbow prisms in the water and also because the local hummingbirds love to fly in and out of the spray, wetting their tiny bodies.

One way to determine when your plants need water is to dig into the soil with a trowel. If it is dry two or three inches down, it's time to water. Wind or intense heat evaporates moisture quickly; so if these conditions exist, a daily watering may be necessary. Plants in containers dry out more quickly than those in the ground and will need more frequent attention.

It's best not to wait until a plant wilts to care for it. However, if it droops slightly during the heat of the day, don't water it at that time; it may just be relaxing. Check it later in the afternoon, when it's cooler, to see if the soil is dry. Use your trowel and your intuition to stay in tune with your plants and their need for water.

Mulching

The best mulch is organic plant material. It helps retain moisture in the ground, keeps growth of weeds to a minimum, and nourishes the soil. In most well-prepared, planted beds or containers the closeness of the plants when fully mature will provide a natural mulch. However, even in this case, adding mulch provides an extra layer of care and protection to the plants before they are full grown. There are many materials to use: straw, hay, weeds, grass clippings, the hulls of buckwheat, rice, or cocoa beans, aged manure, and compost; pine needles can be used when an acid soil is desired. If you live near the coast, gather seaweed for a fine mineral-rich mulch that is high in potash and free of weed seeds. It may be applied fresh or rinsed before using. Dried seaweed is available commercially.

Mulch is particularly helpful in hot, dry areas or during a drought. It's best applied when the ground is moist and warm. If applied too early in the spring when the ground is still cold, it may seal the coldness into the soil and possibly harm the plants.

Mulch by spreading a three- to eight-inch layer of organic material on the soil surrounding the plant. Leave some space around the stem to discourage insects from feeding on the plant. Keep in mind that a thin layer of finely shredded mulch—rice hulls or compost—may be more effective than a thick layer of loose material. Straw allows more light to reach the soil, which can stimulate growth of weeds and evaporation of moisture.

Weeding and Cultivating

Weeding is sometimes difficult for me because what is considered a weed is often one of my favorite herbs, such as the dandelion! So I've selected certain areas in my garden where I allow wild herb weeds to grow and others where I want only flowers and vegetables. This makes it possible to weed the garden with an easy conscience. Often these herb weeds end up in my salad or herbal medicine chest: chickweed, purslane, dock, plantain, burdock, and many others. Of course, most of my weeds contribute to the compost pile, which ends up back in the garden as nutritious soil.

In some gardening methods weeds are left to grow along with the other plants. But in my garden, the weeds are so prolific they compete with the cultivated plants. I've learned to weed with a knife, cutting the plant just below the soil level. This discourages the weed's growth, while leaving its roots to compost and enrich the earth. The roots of a weed travel deep into the ground and bring up minerals; they also help to aerate the soil. When they decay, water can more easily travel down the pathways they've made into the subsoil. Some weeds, such as clover and sheep sorrel, spread by their root systems and will continue to thrive even when their tops are removed. For these, I use the knife to

pull up as much of the root as possible. Weeding requires concentrating on each plant, and I have come to appreciate it as a quiet, contemplative activity.

Weeding also helps to cultivate or loosen the soil. It's important to check the garden and plant containers frequently to see that the earth hasn't become hardened or caked. When this happens, water isn't being properly absorbed and the plants can become stifled as the soil loses its light, airy quality. Use a small pitchfork or hand tool to break up the ground between the plants, and work carefully so as not to damage the roots.

Pruning

Most plants naturally grow in a shapely manner and generally do not need any radical pruning.

There are several ways, though, in which pruning is helpful to flowering plants. When I cut their flowers in bud or bloom for bouquets, I am also encouraging them to produce new flowers. Regular pruning of dead flowers improves the plant's appearance and also extends its life by postponing the seed-making process.

The shape of the plant can be enhanced by pruning. If the plant is growing tall and thin and lacks a full appearance, pinch the first blossom buds, which will cause side branches to form. If more fullness is desired, branches may be topped. If the plant becomes too bushy, stems from the side can be cut out, leaving the central branches intact. It's also important to remove any damaged or diseased growth.

Most plants are best pruned in the spring before they come into flower. The flowering branches of perennials, such as carnations, shasta daisies, and sweet Williams, however, can be cut back after flowering. These will bloom again in the spring with strong new growth.

Fertilizing

Plants often need to be fertilized, fed extra nutrients that will help them grow. Manure, compost, bone meal, and water-soluble seaweed fertilizer are all excellent. Perennials, plants that bloom for many years on the same root stalk, can receive a two- or three-inch layer of manure or compost both after they have finished blooming and again in the spring when new growth starts. A sprinkling of bone meal in the spring encourages the plant to form blossoms. These organic fertilizers should be lightly worked into the soil around the plant.

Annuals, which grow, bloom, and die in one season, will naturally receive enough nutrients from properly prepared soils. However, they may be mulched with manure or compost and watered occasionally with a seaweed fertilizer. It is particularly important for flowers in containers to be fertilized in this same manner. Their roots cannot travel deep into the soil and depend upon the nutrients you provide them. Remember that plants need food regularly and will respond when well nourished by producing beautiful flowers.

Compost

Compost is the great life-giver to plants. It transforms weeds, discarded kitchen scraps, manure, leaves, grass, and other plant materials into wonderful soil, full of humus. Humus is the dark, earthy substance in fertile soils that is formed from decomposing organic matter. It has a rich aroma that reminds me of the first smell of spring: a combination of gentle rain, warm earth, and budding greenery. Humus, from compost, provides nitrogen, phosphorous, potash, and trace elements for the plants.

Making compost reminds me that the cycles of life are always continuing. From discarded and dead plant matter comes new soil that goes back into the garden to provide flowers and food. Some of these flowers are then turned again into compost to continue the process. Nature itself is always composting on the forest floors, where dead leaves, branches, plants, and even insects, birds, and animals are transformed into soil.

There are many composting methods of varying degrees of complexity. If you have the space, choose a cleared area in the garden to begin a compost pile. Start with a layer of stalky type things, such as large weeds or the vines of peas or tomatoes. Add to this a layer of kitchen discards—vegetables, fruits, stale bread, and crumbled egg shells. Be careful about adding too much citrus rind; it can make the compost overly acidic. Meat, fish, and poultry can attract animals and are best left out.

Continue layering with weeds, leaves, fresh manure, dirt, old flowers, plants, and other organic materials. If you live by the sea, seaweed is terrific for the compost; it breaks down quickly, activating the heap and causing it to heat up. Heat increases the decomposing action and helps to complete the composting. Keep adding to the pile until it gets big, at least four to five feet in height and diameter. It will shrink by one third to one half when it is ready.

Layers of nitrogen-rich fresh manure stimulate bacterial action; the resulting decomposition of the materials causes the pile to heat up. This same process will happen without manure, but it is much slower. Properly prepared compost does not have a bad odor. It can be ready to use in six to eight weeks. I usually have three piles: one of finished compost, one completed pile that is composting, and one new pile that is growing in size.

Air is essential for composting and turning the heap several times while it is heating will help. The pile also should be kept moist, but not soggy. Cover it during rainy weather with plastic or a tarp.

Another method of making compost involves continually adding organic materials to one pile and then removing the finished compost from the bottom of it. But the method I've described is preferable because it works more efficiently.

When earthworms appear in the compost you can be sure that it is ready. They are hard workers in the garden. Their waste, called worm castings, adds humus to the soil. Also, they cultivate as they wiggle and eat their way through the earth.

Compost can even be made in an apartment in a garbage can with perforated sides. Find the method that best suits your needs. My own composting technique is quite casual and works for a small garden. My heap supplies plenty of compost when I need it and has a huge appetite that devours all my kitchen waste and garden weeds.

A VARIETY OF FLOWER GARDENS

A flower garden can be as small as a single clay pot or as large as the acres of tulips in Holland. The size of your garden will be determined by the amount of time and space you can devote to it. I recommend beginning with a small one and expanding it as you gain more knowledge and understanding of plants.

The following ideas for different types of gardens can help you design your own; be guided by them in choosing the flowers that are appropriate for your needs, climate, and landscape. Flower combinations can be adapted to a space or container of any size by increasing or decreasing the number of plants used.

Most of the flowers I've chosen are planted in the early spring to be enjoyed throughout the summer. Annuals, such as marigolds, will die totally after blooming. Perennials, such as columbine and peony, live for more than two years. They will die back in cold areas, their root stock becomes dormant in the winter, then comes back to life in the spring. In warmer areas their foliage remains throughout the winter. Biennials, such as foxglove, will bloom the second year and then die back. In the tropics it's possible to plant almost anytime. In temperate zones spring and fall are the best planting times.

Indulge your imagination when planting flowers and don't be limited by any preconceived images of gardens. Plant in circles; sculpt your garden with soft mounds and curves; use old teapots, boats, fountains, or enameled pots for planters. Grow a number of the same flowers together with a group that has contrasting colors, such as purple lobelia bordering a dense mass of bright red geraniums. You can mix colors for a surprising array. Plant wild flowers, annuals, perennials, and bulbs all together. Create ground covers with intense colors, such as portulaca, gazania, or African daisy.

I love the carefree effect that results when flowers spontaneously reseed themselves—and many do—such as foxglove, forget-me-not, poppy, Johnny-jump-up, rose campion, feverfew, and nicotiana. They come up where the breeze tosses their seeds, often in just the perfect place! These volunteers add a relaxed feeling to a cultivated area.

I try to plant the flowers that will grow well where I live. This is often a matter of experimentation. Books, other gardeners, and local nurseries can help you find out what grows best in your area.

I realized that the flowers that prevailed in my garden were those that could survive the challenges of the sea coast. They have had to endure wind, fog, gophers, snails, and slugs. Once acclimatized, the plants in my garden grow strong and burst into brilliantly blossoming bouquets.

EDIBLE FLOWER GARDEN

An edible flower garden may be grown in a container or garden bed and can encompass both edible flowers and flowering herbs. Its blossoms will complement your favorite dishes. If you plant your garden near your kitchen door, the plants will be right at your fingertips when you're preparing a meal. If you plant it as part of your vegetable garden, it's possible to pick the flowers and the greens for your salad at the same time.

Imagine the appealing look of a planter box bordered with Johnny-jump-ups and nasturtiums, filled in with calendulas and forget-me-nots. They are all delicious flowers and provide a rich-hued display of orange, yellow, purple, and blue. Plant a half barrel with edible blossoms such as purple petunias cascading over its sides, scented geraniums in the center, and multicolored giant pansies in between them. Iceland poppies with their delicately-flavored pastel petals look like graceful dancers surrounded by clouds of sweet-tasting lavender, apricot and yellow violas.

Flowering herbs enliven foods with their enticing flavors. They have also been used in teas for centuries for their traditional healing properties. Most herbs are native to the Mediterranean coast and thrive in full sunlight with poor, well-drained soil. These conditions encourage them to produce strong, aromatic oils. Herbs grown in the shade and watered excessively tend to be weak in fragrance and taste. Use less manure than usual in preparing the soil for herbs, cultivate it well for good drainage, and make sure the spot is sunny and dry. There are some herbs, however, such as angelica, lemon balm, mint, and sweet woodruff, that will grow well in partial shade.

Herbs beautify the garden with their attractive, fragrant foliage and flowers. Plant them along paths, in the spokes of an old wooden wheel, or around a fountain or birdbath. Grow plants of the same herb grouped together, or scatter them among your flowers and vegetables. Plant chives with their soft purple ball-shaped flowers, calendulas with their orange glow, pineapple sage in striking red bloom, and lavender with tall spikes of fragrant blossoms. Many flowering herbs—basil, chives, chervil, coriander, parsley, sweet marjoram, thyme—can be enjoyed in pots either outside or inside. Inside, during the winter, a single pot can hold a nasturtium growing up a sunny window.

Annual flowering herbs grow quickly in one season, and their seeds germinate easily. Many will, in fact, reseed themselves. They may be planted directly in the ground after frost or many may be started in flats indoors. However anise, chervil, and coriander, as well as the biennial, caraway, have deep-growing taproots and cannot be easily transplanted without damaging this long root that grows directly from the stem. These should be sown right into the garden or in peat pots that can be planted without disturbing the roots. Other annual herbs include basil, borage, calendula, dill, German chamomile, and garden cress.

Perennial flowering herb seeds are slower to germinate because of their hard outer seed covering. It is best to freeze and thaw them several times in the freezer before planting; this helps speed up germination. Plant them immediately after the freezing treatment in flats inside or outside rather than directly into the ground. Be patient and give them plenty of time to sprout.

Many perennial herbs, such as rosemary and lavender, can be propagated by bending a branch of the mature plant to the ground and covering it with soil. It will eventually take root and become a separate plant.

When the plants are large enough, herbs may also be split by root division. Simply remove a small section of the herb including stems, leaves, and roots and transplant it into the soil. It will grow into a complete and separate plant. This is best done in the early springtime, though in temperate zones root division may also be done in the fall.

Flowering perennial herbs include bee balm, catnip, chives, comfrey, garlic, fennel, hyssop, lavender, lemon balm, mint, oregano, rosemary, sage, scented geranium, sweet marjoram, thyme, watercress, and yarrow. Parsley and angelica are biennial herbs, flowering in their second year. The seeds are very slow to germinate, sometimes taking one month, but can be planted directly into the ground as long as you remember to water them.

Refer to the list of edible flowers (see pages 133–135) to help you create a delicious garden of flowers and flowering herbs.

AROMATIC FLOWER GARDEN

Imagine walking on a summer night into a flower garden heavily perfumed with honeysuckle, jasmine, and nicotiana—a haven of sensuous delight. Powerful aromas caress you and with a deep breath you drink them in.

I've often been met by a tantalizing fragrance carried on the breeze. Acacia, Spanish broom, mock orange, lemon, black locust, orange, and sweet peas send their scents far out like messengers. Yet other flowers keep their perfume closer to themselves and must be touched or sniffed to be enjoyed.

Place pots of aromatic plants where they will be most appreciated. You might decorate your living room with containers of narcissus that bring the fresh essence of spring indoors. Outside fill the empty spaces in your garden with bouquets of scented geraniums. Move large potfuls of stocks and nicotiana next to a favorite bench to inhale their rich perfume in the moonlight. Line the steps up to your front door with freesias and other blooming bulbs to welcome you and your guests fragrantly.

My vision of an aromatic garden is a small area with paths of stepping-stones that have creeping thyme planted between them. As you walk, each step sends up a refreshing scent. The paths are bordered with lavender so that you can brush it with your fingertips as you pass. In the center is a circular lawn of low-growing Roman chamomile that surrounds you with its calming, fruity aroma when you sit on it. Vines of clematis, honeysuckle, and jasmine trail luxuriously over fences. An arbor of "sweetheart" roses blooms with tiny pink buds. In the spring freesias, daffodils, narcissus, violets, hyacinths, iris, and lilacs completely fill the garden with a potpourri of scent. They will be followed later in the spring and in the summer by mock orange, carnations, stocks, heliotrope, sweet peas, nicotiana, lilies, and roses.

Following is a list of plants, shrubs, and trees with fragrant flowers to use when creating an aromatic garden.

Acacia	Hyacinth	Night-blooming jasmine
Apple blossom	Iris	Orange
Basil	Jasmine	Petunia
Bee balm	Lavender	Pink
Black locust	Lemon	Plumeria
Broom	Lemon balm	Rose
Carnation	Lemon verbena	Rosemary
Ceanothus	Lilac	Sage
Chamomile	Lily	Scented geranium
Clematis	Lily of the valley	Star jasmine
Daffodil	Lotus	Stock
Daphne	Magnolia	Sweet alyssum
Dill	Mignonette	Sweet pea
Fennel	Mint	Sweet William
Forsythia	Mock orange	Thyme
Freesia	Moonflower	Tuberose
Gardenia	Narcissus	Violet
Ginger	Nasturtium	Wallflower
Heliotrope	Nicotiana	Water lily

DYE FLOWER GARDEN

There are many flowers that can be used for natural dyeing. Experiment with your favorite flowers to discover what colors they yield. One advantage of growing flowers for this purpose is that they can also be enjoyed in other ways: for example, coreopsis, cineraria, and rudbeckia are especially colorful; daffodils, hyacinths, and lilacs are aromatic; calendula, fennel, and hibiscus provide food and tea; snapdragons, scabiosa, and daisies make excellent cut flowers. Because large quantities of flowers are needed for dyeing you will want to grow many plants of the desired varieties. Keep the flowers cut so that more will grow. Dry the flowers as you gather them until there are enough to use for dyeing. Offer to help your friends keep their flowers pruned and save the blossoms.

Consider the first year of a dye flower garden a trial period during which you'll get to know the flowers that produce the colors you like best. If you love the rusty oranges that coreopsis or yellow dahlias yield, you can plant a whole garden bed or large planter box with them the next year. Grow spring daffodils and gather them to see what shade of yellow you obtain in the dye pot. Keep a mature, yellow marguerite bush well pruned and you'll easily have enough blossoms to dye yarn a goldish yellow. Blue lupine flowers turn wool different intensities of green. My purple stock that spice the air all summer will dye wool an interesting shade of blue. One year I dried all my marigolds and put them in the dye pot with some calendulas. The resulting yarn was a rich brassy color. Purple asters dye wool a greenish-gold. Remember that the colors will vary according to climate, soil, plant health, and other unknown factors. (See Chapter 3, "Flower Dyeing—Color from Nature's Flowers" for a listing of dye plants for your garden.)

EVERLASTING FLOWER GARDEN

Everlasting flowers are those with straw-like petals that dry well when you hang them upside down. These flowers can keep their color and shape for many years and are very easy to grow. In temperate climates many of them will reseed themselves year after year. They grow best in soils that drain well but are not too high in nitrogen content. When preparing the earth for everlasting flowers use less manure than usual; too much can cause weak flower stems and poor color. Potash, from ashes, helps the plants to grow stronger stems and brighter flowers. Full sun and adequate watering are important. Plant in early spring after the possibility of frost. Sow them directly into the ground or into flats for transplanting later. A border of the clover-like blossoms of pink and purple globe amaranth filled in with the bold oranges, wines, and yellows of strawflowers or the softer white, rose, and lavender shades of statice make an effective combination in a large container. A few tiny white baby's breath flowers will add a light airiness to the planting.

When gathering flowers from the plant, cut the stem to a strong point of new leaf and bud growth. This encourages new stalks and more flowers. Most everlastings have stems that dry well. However, you might want to replace the stems of strawflowers, for example, with florist's wire.

Chinese lantern, globe thistle, yarrow, and one variety of baby's breath and statice are perennial plants. Honesty is a biennial, but all the other everlastings are annuals. A list follows of the most common everlasting flowers.

Acroclinium	Ornamental grasses
Baby's breath	Rhodanthe
Bells of Ireland	Starflower or Star everlasting
Celosia	Statice
Chinese lantern	Strawflower
Globe amaranth	Winged everlasting or Ammobium
Globe thistle	Xeranthemum
Honesty or Money plant	Yarrow, golden
Love-in-a-mist	

CUTTING FLOWER GARDEN

I've always liked to imagine myself in the future as an older woman growing a cutting flower garden to which people would come to pick their own bouquets. I would enjoy the exercise of growing flowers and the company of flower lovers.

The traditional cutting garden belonged to the wealthy estates of an earlier age. It was located in an area away from the main flower garden and the flowers were grown specifically to be cut for use in the house. Today it's much more realistic to have one flower garden or to mix flowers with vegetables.

A cutting garden is made up of flowers that will last well when gathered for arrangements. Plant beds of gayly colored dahlias, rose-bushes, delphiniums, day lilies, and columbines. Chrysanthemums mirror the colors of the trees in the fall, while daffodils, tulips, and forsythia greet the spring. Grow combinations of flowers that set off their color and shape—graceful pink cosmos bordered by stately carnations and snapdragons. Plant a mixed bouquet of soft blue forget-me-nots, purple violas, beautiful pink linaria, and glowing yellow alyssum that edge some taller pink or white marguerites, yellow daffodils, orange and yellow calendulas, blue bachelor's buttons, and rose campion with its silver foliage.

An ideal cutting garden will provide blossoms in an array of colors from early spring bulbs to the last rose of winter. It can be planned with this in mind by alternating plantings of annuals and perennials with different blooming times. (See "Flowers That Arrange Well" in Chapter 3 for a list of flowers best suited for a cutting garden.)

WILD FLOWER GARDEN

Imagine transforming your garden into a meadow of wild flowers, letting the look of nature return to your landscape. Even in a limited space, pots or baskets of wild flowers have a colorful, natural appearance.

Wild flowers are easy to grow, though sometimes their seeds take a while to sprout. You can speed up their germination by storing the seeds with an equal amount of damp sand in the refrigerator for a few months. This process is called stratification. It simulates the cold, wet winter dormancy after which the hard outer seed coat begins to soften, encouraging the embryo to develop and the growing cycle to begin. When the seeds become swollen and split, they may be planted in flats or outside. Be patient, some seeds will be ready in three to four weeks; others may take four months. Most wild flower seeds benefit from this treatment.

It's important to prepare the ground before planting. Deep digging isn't necessary, but the soil should be loose and drain well. For my first attempt at growing wild flowers I simply threw the seeds on the ground. That didn't work at all. The next time I dug the soil lightly, added some compost, planted the seeds, and covered them with a thin layer of soil. They blossomed into a bouquet of orange California poppies, purple lupine, and pink clarkia.

Plant the seeds when rain can be expected, in the early spring after frost or, in temperate western climates, in the late fall. Wild flowers do require water, though some are drought-resistant. If there is a dry spell in the midst of the rainy season, watering is important. Most annual wild flowers will reseed themselves prolifically. After the first year they will need minimal care.

Birds love wild flower seeds and will happily eat all that are planted. If birds are a problem, cover the ground with a net or light canvas that will let the sunlight through until the seeds germinate. It's best to grow the flowers away from grasses whose roots can inhibit their growth.

Wild flower seed mixes are available for particular localities from seed catalogs or nurseries in your area. You can also gather wild flower seeds from the countryside. Cut the dried flower heads from the plants about one month after flowering or when the seeds appear mature. If there is a chance that the seeds may scatter before you collect them, put a fine mesh bag over the flowers so their seeds will fall into it. Always sow more wild flower seeds than you will need for their germination is often incomplete. Below is a list of some common wild flowers to grow for a pleasing display. Almost all of these can be easily started from seed.

Aster	Coreopsis	Mallow
Baby blue eyes	Daisy	Mullein
Black-eyed Susan	Evening primrose	Penstemon
Blazing star	Farewell-to-spring	Quaking grass
Blue-eyed grass	or Godetia	Queen Anne's lace
Blue flax	Fireweed	Saint-John's-wort
Buttercup	Forget-me-not	Siberian wallflower
California poppy	Foxglove	Teasel
Chicory	Goldfields	Tidytips
Chinese houses	Indian paintbrush	Violet
Clarkia	Linaria	Yarrow
Columbine	Lupine	

CONTAINER FLOWER GARDEN

For the city dweller or any gardener with limited space and time, containers are a blessing. A balcony, deck, fire escape, or the side of a driveway can become a fertile growing area. With a variety of containers, indoors or out, it's possible to grow flowers, vegetables, and even fruits.

One winter I decided to give my garden beds a rest in order to replenish the soils with nutrients that had been used up during the growing season. I planted winter flowers and vegetables in redwood boxes on my deck. In our mild Northern California winter I grew crisp red and green lettuce, fat bunches of parsley, warming orange and yellow calendulas, purple violas, ruby red chard, exquisite lilac and green-leaved miniature flowering kale. All these brightened many gray days and provided delicious food all winter long! There are many flowering plants that thrive in containers and many new dwarf varieties are actually suited to this culture. They require a minimum amount of care: watering, fertilizing, and the removal of dead flowers. Use clay pots, wooden planters, half wine barrels, old porcelain bath tubs, baskets, driftwood logs, teapots, antique or new pottery, copperware or other imaginative containers.

Drainage is important for successful plants. The soil should be porous enough and the pots should have adequate enough drainage to allow water to flow through easily. For a good soil mixture refer to the discussion of planter boxes (see page 52) earlier in this chapter.

The container needs to be both deep and wide enough to allow room for complete root growth. Plan the size of the container to fit the mature plant; you can grow flowers much closer than you would in garden beds. Depending on the plant, you may need to repot every few years. Renew the soil in containers after annuals or other plants have completed their cycle of growth. Remember that container plants will need water more frequently than those in the garden. Mulch will help retain moisture and liquid seaweed fertilizer once a month will keep plants healthy.

I love to design richly colored container plantings. One of my favorites has feathery pink cosmos in the center, edged with the clear yellow and orange hues of nemesia, and filled in between with little purple Johnny-jump-ups peeking through the foliage. Another appealing combination for shadier locations is a full border of royal blue "crystal palace" lobelia surrounding deep rose flowered fibrous begonia. One year I grew velvety magenta petunias billowing around burnt-orange cosmos. Double stocks, mounds of giant pansies, and an edging of scented lilac sweet alyssum make a beautiful display. Or plant a large round shallow pot with one deep crimson primrose and surround it with soft clusters of delicate pink fairy primrose.

Mass together the same kind of multicolored seasonal flowers in separate pots. Groupings of spring bulbs, chrysanthemums, or cyclamen add vitality to a deck or balcony. Showy scarlet sage bordered with lemon yellow alyssum is an intensely colored combination. Fuchsias and tuberous begonias are graceful hanging in a shaded spot. Dusty miller has a silver radiance in the moonlight and blooms abundantly with purple blossoms. Below is a list of some flowers that grow well in containers.

Ageratum	Cyclamen	Nicotiana
Alyssum	Dahlia	Pansy
Anemone	Daphne	Petunia
Aster	Dusty miller	Phlox
Azalea	Fairy primrose	Portulaca
Baby's breath	Fuchsia	Primrose
Bachelor's button	Gardenia	Rose
Begonia	Geranium	Salpiglossis
Bird-of-paradise	Gloxinia	Scarlet sage
Bleeding heart	Iceland poppy	Scented geranium
Bougainvillea	Impatiens	Schizanthus
Calendula	Ivy geranium	Snapdragon
Camellia	Johnny-jump-up	Stock
Campanula	Lantana	Sweet alyssum
Candytuft	Lavender	Sweet William
Canterbury bell	Linaria	Verbena
Carnation	Lobelia	Viola
Celosia	Marguerite	Wallflower
Chrysanthemum	Marigold	Zinnia
Cineraria	Nasturtium	
Cosmos	Nemesia	

SPRING BULBS

Bulbs provide a hidden garden that blossoms faithfully each spring in a variety of colors and scents. By summer most bulbs are forgotten and dormant under the ground. Each year they produce more flowers and multiply into more bulbs. They require a minimum of care after planting: watering if there is a dry spell and fertilizing with bone meal. Bulbs will even continue to flourish with no attention at all, fed by the rains and sunshine.

A bulb contains within its compact form all that is needed for a complete cycle of growth: embryo, leaves, stems, flowers, and nutrients. When first planted in late summer or fall the bulb is dormant. Once in the ground the roots begin to grow right away and continue to grow until there is a freeze. When the sun warms the ground in the spring, root growth resumes, and the leaves begin to grow toward the light. After blooming, the leaves and roots absorb food to store in the bulb until the next year. During this time the bulb also reproduces. Because

the bulb still grows underground after blossoming, it's important to remove old blossoms in order to inhibit seed growth that would take energy away from the bulb. However, the foliage should be left on the plant until it is totally dry and withered; it nourishes the bulb and promotes the underground growth.

After many years the bulbs may have multiplied so thickly that they stop flowering well. If this occurs, separate them when they are dormant by pulling the large bulbs apart. Do not separate small bulblets from the mother bulb; they are receiving nourishment from it. Store the bulbs in a cool place and replant them in the fall. I use the word bulb in general to describe all plants that grow from bulb-like parts. Actually, flowers that grow from true bulbs include daffodils and hyacinths, while crocus and gladiolus grow from corms; bearded iris and calla from rhizomes, and cyclamen and begonias from tubers.

There are many bulbs that can endure freezing winters. These are referred to as "hardy" bulbs and include snowdrops, crocus, hyacinth, daffodils, tulips, fritillaria, Dutch iris, amaryllis, and grape hyacinth. In temperate frost-free areas tulips and hyacinths do best if refrigerated six to eight weeks before planting. Other bulbs are called "tender" because they cannot endure a frost. These include dahlias, gladiolus, tuberous begonias, freesias, anemones, and ranunculus. These must be dug up before the first frost and replanted in the spring. In frost-free areas these bulbs may remain in the ground.

Hardy bulbs are best planted in late summer or early fall. Prepare the ground so that it will drain well and provide nutrients for the bulb. Individual holes can be dug with a spade, trowel, or bulb planter. Add one teaspoon of bone meal and a handful of compost or aged manure and mix these with the soil in the bottom of the hole. Plant the bulb in the ground to the depth of about three times its diameter with the pointed end up, then cover it with soil. Another method is to prepare a whole bed and dig the holes directly in it. Or, a small area can be dug out, fertilized, then planted with ten to twelve bulbs at once. Space the bulbs according to their size: larger bulbs, eight inches apart; medium-sized ones about six inches apart; and smaller ones three to four inches apart. Bulbs grow best when planted in groups of at least six of the same kind. Water the area deeply. If there is a dry period, water once a week until the first frost or until it rains. When growth begins in the spring, be sure the bulbs stay well watered. A sprinkling of bone meal at this time will encourage healthy blossoms.

Daffodils are well suited for "naturalizing"; this refers to planting the bulbs so that they blend into the natural landscape. Daffodils will multiply freely each year and are particularly effective in a wooded setting or grassy meadow. My father planted the woods around our home with hundreds of daffodils that naturalized in the twenty-five years that he lived there. Spring was always resplendent with vivid shades of yellow as all the varieties of daffodils broke through the brown of winter leaves. It seemed like magic! Some of the children of those same bulbs are now in my garden. One way to decide where to put bulbs for naturalizing is to throw them around you and plant them where they land. Just be sure to find them all!

Bulbs can be a dynamic part of the garden every spring. Create a flowering sea of deep blue grape hyacinths with islands of red and yellow tulips. Narcissus and hyacinths flourish in pots. Massed together they liven up a deck or balcony. Plant shady, wooded areas with showy clusters of daffodils, fritillaria, wood hyacinth, and dogtooth violet. Bulbs grouped in large beds of one color and type and edged with a contrasting color are especially attractive. Plant bulbs with other kinds of flowers such as golden daffodils with softly colored violas. Or grow perennials near your bulbs so that they fill in the spaces left after the bulbs have bloomed. Design bulb plantings for a fragrant and long-lasting display. Below is a partial list of the most common bulbs. The majority of them bloom in the spring; however, begonias, canna, dahlias, gladiolus, lilies, and tigridia usually flower in the summer while cyclamen and montbretia provide fall color.

Allium	Dutch iris	Puschkinia
Amaryllis	Freesia	Ranunculus
Anemone	Fritillaria	Siberian squill
Begonia, tuberous	Gladiolus	Snowdrop
Calla	Glory-of-the-snow	Sparaxis
Canna	Grape hyacinth	Spring snowflake
Clivia or Kaffir lily	Hyacinth	Tigridia
Crocus	Iris, bearded	Tulip
Cyclamen	Lily	Winter aconite
Daffodil	Lily of the valley	Wood hyacinth
Dahlia	Montbretia	
Dogtooth violet	Narcissus	

FLOWERING VINES AND CLIMBING PLANTS

Flowering vines and climbing plants create a lovely addition to any garden; they cover large areas and blossom for many months. My own garden has a passion vine with brilliant four-inch red flowers that passionately attempts to coil and climb over everything it can reach. Aromatic jasmine grows on one side of it and honeysuckle grows on the other. This combination makes a contrasting and fragrant backdrop throughout the year.

I remember clearly many of the vines that I have seen over the years. I recall a deep purple clematis in a friend's garden; the large flowers looked like stars against the green foliage. My memories of Mexico bring to mind white buildings covered with reddish-pink bougainvillea illuminated by the hot sun. In Hawaii I've seen tall, colorful walls of these blossoms with orange, pink, yellow, and rose-

colored bracts. And I remember wisteria growing around the edge of a neighbor's covered patio, the dangling sweet flowers gracefully framing it every spring.

One garden I've enjoyed is bordered by a whole *hedge* of honeysuckle, which delights everyone who walks past it. Another favorite flower memory is of a trumpet vine with its large orange flowers completely surrounding a friend's window. The steps to her house are planted on either side with star jasmine. Walking to her front door is an exhilarating experience. Aromatic giant Burmese honeysuckle with its three-inch golden yellow flowers vines its way through another friend's bathhouse and scents the air for those who swim in her pool.

Heavenly blue morning glory also has an exuberant growth. I've been surprised to find huge falls of the azure flowers in the alleyways of city streets.

There are so many ways flowering vines can enhance your garden. They will vigorously cover unsightly fences, create privacy, spill over a wall, or climb up a post.

Many flowering vines and climbing plants, such as star jasmine and bougainvillea, are evergreen, providing year-round foliage and seasonal flowers. Others are deciduous, losing their leaves every winter and growing them back in the spring. Wisteria and clematis are among this type. Several of them, including honeysuckle and bougainvillea, need warmth and protection from frost and wind.

Vines climb in different ways. Some twine around supports or around themselves, others have tendrils that wrap around whatever is nearby, some can cling to surfaces, and several must be totally supported. Be sure to secure those vines well, with rope, wire, mesh, or staples—whatever works best. After the first year they will usually anchor themselves. Discover the best flowering vines and climbing plants for your area and watch your garden come alive with their blossoms. Consider pruning them to keep them in shape.

Bougainvillea	Coral vine	Orchid vine
Black-eyed Susan vine	Cup-and-saucer vine	Passion vine
Canary bird vine	Cup of gold vine	Potato vine
Cardinal climber	Dutchman's pipe	Scarlet runner bean
Chilean bellflower	Honeysuckle	Sweet pea
Chilean jasmine	Jasmine	Silver-lace vine
Clematis	Mexican flame vine	Trumpet vine
Climbing hydrangea	Moonflower	Wisteria
Climbing rose	Morning glory	

INDOOR FLOWER GARDEN

Indoor plants provide the luxury of flowers year round. To thrive they need warmth, water, moisture, and fertilizer. Flowers also need bright light, but it is best to keep them out of the direct, hot sun in a window. To keep them from drying out, mist the plants or have them sit in a shallow pan filled with pebbles and water. Dust should be removed regularly from their leaves with a wet sponge.

Some potted plants can live outside all summer, then come in for the winter. My parents had a vigorous geranium with colorful red blossoms in a large pot outside; it continued its flowering show inside during the cold weather. Perennial herbs in pots will also grow indoors in the winter. African violets like the brief morning light of winter and filtered light in the summer. They are best watered from the bottom. Gardenias fill your home with tropical fragrance if they are kept warm and out of direct sunlight and drafts. Cyclamen—unusual-looking inside-out flowers that come in shades of rose, pink, crimson, and white—bloom for many months, like to be kept moist, and thrive with bright days and cool nights. Direct sun will bleach their leaves white. Keep the old flower stems pinched off to encourage new blossoms.

Spring bulbs, such as hyacinths, narcissus, tulips, grape hyacinths, and freesias have a special, fragrant appeal indoors. Plant them in pots with the bulbs fairly close together, cover them with soil, and moisten. Grow hyacinths in a "hyacinth glass" designed so that just the base of the bulb touches the water. You can actually see the bottom of the glass fill with roots and the bulb begin to sprout—an excellent way to learn how a bulb grows. Add a bit of charcoal or a few drops of bleach to keep the water sweet.

Narcissus are best grown in a shallow pot or dish about three inches deep. Fill it with pebbles and place the bulbs about one quarter of an inch apart in the pebbles so that their bottom halves are covered. Add enough water to make the bases of the bulbs wet and keep the water at this level. Leave all these forced bulbs in a cool, dark spot until the roots have grown and the bulbs have shoots one or two inches tall. Then put them in a bright window, water them, and watch them burst into bloom. After they flower, cut off the stalks, keep the plants moist, and remove the foliage when it dies back.

These bulbs are usually most productive when grown in a pot for one season; the flowers will be weaker the next year. When they are dormant remove them from their containers and plant them in the garden to blossom and grow for many more years.

Many annuals, which need light and moderate to cool temperatures, are well suited for growing inside. Line your windowsill with pots of cheerful morning glories, nasturtiums, petunias, or marigolds. Plant different shades of lobelia to trail down a pot in a purple and blue waterfall around bright orange calendulas. Grow some schizanthus, also known as poor man's orchid, with its clusters of exquisite blossoms in pinks, amethysts, and yellows. Mine spill over the edge of the container when they are in full bloom, so plant an upright flower such as sturdy bachelor's buttons with them. Experiment with combinations of salpiglossis, love-in-a-mist, Johnny-jump-up, viola, pansy, celosia, or forget-me-not. When the annuals have finished flowering you can compost them with an easy conscience; they have finished their life cycle and will not flower again.

Try different flowering favorites to see how they grow in your home. They can also be started outside, until they flower, and then be brought inside. Below is a list of some flowering plants with which to create your indoor garden.

African violet	Calla	Dutch iris
Amaryllis	Canna	Dwarf citrus
Azalea	Cape primrose	Exacum or Persian violet
Bachelor's button	Celosia	Flowering maple
Begonia	Chrysanthemum	Forget-me-not
Black-eyed Susan vine	Cineraria	Freesia
Bougainvillea	Clivia or Kaffir lily	Fuchsia
Bromeliad	Columnea	Gardenia
Calceolaria	Crocus	Geranium
Calendula	Cyclamen	Ginger

Gloxinia	Love-in-a-mist	Pansy
Grape hyacinth	Marigold	Passionflower
Hibiscus	Morning glory	Petunia
Hyacinth	Narcissus	Poinsettia
Impatiens	Nasturtium	Ranunculus
Johnny-jump-up	Nicotiana	Salpiglossis
Kalanchoe	Orchids:	Scented geranium
Lantana	Cattleya,	Schizanthus
Lily of the Nile	Cymbidium,	Tulip
Lipstick plant	Phalaenopsis	Viola

SHADE FLOWER GARDEN

I have soothing memories of hot summer afternoons in my family garden. I loved lying under the shade trees on the cool grass and lazily watching the leaves, silhouetted against the sky, barely moving in the occasional breeze. The sunlight was soft and filtered through the branches. At those moments I felt enveloped by a comfortable stillness that led to flowering daydreams.

Shade seems to heighten the lush greens and vibrant colors of the plants. Have you noticed how vivid pink- and rose-colored impatiens look in a shady garden? One summer I saw a striking container-garden a woman grew on the shade porch of her house. Hanging next to each other from the rafters were baskets overflowing with tuberous begonias, fuchsias, and impatiens. The magentas, oranges, pinks, and wines of the flowers were so electric they almost seemed to glow!

Certain flowers grow better in cooler, shady areas than in hot sunlight. Others will not thrive without a high intensity of light and warmth. A shady flower garden may get as little as one or two hours of sun a day. Half shade refers to three or four hours of sun. Deep shade is filtered light through branches and leaves. Most shade-loving plants can tolerate a few hours of sun a day, provided it is not during the hottest midday hours; early morning or late afternoon are the best. Interestingly, in cool, summer coastal areas many shade plants grow well when planted in full sun because the intensity of the light and heat is modified by the ocean.

A shade garden planted with clusters of impatiens, purple-red fuchsias, and lush ferns is calming and restful. Plant masses of richly colored cinerarias, primroses, or cyclamen in garden beds, boxes, or pots. One of the most beautiful gardens I've seen was landscaped with cloud-like bushes of soft pink, lavender, apricot, and creamy white azaleas and rhododendrons under the partial shade of mature trees. These encircled a pond where a family of swans spent its time swimming a graceful water ballet.

Combine billowing blue hydrangeas, stately pink foxglove, and ample borders of rose-colored fibrous begonias. My own garden has a statue of a serene Buddha surrounded by impatiens and begonias, with

pink and mauve fuchsias hanging over him. Create small beds of sweet-scented violets and golden narcissus under trees to perfume the air as you stroll through your garden.

The following are some of the many flowering plants that thrive in the shade. All have different requirements for the amount of shade needed; investigate their individual needs before planting.

Ajuga	Day lily	Mignonette
Anemone	Flowering maple	Monkey flower
Azalea	Forget-me-not	Monkshood
Begonia	Foxglove	Narcissus
Bergenia	Fuchsia	Nicotiana
Bird-of-paradise	Globeflower	Periwinkle
Bleeding heart	Gloxinia	Primrose
Calla	Hellebore	Rhododendron
Camellia	Hepatica	Schizanthus
Campanula	Hosta	Scilla
Cardinal flower	Hydrangea	Shell ginger
Cineraria	Impatiens	Shooting star
Clivia or Kaffir lily	Iris	Star jasmine
Columbine	Jacob's ladder	Trillium
Coralbells	Kenilworth ivy	Viola
Cyclamen	Lady's slipper	Violet
Cymbidium orchid	Lily of the valley	Wild ginger
Daphne	Meadow rue	Wood sorrel

FLOWERS AS COMPANION PLANTS

In companion planting assorted flowers and vegetables are grown together in one area. Flowers planted with vegetables, fruits, and herbs throughout my garden help to discourage insects, attract bees, and help each other to grow healthy and strong. Exactly why this happens is not totally understood, but observation and testing have confirmed the results. In some cases the roots of a plant give off substances that affect its neighbors. Marigolds exude a compound from their roots that keeps nematodes away, and the strong odor of their flowers offends certain insects. Most aromatic flowering plants are repellent to the cabbage moth. Garlic and yarrow planted among herbs are said to increase the strength of the herbs' essential oils.

Insects are particular about what they eat and will be easily discouraged from devouring plants they like when they find distasteful plants nearby. They particularly dislike the onion family and marigolds; these can be used to edge a small garden bed like sentries. Nasturtiums are good to plant around fruit trees as they attract aphids and therefore keep them away from the trees. Borage and marigolds are known to defy the tomato hornworm and to attract bees. Basil also protects tomatoes from the hornworm and improves the plant's growth and flavor. Tansy has bright yellow flowers, a strong odor, and a bitter taste; it does not invite cucumber beetles, Japanese beetles, and cutworms. It also keeps away ants and protects fruit trees and roses. In addition to marigolds—scarlet sage, dahlias, calendulas, and garlic repel nematodes. Petunias are helpful planted at random in the garden as they protect beans and discourage aphids. The gopher plant can be used to help keep gophers and moles away. An edging of garlic chives with lovely purple flowers is good for roses, ornamentals, and fruit trees. Calendulas are a friend to almost all plants. Aromatic flowering herbs— lavender, thyme, sweet marjoram—are good to scatter throughout the garden as their scents repel many pests.

Pyrethrum flowers are the base of a commercial pesticide. White pyrethrum *(Chrysanthemum cinerariifolium)* is a perennial that grows to about one foot and is covered with daisy-like blossoms; it belongs to the Chrysanthemum family. Feverfew, similar to pyrethrum though not as strong, has small white daisy-like flowers, is very easy to grow, and reseeds itself abundantly. One initial planting will provide you with transplants to share.

Use the dried flowers of pyrethrum or feverfew to make natural insecticides. In the blender blend about one half cup to one cup dried blossoms to a powder, add two or three cups water, and mix well. Let it sit overnight and strain it the next day. For a consistency that is easier to apply, add about one quarter cup of liquid soap. Spray this mixture on insect-infested plants.

Experiment with these flowers and others using interplantings and liquid sprays. One way to test their effectiveness is to plant one bed of the same crop with companion flowers and one without. Or surround only one of several apple trees with nasturtiums. Observe how the plants and trees react. Remember that healthy, happy plants will resist disease and insects; flowers planted nearby can help by being their friends in times of need. Lists of flowers and their accompanying companion plants follow.

FLOWER	COMPANION PLANT
Basil	Tomato
Borage	Strawberry
(attracts bees)	Tomato
	Squash
Calendula	Almost all plants
Chamomile	Cabbage
	Onions
Chives	Fruit trees
	Roses
	Ornamentals
	Carrots

FLOWER	COMPANION PLANT
Dill	Cabbage
	Carrots
Feverfew	Many plants
(acts as an insecticide)	
Garlic	Roses and almost all plants
(increases strength	(except beans and peas)
of essential herb oils)	
Geranium, white	Roses
Marigold	Almost all plants
(attracts bees)	
Mints	Cabbage
	Tomato
Mustard	Cabbage
Nasturtium	Tomato
	Radish
	Cabbage
	Cucumber
	Fruit trees
	Squash
	Beans
Petunia	Fruit trees
	Roses
	Beans
	Many others
Pyrethrum	Almost all plants
(acts as an insecticide)	
Radish	Squash
	Melon
	Cucumber
Rosemary	Carrots
	Cabbage
	Beans
Rue	Roses
	Berries
	(dislikes basil)
Sunflower	Cucumber
Tansy	Fruit trees
	Roses
	Berries
	Squash
Yarrow	Herb plants
(increases strength of essential oils)	

BLOSSOMS AND BLOSSOMS OF FLOWERS

Blossoms and blossoms of healthy flowers are the bounty of your first garden of strong, vital plants. You have learned to dig into the earth, create healthy soil by adding nutrients to it, make raised beds, start seeds, and nourish them into mature flowers. You now have a sense of the many kinds of flowers you can use in designing your garden. You can delight your senses with different aromas, create meadows of wild flowers, find just the right plant for the shade, fill your small balcony with blossoming containers, or plan a spring bulb garden that will reappear year after year. As you perfect this art of gardening you will begin thinking about what to do with all the flowers you've grown.

The next three chapters will show you many ways to bring blossoms into your daily life. Chapter 3, Creative Flower Crafts, presents a variety of pressed, dried, aromatic, and long-lasting creations based on flowers. Chapter 4, Natural Flower Foods, provides unique recipes that incorporate edible flowers. In Flower Alchemy, Chapter 5, you'll be introduced to many flower body care products including salves, lotions, oils, and facials. Your home will soon be filled with tasteful, artistic, and healthful flower creations.

3
CREATIVE
FLOWER CRAFT

Your rosebush is bursting with plump pink blossoms, there are more marigolds than you can count, and the strawflowers are beginning to bloom. What are you going to do with all of them? Of course, you'll appreciate them in your garden and invite friends over to see them. But then what? Just let them wither on the stalks? Why not make attractive flower arrangements for your house or bring someone a bouquet as a gift?

Perhaps you also have a desire to preserve the flowers' beauty a bit longer. If so, there are many lovely things you can create with your flowers so that you can keep and enjoy them long after they are gone from your garden. Dry them for everlasting displays, press them to use in cards, books, pictures, or herbaria. Make festive garlands or wreaths. Create aromatic potpourris, sachets, pomanders, and pillows. Use flowers for dyeing yarn soft, natural colors. Your bountiful harvest of blossoms will beautify and scent your home all year long.

During the Middle Ages, potpourris, sachets, and pomanders were used to hide the unpleasant aromas of daily life and to protect against disease. In Victorian times, people began to create flower crafts for pleasure and beauty. They were fond of domesticating nature by bringing it indoors and made elaborate dried and pressed flower arrangements. The life-style then also gave birth to the language of flowers; they created meaningful bouquets of blossoms to convey intimate messages to friends and lovers.

In early America, making goods by hand was a matter of necessity rather than choice. A housewife was busy providing the basics of food, clothing, and shelter for her family. She only had time to dry wild flowers or grasses to decorate her home.

Today crafts have again found their place in American households. Increased leisure time makes it possible to learn some of the handicrafts that were once the skills of daily life. There is a joy in creating your own original flower crafts and working with the simple materials nature provides.

FLOWER ARRANGING

A gracefully arranged bouquet is one of the simplest and most delightful ways to bring flowers into your home. The flower arrangements I make are inspired by the flowers available each season. I see which flowers, flowering herbs, and leaves are in the garden or at flower shops, then combine them into full bouquets. Early spring calls for fragrant daffodils, hyacinths, narcissus, and sprigs of rosemary or peppermint. One of my fondest memories is of the huge bouquets of lilacs my mother would put in my bedroom; their enveloping aroma would soothe me to sleep and when I awoke I was reminded that warm days had arrived.

Later in the season, gather columbines, lavender spikes, pinks, roses, baby's breath, scented geraniums, sweet basil, and thyme for colorful perfumed displays. I like to use teapots, silver serving dishes, crocks, and old colored-glass bottles as well as elegant vases for arrangements. One flower in a glass bowl can be eloquent; I sometimes float a gardenia in a brandy snifter for an understated but stunning effect. Display a single rosebud, carnation, or calendula in a small vase or bottle. A woven basket can conceal a tin can or glass jar full of flowers that spill over its edges.

Sometimes a glass or metal florist's "frog" (a small, heavy holder with holes or sharp prongs), bent chicken wire, or florist's clay is needed to help hold the flowers upright. If you have access to lots of short-stemmed flowers, such as dahlias or roses, use a large shallow bowl, bend chicken wire to fit near the top, and fill the bowl with water. Fit the spaces in the wire with the flowers; the entire surface will be floating with color.

I shape arrangements naturally and easily. Tall flowers can rise from the center of a container. Move the shorter ones down to trail over the edges. Fill in the bouquet with light open flowers—baby's breath or flowering grass. Add rosemary, lemon balm, or other herbs for their scent and foliage. Make the bouquets full but be sure they aren't crowded.

Wild flowers look best unarranged, as in nature. One day I was walking to a friend's house for dinner and decided to pick a bouquet of wild flowers and herbs I found along the way. I gathered yarrow, broom, star tulip, self-heal, iris, dandelion, wild honeysuckle, clover, wild rose, mugwort, sagebrush, and ferns. The arrangement developed in my hand as I added each new flower and leaf. They were ready to put in a container just as I had gathered them. It's this kind of spontaneity that most often inspires me when I arrange flowers.

IKEBANA—JAPANESE FLOWER ARRANGING

In Japan, flower arranging, *ikebana*, is an art like painting or sculpture that is taught from childhood; historically it was man's work and even the soldier or *samurai* would learn it. It was said that *ikebana* originated with Buddhist monks who would gather the flowers and broken twigs that lay on the ground after a storm. Revering the holiness of all life, they carefully arranged them into bouquets. Thus, *ikebana* was born and still flourishes after fourteen hundred years. The Japanese have always expressed a love of nature in their art, and *ikebana* reflects this by representing the harmony of nature.

There are many styles of *ikebana*. Each has specific requirements as to the placement of every branch and flower, the design, color relationships, and the container used. Each component in the arrangement has a special name. In many larger cities courses in *ikebana* are available; practical books can also serve as guides in learning this traditional art form. Its technique can serve as an inspiration for creative flower arranging.

PREPARING FLOWERS FOR ARRANGEMENTS

There are a few guidelines to follow in preparing successful flower arrangements. The best times to gather flowers are early morning, before the sun rises, and late afternoon, when they are at their peak. When you cut flowers off a plant you are pruning it and increasing the plant's ability to produce more flowers. If the blossoms are left to create seed, it will cause the whole plant to stop flowering. As a general practice, only gather flowers where there is an abundance of them and always leave some on the plant. Use a sharp tool to cut the stalk cleanly; do not tear it. For a longer-lasting bouquet pick some flowers that are in bud and some that are nearly open.

Carry a bucket or jar of water with you to put the flowers in immediately after cutting. They may be left in this container for a few hours. Before making your arrangement recut the stems at an angle. This allows for more absorption of water. Gently hammer the ends of those flowers that have woody stems, such as lilacs, in order to split them. Use a match to lightly burn the cut ends of blossoms with a milky sap, such as the poppy, to seal them. Remove leaves that would be submerged. Change the water in vases every few days and recut the stems at the same time. A couple of drops of bleach will sweeten the water and keep it from smelling. Be careful not to add too much. Keep the arrangement out of direct sunlight.

FLOWERS THAT ARRANGE WELL

Following are lists of selected cultivated, wild, and herb flowers that are particularly suited for arrangements because of their ability to last when cut. They also offer a wide variety of colors, shapes, and aromas. They are the flowers you will want to grow in your own garden if you are fond of making floral displays.

CULTIVATED FLOWERS FOR ARRANGEMENTS

Anemone	Bells of Ireland	Celosia
Anthurium	Bird-of-paradise	Chrysanthemum
Aster	Calendula	Cleome
Baby's breath	Camellia	Columbine
Bachelor's button	Carnation	Coreopsis

Cosmos	Larkspur	Rose
Daffodil	Lilac	Rose Campion
Dahlia	Linaria	Rudbeckia
Daisy	Marguerite	Safflower
Delphinium	Marigold	Salpiglossis
Dusty miller	Narcissus	Shasta daisy
Forget-me-not	Nasturtium	Snapdragon
Forsythia	Nicotiana	Statice
Freesia	Orchid	Stock
Fuchsia	Painted daisy	Strawflower
Gaillardia	Pansy	Sweet pea
Gardenia	Peony	Sweet William
Geranium	Petunia	Tulip
Geum	Phlox	Viola
Gladiolus	Pincushion flower	Wallflower
Heather	Poppy	Yarrow
Hollyhock	Protea	Zinnia
Iris	Ranunculus	

WILD FLOWERS FOR ARRANGEMENTS

Blue-eyed grass	Mullein	Sorrel
Cattail	Mustard	Tansy
Dock	Pearly everlasting	Thistle
Forget-me-not	Plantain	Violet
Goldenrod	Queen Anne's lace	Wild onion
Indian paintbrush	Saint-John's-wort	Wild rose
Mugwort	Scotch broom	Yarrow

FLOWERING HERBS FOR ARRANGEMENTS

Basil	Mints:	Scented geraniums:
Bergamot	Apple	Apple
Dill	Orange	Lemon
Feverfew	Peppermint	Nutmeg
Garlic chive	Spearmint	Peppermint
Hyssop	Rosemary	Rose
Lavender	Rue	Sweet marjoram
Lemon balm	Sage	Thyme
Lemon verbena	Santolina	Wormwood

MAY DAY BASKETS

A tradition I like to revive is that of bringing fresh flowers to friends on May Day. These bouquets are harbingers of spring and the yearly renewal of life. The custom originated in Roman times when a spring festival was dedicated to Flora, the goddess of flowers. This was held just before May first to celebrate the end of winter and to ask for the goddess' favor for a bountiful spring. The Romans brought the custom to England, where it became known as May Day. Part of the celebration was to leave baskets or garlands of flowers on the doorsteps of houses. To make your own May Day basket, gather flowers and fill a small straw basket with them. Tie a ribbon on it and give it to a friend in celebration of a happy spring.

TUZZY-MUZZY AND THE LANGUAGE OF FLOWERS

During the Victorian era in England, speaking with flowers became the rage; each blossom in a bouquet had a specific meaning. This language of flowers came from France in the early nineteenth century, a time when French artists were painting lavish florals. It arrived in England during the time of George IV and reached its peak in 1840 during the reign of Queen Victoria. Flower language came to America several years later. Dictionaries of this language became very popular. One could express devotion, passion, anger, jealousy, and other

feelings or thoughts through the use of bouquets or of cards portraying the appropriate blossoms. A problem arose when flowers would be listed in dictionaries with different meanings. To interpret a friend's or lover's message correctly it was vital to use the same flower dictionary.

A popular form of expression was the tuzzy-muzzy, or nosegay. The artfulness of these bouquets of flowers and herbs came in carefully choosing and arranging the appropriate ones for specific messages. The stems of the flowers were covered in lace or a doily and tied together with a ribbon. A bouquet of pansies, peppermint, and honeysuckle indicated thoughts of warm feeling, love, and affection. Lavender, love-in-a-mist, and foxglove told of distrust, perplexity, and insincerity. Different varieties and colors of roses had particular meanings: A white one alone would say I am worthy of you; a red rosebud meant pure and lovely; and a Carolina rose declared that love is dangerous. To send a white and red rose encircled by ivy was to speak of unity and marriage. A wilted white rose with garden anemone told of the end of a relationship. A red tulip surrounded by purple lilacs was a declaration of deep love after the first emotions of love. White lilacs, white lilies, and white rosebuds complemented innocence, purity, and girlhood. Lily of the valley meant the return of happiness, and spring crocus signified youthful gladness—good reason to celebrate.

Imagine the extremes to which this may have been carried. Admirers communicated without identifying themselves. There were secret love affairs, passion was spoken through flowers, unhappiness and remorse were expressed with blossoms. How indirect and very romantic! The flower garden became more than a simple source of enjoyment; it was a compendium of sentiments. Flowers were grown to express the deepest of feelings.

A drawing or painting of flowers held hidden meanings that made it more than just a still life. Poems were written using the language of flowers. Kate Greenaway, the English illustrator of children's books, published her *Language of Flowers* in the late nineteenth century. This book remains in print today to serve as a guide to anyone who might want to revive the charming custom of sending flower messages.

DRIED FLOWERS

My favorite way to use dried flowers is to hang bouquets of them upside down from a beam, over a window, or on the wall. High above my stove is a wooden beam from which I've hung full bunches of strawflowers, roses, statice, and baby's breath. I keep about ten bouquets in a space of four and one half feet; they brighten my whole kitchen. When I include aromatic flowering herbs in my dried bouquets their healing scents fill the whole house.

The Upside-down Method

The easiest way to dry flowers is to tie a bunch together and hang them upside down in a cool, airy place out of direct sunshine. If they can't be kept out of strong light, paper bags, left open at the bottom, may be placed over them. Remove the foliage to avoid the shedding of dried leaves when working with the flowers later. Make the bouquets small enough so they will dry well, but large enough to look full and colorful.

Roses respond well to this method. I still have my birthday bouquet of long-stemmed red roses from five years ago. I turned them upside down to dry them, then hung the dried blossoms right side up on the wall. Dried bouquets are attractive in a vase, old antique jar, or similar container. Little dried rosebuds and roses find their way into many shelves and nooks in my house. Their simple beauty adds a charming touch to a spice shelf or a bathroom mirror. You can also string rosebuds and suspend them from beams or across windows.

There are many flowers that hold their shape and color well when dried in this way. They include the everlastings—strawflowers, statice, and globe amaranth—whose petals are already nearly dry. I once grew a small garden of these flowers and they provided many blossoms for making wreaths and bouquets for myself and my friends. Cut everlasting flowers before they are in full bloom; they will continue to open indoors. Gather them on a warm, dry day to avoid picking them with moisture, which might cause mold.

FLOWERS TO DRY UPSIDE DOWN

Acacia	Hollyhock	Safflower
Acroclinium	Honesty or Money	Scotch broom
Artichoke	plant	Sea holly
Baby's breath	Hydrangea	Starflower or Star
Bells of Ireland	Lamb's ears	everlasting
Cardoon	Lavender	Statice
Cattail	Love-in-a-mist	Strawflower
Celosia	Mullein	Sunflower
Chinese lantern	Onion	Tansy
Cupid's dart	Pampas grass	Teasel
Dock	Pearly everlasting	Thistle
Garlic	Pennyroyal	Wild buckwheat
Globe amaranth	Poppy seed heads	Winged everlasting or
Globe thistle	Protea	Ammobium
Goldenrod	Quaking grass	Xeranthemum
Grasses	Queen Anne's lace	Yarrow
Heather	Rhodanthe	

GATHERING AND DRYING
FLOWERS WITH DESICCANTS

I enjoy capturing a blossom at its moment of perfection and preserving it to display in the middle of winter. Several methods may be used to dry flowers that might otherwise be but a summer's memory. Sand, silica, and borax are desiccants—drying mediums—that are quite easy to use. They pull all the moisture out of the flower in a slow but thorough dehydrating process.

Gather flowers at their peak of beauty on a dry day after all the moisture has evaporated from the plant. Wilted, wet, or damaged flowers will not dry well. The colors will change as they dry: the reds, pinks, and purples will darken; the whites will brown a bit; the deep purples and reds will turn nearly black. Yellow to orange flowers keep the vibrancy of their colors the best.

Use a container large enough and deep enough to hold the desiccant and the flowers you want to dry—a small cardboard box, shoe box, or large tin. For example, if the flower, head and stem, measures 6 inches you will need a box about 10 inches deep. Remove the foliage from the stems, and put a 1- to 2-inch layer of sand or other desiccant in the bottom of the container. Arrange the blossoms on this base and carefully begin to "rain" the sand, silica gel, or other medium over the flowers until they are thoroughly covered. Place the box in a warm, dry location where it will be undisturbed. Be sure to cover it tightly if you use silica gel, which absorbs moisture from the air. Leave one blossom toward the top where it can be easily tested for dryness; the flowers will feel "crisp" when properly dried. Gently remove each blossom and dust it off with a soft paintbrush. At this point the flowers may be sprayed lightly with a flat lacquer, but I prefer to leave them natural.

Flowers with heavy heads and weak dried stems, such as tulip, rose, calendula, and pansy should have their stems replaced with florist's wire before drying. Put the wire through the calyx and the flower head; when it is through, bend it slightly and pull it down so that it is hidden and holds well.

There are some specific guidelines for arranging flowers in the boxes. Rose, tulip, camellia, columbine, iris, peony, pansy, violet, and daffodil dry best when arranged with their "blossoms straight up." Cut the stems to an inch, or, if a long stem is desired, use a deep box and a flexible yet strong florist's wire and green florist's tape to wrap around it. These are available at most florist shops, craft stores, and plant nurseries. Bend the wire to facilitate the drying process. Make a small hole in the drying medium; place the upright flower in it and sift the sand or other desiccant over it until well covered.

Other flowers dry well with their stems up and their blossoms pointing down. Large clusters and many composites—hydrangea, daisy, calendula, rudbeckia, cosmos, dahlia, and zinnia—dry well in this position. Place the flowers with their stems up on the drying medium

and sprinkle it over them until the flowers and stems disappear.

Still other flowers, especially those with long clusters, can be dried "laying down." These include hyacinth, bougainvillea, stock, lilac, honeysuckle, snapdragon, and sweet pea. Place the flowers on a layer of desiccant and cover them carefully.

Smaller flowers, such as buttercup, lily of the valley, orchid, pinks, and marigold can be dried at an "angle." They can retain more of their own stem than those dried in the other positions. Make an indentation on an angle into the drying medium with your finger into which the stems can be placed. Then gently cover the flower heads with the desiccant, working slowly and attentively.

Sand

The use of sand is one of the oldest methods of drying flowers. The sand should be fine and light, sandbox quality. It may be found on white sand beaches, around lakes, or riverbeds. Sand can usually be purchased at plant nurseries or other garden supply stores. Experiment with the lightest sand available to you; screen out large pebbles or rocks before using. A friend who lives right on the seashore in British Columbia, Canada brings sand in from the beach, removes any large twigs or rocks, and then preserves the beautiful flowers of Vancouver Island. Flowers keep their color well when this method of drying is used and may be kept in the sand a long time without risking damage.

Silica Gel

Silica gel is a chemical product that closely resembles sand in texture, but has little blue grains in it. The blue disappears when all the moisture in the flowers has been absorbed; this way you can tell when the flowers are dry. Remember to store it in an airtight container before and after use.

Putting your flowers with silica gel in a barely warm oven speeds up the drying process, but takes ten to thirty hours of baking, depending upon the size of the flowers. Silica gel may be reused by drying it out in a warm oven.

Borax and Other Methods

A mixture of two parts borax to ten parts cornmeal will dry flowers effectively but cannot be reused. I've also heard that kitty litter, sawdust, and powder can be used as desiccants, but I've found that sand, silica gel, and borax are superior.

FLOWERS TO DRY WITH DESICCANTS

The following flowers are particularly suited for drying with desiccants because their large, soft petals easily yield their moisture to the drying medium without losing their shape or color. Most of these flowers would just wilt and shrivel up were they to be hung upside down to be air dried. Some of them, such as the rose and hydrangea, are suited to both methods, though only desiccant-dried roses will retain their full-bloom appearance. Experiment. Many flowers will dry well using this method.

Ageratum	Dahlia	Lily of the valley
Anemone	Daisy	Love-in-a-mist
Aster	Day lily	Magnolia
Azalea	Delphinium	Marigold
Bachelor's button	Fuchsia	Orchid
Black-eyed Susan	Geum	Pansy
Bougainvillea	Gladiolus	Peony
Calendula	Hollyhock	Rose
Camellia	Honeysuckle	Snapdragon
Carnation	Hyacinth	Stock
Chrysanthemum	Hydrangea	Sweet pea
Columbine	Iris	Tulip
Cosmos	Larkspur	Violet
Daffodil	Lilac	Zinnia

DRIED FLOWER ARRANGEMENTS

Dried flowers can be mixed with other plant materials, silver dollar eucalyptus and grasses, for example, to make long-lasting arrangements. Effective bouquets can be created around a particular theme. I like to make them with flowers all of a single color tone or by using a whole mass of one variety of flower. The larger, heavy blossoms look best placed lower in the arrangement, with the smaller blossoms mixed around and above them. I find it helpful to create a basic shape first, then add the central flowers. Fill the bouquet in with leaves, ferns, grasses, or berries for volume and design, to contrast with or complement your flowers.

I've also made arrangements enclosed in glass or Plexiglas boxes or domes. This is a good idea if you're using desiccant-dried flowers, which tend to regain moisture and wilt when displayed in a damp place.

One bouquet of dried flowers can transform a room with its color. A basket filled with a solid mass of purple, yellow, white, and pink statice is a striking arrangement. I made a large flower bouquet in half of an old, intricately woven Afghan saddlebag; its brilliant hues liven up a plain wall. Dried bouquets, hung upside down or right side up, can be effective decorative accents in corners or on walls or shelves.

PRESSED FLOWERS

Pressing flowers is a way to preserve both botanical specimens and favorite garden blossoms. I have a fifty-year-old book, *Flowers from the Holy Land,* of pressed flowers that had been carefully mounted and arranged. A thin piece of tissue protects each page; the flowers are still colorful and well preserved. This book inspired me to write and design several small handmade books of pressed blossoms and poems. Flowers and words blended together to make each page an exciting creation. There are many ways to use pressed flowers, but first you'll want to gather them carefully to preserve their fresh look.

COLLECTING FLOWERS FOR PRESSING

Collect flowers to be pressed after a few days of dry weather on a clear day when the dew has evaporated. If the flowers are damp, they may turn black or brown when pressed. When gathering or traveling, take along a phone book or magazine to put the flowers in until you get home to the press. I've often found lovely flowers when I've been out for a walk and unsuccessfully tried to preserve them in my hand or in a scrap of paper in my pocket. It's important to press flowers as soon as possible after picking them. Label the page on which you dry them with their name, the date, and where they were found.

The Flower Press

A press can be made from newspapers or phone books, but the most effective press is a layered arrangement of wood, cardboard, blotter, and paper that is quite easy to construct. Start with two pieces of plywood large enough for most flowers or plants; mine are 12 by 15 by ¾ inches. Place one piece of plywood on the table, then put on top of it a piece of corrugated cardboard, a blotter, a folded newspaper, another blotter, and another piece of corrugated cardboard, all about the same size as the plywood. Continue layering as needed, placing the flowers to be pressed between the folded newspapers. Top with the remaining piece of plywood and press tightly together with rope, belts, C-clamps, long bolts with wing nuts, or a heavy weight. The corrugated cardboard provides air circulation; the blotters absorb moisture; the newspaper provides an absorbing neutral medium; the plywood provides firmness, and the clamps or rope provide the pressure. Put the press in a warm place. It may be necessary to change the blotters if they become too damp. Flowers will press well and keep their color provided they are gathered properly and kept out of direct light. When the flowers are completely dry, store them in newspaper, envelopes, or in a book, with their names and dates recorded.

Arranging for Pressing

Arrange the flowers on the newspaper in the form you want them to maintain. Try bending, curving, and arranging blossoms naturally and artistically. Gather flowers in their many stages of development; in bud, partially opened, and in full blossom. Don't forget some leaves. Sometimes it's necessary to break the flower apart with flower heads, stems, leaves, and buds all dried separately. There are hundreds of flowers to press; large, many-petaled, succulent, or thick flowers are more difficult to use.

FLOWERS TO PRESS AND OTHER SUGGESTIONS

The following flowers are particularly good for pressing because they hold their color well when dry, are easy to work with, and do not contain a lot of water. Experiment with others that grow in your area.

Pressed flowers preserved in books retain their color much longer than those exposed to light. I love the soft tones that develop as they age; the pinks that darken to lavender or purple, the yellows that lighten, and the greens that turn to brown. Pressed blossoms with their subtle hues are yet another aspect of the flowers' beauty.

WILD FLOWERS

Azalea	Fireweed	Poppy
Bindweed	Forget-me-not	Radish
Blue-eyed grass	Geranium	Rose
Broom	Indian paintbrush	Saint-John's-wort
Buckwheat	Larkspur	Scarlet pimpernel
Buttercup	Mallow	Sun cup
Chicory	Mustard	Wood sorrel
Clarkia	Penstemon	
Daisy	Phlox	

GARDEN FLOWERS

Baby's breath	Hibiscus	Pinks
Bachelor's button	Hollyhock	Poppy petals
Bougainvillea	Hydrangea	Primrose
Cineraria	(MY FAVORITE)	Sage
Clematis	Johnny-jump-up	Schizanthus
Coralbells	Lobelia	Sweet alyssum
Cosmos	Marigold	Viola
Daisy	Pansy	Violet
Delphinium	Phlox	

PRESSED FLOWER CRAFT

When the outdoor activities of spring and summer begin to slow down, it's time to take out your collection of pressed flowers. There are many things you can make with them, such as one-of-a-kind books, journals, traditional herbaria, attractive framed arrangements, cards, and calendars.

Books and Journals

There were several steps in the creation of my pressed flower poetry books; here is how I made one of them. First, I chose twenty poems I had written. Then I had my sister make a small hand-bound book. Next, I looked through all the flowers I had pressed to see how they could be used. The design was laid out, and the poetry was written in. Each page became a painting, an expression of mood and feeling. I had lovely, soft blue and lavender hydrangeas and pink, red, and orange bougainvillea.

I arranged them in a free-form design around the poem so that the page was full of blossoms.

To glue the flowers on the page you will need water-diluted white glue that becomes clear when dry, an ink roller, rolling pin, or bottle, a paintbrush, waxed paper, and paper towels. Place the flowers carefully face down on the waxed paper and paint the back of them with glue. Or put a layer of glue on a piece of glass and place the flowers on it. If a flower is too wet or too dry, it comes apart. It's a delicate process and must be done with care.

Once the flowers are coated, lay them on the page. They're not easy to move, so have the design well planned and marked lightly with a pencil. When all the flowers are on the page, cover with paper towel and run the ink roller over it to take up any extra glue. Place a layer of waxed paper between each page until the glue is dry. Continue in this way— arranging, gluing, rolling, and so on until the book is complete. I've made several of these special one-of-a-kind books, using inexpensive blank books that I have covered with beautiful material. They are very rewarding to create and to give!

Another way to use pressed flowers is in a journal, reflecting the mood of a day or month or season. Journals are personal and flowers can help to recapture a peaceful walk in the woods or a friendly visit to a neighbor's garden. The book might simply contain pressed flowers from the garden or from out in the wild, the theme varying with the season, location, variety, or color.

Herbaria

An herbarium is a collection of pressed flowers or plants well mounted on heavy white paper with specific botanical information—the date, the location where the specimen was found, and often, its historical uses. There are extensive herbaria that catalog many of the plants that exist on earth. For example, the herbarium of The New York Botanical Garden in the Bronx has four and a half million plant specimens carefully preserved. Herbaria provide accurate and helpful information for the botanist, herbalist, scientist, and other plant enthusiast.

Interest in recording and keeping plant specimens began with the publication of the first herbals in the fifteenth century. Plants were then of great notice for medicinal as well as botanical purposes. People wanted to know more about them and compare them with the flora growing in their own areas. It wasn't until the mid-sixteenth century that preserving plants in an organized manner became increasingly important and the first herbarium was begun by an Italian botanist, Andrea Cesalpino. Other European botanists followed his example. Herbaria grew in popularity and also in accuracy as the need to classify plants more specifically became established. They were useful in examining and ordering plants according to their evolutionary development. From these early models, vast herbaria have been created in many universities, museums and private collections. Studying them provides a greater understanding of the many ways plants have been and can be used.

Your personal herbarium can catalog the flowers in your garden or the wild ones in your area. I made one to record my flower dye experiments. Every plant was pressed with details of the experiment and samples of the dyed wool, silk and cotton fibers. An herbarium might also show the members of a particular botanical family; such as the rose, mustard, or pea family. Or it can simply contain your favorite flowers.

The first step in making your own herbarium is to press the flowers. When they are ready, heavy paper is needed for mounting; it can be colorful construction paper, heavy white paper, or any good quality paper that is strong. Glue the pressed flowers onto the page as described in the previous section on books. Each page can be designed and executed distinctively, using calligraphy for the common name, Latin name, location, date, and uses. Your herbarium pages may then be compiled into a book or attractively framed to display in your home.

Pressed Flower Pictures

One of my very special possessions is a tiny wild flower mounted on velvet in a round, silver frame that was pressed in Denmark during a friend's childhood. It must be thirty years old now and has unique and personal charm.

To make a flower picture find a suitable frame. I love antique frames that have been passed down through the years. It's often a good idea to make your first picture small. Next decide on a background; white or colored paper or any single color cloth, such as velvet. Using the glass as a guide, cut this to fit the frame. Then glue the material onto strong cardboard. Arrange the flowers in a creative design, keeping in mind color, shapes, sizes, and overall composition. Fill in the picture with leaves and weeds. Finally, using a water-soluble white glue, secure the flowers, leaves, and stems carefully to the surface. When dry, put the picture in the frame, cover it with glass, and remember to hang it on a wall out of direct sunlight.

Pressed Flower Cards and Calendars

The easiest method of making cards with pressed flowers is to design an arrangement and glue it directly onto the front of a folded piece of heavy paper or card stock. Choose complementary colors to set off the flowers. One card I made was a poem written on rice paper. Pressed hydrangea blossoms surrounded it, falling lightly down the page. The cover I made for it was with different rice paper and more flowers. Its oversized envelope was sealed with one blossom. Play with creating your own cards; large or small the results will be appreciated.

A calendar is a wonderful way to herald the arrival of each month with its own flowers. Use a medium to heavy weight paper and leave an area for each month for single or multiple flower arrangements. Early spring might be illustrated with violets and forget-me-nots. June might blossom with pansies and cosmos. The flowers can be gracefully arranged over the entire page. A special flower may be placed on a date to remind you when it usually blooms or of an important date. Make the calendar as simple or complex as you like, always allowing the special qualities of the flowers to inspire you.

There are other things you can create with pressed flowers, such as bookmarks or place settings. Send a sweet message by enclosing a nicely pressed blossom in a letter or gluing it to stationery and then adding a drop of scented oil.

GARLANDS

Ancient Greek literature tells of maidens wearing garlands of hyacinths at weddings and guests being given garlands of violets and other aromatic flowers before banquets. In his *Metamorphoses* Ovid wrote of a woman:

. . . her hair is smoothed with a comb: now she decks herself with rosemary, again with violets and roses, sometimes with lilies.

Flowers served as fragrant substitutes for costly perfumes. The Romans also used garlands for their special occasions—weddings, ceremonies, and sacred celebrations. Flowers were grown specifically for making garlands and there were skilled artisans to create them.

There is a Greek myth that tells how garlands of bay laurel came into existence. The graceful nymph Daphne was amorously pursued by Apollo, the god of art and beauty. He had boasted to Cupid, the god of love, who in anger struck them both with his arrows—one to fall in love and one to reject love. Daphne fled from Apollo's advances (due to Cupid's tricks) and prayed to her father to save her. By the time Apollo caught her, she had been transformed into an elegant tree—the bay laurel. This became sacred to Apollo and from that time on he wore a garland of laurel. Laurel garlands were given as prizes to the winners in the Pythian games in Apollo's festival, and have since been the symbol of victory.

Garlands were also given to Roman actors and actresses after pleasing entertainment. This custom is continued today when performers receive bouquets of flowers in appreciation of a fine performance.

The English were fond of garlands; Gerard in his seventeenth-century *Herbal* mentions them frequently. He speaks of sweet violet garlands "which are delightful to look on and pleasant to smell." He also describes the benefits of wearing a rosemary garland:

> If a garland [of rosemary] . . . be put about the head it comforteth the brain, the memory, the inward senses and comforteth the heart and maketh it merry.

One of the loveliest ways to celebrate spring is to wear a garland of fresh flowers woven into a headband and tied with long streamers of colorful ribbons. Sandro Botticelli's late fifteenth-century painting "Primavera" shows Flora, the goddess of flowers, in a long flowered dress with blossoms in her hair and a similar garland around her neck.

Begin a garland by gathering the supple branches of willow, bay, or fern. Braid them together in a circle large enough to fit around the head. Then add the flowers by simply weaving their stems into and out of the base. Long ribbons can be tied on to help hold it together and to add a touch of floating color. Another method is to use everlasting flowers attached to a thin wire circle. Fit this to your head and add ribbons to it. This type of garland is made in the same way as a wreath; I'll describe that technique in detail a little further on.

The Hawaiians have a tradition of giving a sweet-smelling *lei* to people arriving at or leaving their islands. These are three to four feet of flowers strung together with thread or light cord, then tied to hang around the neck like a long flower necklace. *Leis* are made from the aromatic pikake, plumeria, tuberose, orchid, and carnation. Once the blossoms fade, they can be dried to add their fragrance to potpourris.

WREATHS

Wreaths are ancient symbols; Egyptian art shows that they accompanied the dead on their voyage to the other world. Throughout the ages the weaving of plants and flowers in circular form has been a material expression of the continuing cycles of the seasons, of birth, death, and rebirth.

I learned to make wreaths from a friend who creates them each year from the herbs and flowers she grows. Begin your own by gathering together the materials you will need. Flexible but strong wire, such as a lightweight clothes hanger or baling wire, is used as a base. Then pick only fresh flowers and herbs; dried plant material is too brittle to use. My first wreath was made from eucalyptus buttons, purple acacia leaves and blossoms, heather flowers, lavender spikes, and scented geranium leaves. After many years it's still hanging in my kitchen. Everlasting flowers make colorful wreaths. Cut them before they are fully open; they will continue to bloom after they are woven into the wreath. Straw or pine needles attached to the wire make a firmer and wider base for the wreath. You will also need heavy green string, chenille yarn, or other strong cord to bind the flowers onto the base. When all the materials are gathered begin the wreath.

Steps in Wreath-making

1. Plan a small wreath, three to four inches in diameter. Finished wreaths look much larger than the size of the wire circle on which they are mounted and require a lot of plant material. Bend the wire around a circular form, a bowl, large can, or saucepan, to the desired size. Use pliers to twist the ends over each other to fasten them.

2. Make small, but full, bunches three to four inches long, of the plant material you will tie onto the base; begin with about fifteen bunches. For a strawflower wreath, use about four or five straw-flowers per bunch.

3. Cut a long piece of heavy green string or green chenille yarn and tie it onto the frame.

4. If you are using pine needles or straw as a base, tie handfuls of it onto the wire, securing it with string or yarn, until the wire is covered. Then tie another string onto them.

5. Wrap the stems of one bunch of flowers tightly onto the frame with the string. Start at the point on the frame where the string is attached. Place the next bunch of flowers over the wrapped stems of the first and attach it tightly to the frame by winding the string around the stems. Fit the bundles close together. The flowers of the second bunch should cover the wrapped stems of the first.

6. Continue securing the plant material until the wreath is complete. The last bundle is sometimes difficult to wrap; proceed carefully.

7. Tie the string in a knot close to the wire and make a loop from which the wreath can hang.

8. When the wreath is assembled it's usually necessary to adjust it by twisting the flowers and plants around a bit. This makes it full and balanced and will hide any visible string. If necessary, add a dried flower or leaf branch.

Making a wreath takes patience; plan to take your time and enjoy the rhythm of wrapping and tying. Hang the completed work on a wall or door out of the sun. If it is made from long-lasting flowers and plant materials you will delight in its gaiety and beauty for many years.

WREATH MATERIALS

Acacia	Globe amaranth	Rose
Acroclinium	Globe thistle	Rosemary
Baby's breath	Grasses	Safflower
Bay	Heather	Sage
Bells of Ireland	Holly	Santolina
Broom	Honesty	Scented geranium
Celosia	Hydrangea	Sea holly
Chinese lantern	Lamb's ears	Starflower or Star everlasting
Cupid's dart	Lavender	Statice
Dock	Pennyroyal	Strawflower
Eucalyptus	Pyracantha	Wild buckwheat
Evergreens	Rhodanthe	Yarrow

ROSE BEADS

Handmade beads created from rose petals can be passed down from one generation to the next, just like fine pearls. Any fragrant rose petals will work, but the best are the old-fashioned damask, cabbage, or musk rose. Gather the petals early in the morning on a clear, warm day after the dew has dried. Use a mortar and pestle to grind or crush the petals. Spread these on waxed paper to dry. Then return them to the mortar and add water or oil to form a paste. You don't want it too thin, so add the liquid drop by drop; it should have a thick dough-like consistency. Decide on the size of the finished bead and with your fingertips dipped in rose oil roll a piece of the mixture into a ball twice the size of the bead you want. Set the bead on waxed paper to dry. Before all the moisture is evaporated pierce it with a needle or fine wire to make a hole for stringing. Return the beads to the paper to finish drying. Turn them frequently.

In a few days they will be ready. For a nice polish put them in a cloth bag and gently rub them together. Then string and enjoy. If the beads lose their scent, sprinkle a few drops of rose oil on them. They will turn a deep wine color and smell of summer's finest fragrances.

A BASKET OF ROSES

One year I decided to create a basket of roses to give as a gift to friends. The project began with the first rose blossom and continued all summer. I gathered and dried petals from my garden, from friends' gardens, and found prunings in an urban neighborhood. From the fresh petals I made rose beads, rose jam, rose treats, rosemary honey facial, rose facial vinegar, and rose water. Dried petals were mixed with other aromatics in potpourris, sachets, pillows, and baths. I picked and dried small rosebuds to string. The choicest long-stemmed blooms were hung upside down in bunches to dry, later to be turned right side up in a dry bouquet. In the fall I gathered rose hips and strung them into necklaces, then hung them to dry in a warm place out of the sun.

All this was arranged in a lovely handwoven basket with the dried roses carefully laid on top. Imagine the delight of your friends to be so indulged with roses and your own pleasure in gathering and creating the rose-gifts. All these recipes can be found in this chapter and the two following. Start collecting roses now for your rose basket!

POTPOURRIS AND SACHETS

Luxuriate in the sheer pleasure of sweet floral aromas. Potpourris and sachets can scent rooms or be tucked into drawers, closets, beds, linens, suitcases, or purses.

Potpourris and sachets originated in the Middle Ages when it was the custom to walk down the street with a small bag of herbs covering the mouth and nose in order to mask the odors of insufficient sanitation. It has been borne out in modern times that certain strong fragrances can be antiseptic and can help to protect those who use them from infection and disease. Different aromas affect us in different ways (see Chapter 6), so a potpourri or sachet can be created for a specific mood or need.

The word potpourri means a mixture of many ingredients; today we know it as a specific mixture of aromatic flowers and herbs. The ingredients for sachets are similar, though potpourris have dried flowers, without any scent, added to them for color. Sachets are small cloth bags filled with a combination of aromatic flowers and flowering herbs. They can be placed in dressers and closets in order to scent clothes and to keep moths or other insects from woolens. Potpourris are stored in containers, such as jars or baskets, in order to scent a room. One of the nicest ones I've seen was a basket that covered a bathroom shelf; it was brimming with aromatic flowers and dried roses of all sizes.

The secret of these creations is to blend a harmonious perfume from many different aromas. It is the perfect combination of fragrances that makes for a unique and delicious potpourri or sachet. Many flowers can be bought already dried, but collecting and drying your own is a pleasure in itself. You can begin gathering them in early spring with the first violets; continue into the summer with roses, honeysuckle, jasmine, lavender, rosemary, sweet woodruff, and pansies, and end with the rich autumn colors of calendula and chrysanthemum. Gather them on clear dry days when the dew has evaporated and at least two days after a rainfall. In the morning, flowers are said to be most filled with their essential oils. Pick the freshest, fullest flowers; avoid ones that are damaged.

Dry flowers whole or remove the petals and spread them in a thin layer on wicker trays or screens. Set these in a warm, dark place to dry. Shake them daily and, if necessary, cover them with light cheesecloth or a screen to keep off the dust. When totally dry, bottle the petals immediately in an airtight container until you are ready to make a potpourri or sachet. Flowering herbs can be dried by hanging them in small bunches upside down in a warm, dry place or laying them on baskets or screens. Store them in a cool, dry place out of direct light.

Potpourris are made of three main ingredients: flowers and herbs contribute their aroma and color; essential oils heighten scents; fixatives preserve the fragrance and the petals.

The enjoyment of making potpourris and sachets is in experimenting and finding your own special blends of scents. I have a potpourri that is still strong after ten years; some can even last as long as thirty to forty years. It seems their quality increases as they age; they mellow and ripen like fine wines with rich bouquets. Below are lists of specific flowers, herbs, essential oils, and fixatives to use in potpourris and sachets.

AROMATIC FLOWERS AND HERBS FOR POTPOURRIS AND SACHETS

Different aromas create the tone of a potpourri. For example it may have the scent of sweet blossoms, fragrant fruits, flowering herbs, or spicy scents. I have divided the following aromatic flowers and herbs into these categories. In some cases they may overlap; carnation and stock are sweet blossoms with spicy scents. Use your own sense of smell to determine the aromas you want to combine.

SWEET BLOSSOMS

Acacia or Mimosa	Lily	Scented geranium
Frangipani or Plumeria	Lily of the valley	Sweet pea
Freesia	Linden	Sweet William
Gardenia	Lotus	Tuberose
Heliotrope	Magnolia	Violet
Honeysuckle	Mignonette	Wallflower
Hyacinth	Narcissus	Ilang-ilang
Jasmine	Nicotiana	
Lilac	Rose	

FRAGRANT FRUITS

Apple	Lemon balm	Lime
Lemon	Lemon verbena	Orange

FLOWERING HERBS AND LEAVES

Bee balm	Orange mint	Sweet marjoram
Chamomile	Pennyroyal	Sweet woodruff
Clary sage	Peppermint	Thyme
Costmary	Rosemary	Yarrow
Fennel	Sage	
Lavender	Spearmint	

SPICY SCENTS

Carnation	Ginger
Clove	Stock

COLORFUL FLOWERS FOR POTPOURRIS AND SACHETS

These flowers may be dried whole or broken into petals to brighten potpourris.

BLUE

Bachelor's button	Forget-me-not	Pansy
Borage	Hydrangea	Primrose
Delphinium	Larkspur	Viola

YELLOW TO ORANGE

Buttercup	Marigold	Rudbeckia
Calendula	Mullein	Tansy
Chrysanthemum	Nasturtium	Tiger lily
Daffodil	Pansy	Viola
Daisy	Poppy	
Gaillardia	Primrose	

PINK TO PURPLE

Aster	Hydrangea	Mallow
Bougainvillea	Johnny-jump-up	Pansy
Clematis	Larkspur	Poppy
Columbine	Lobelia	Viola
Hibiscus		

RED TO WINE

Bee balm	Hibiscus	Primrose
Bougainvillea	Hollyhock	Snapdragon
Cardinal flower	Nasturtium	Sweet William
Fuchsia	Poppy	

ESSENTIAL OILS

The following essential oils may be added to a potpourri or sachet to intensify its fragrance. Use them to complement or emphasize the aromas of the flowers and herbs. Because oils are very strong, add them drop by drop and stir the mixture well to test the aroma after adding each drop. These oils have scents that evaporate quickly. A fixative helps to absorb the aroma and makes it last longer in the flower mixture. A few drops of an essential oil will revitalize your creation if its scent begins to fade. Almost all of the following essences are readily available as pure, natural plant extracts except the sweet blossom essences. You can buy these as pure flower fragrances. They are very expensive, but they are so concentrated that you'll only need to use a little bit at a time.

SWEET BLOSSOM ESSENCES

Acacia or Mimosa	Hyacinth	Narcissus
Carnation	Jasmine	Rose
Frangipani or Plumeria	Lilac	Rose geranium
Gardenia	Lily of the valley	Violet
Heliotrope	Lotus	Ilang-ilang
Honeysuckle	Magnolia	

FRUITY ESSENCES

Apple blossom	Lemon verbena
Bergamot	Lime
Citronella	Neroli or Bitter orange
Grapefruit	Sweet orange
Lemon	Tangerine
Lemongrass	

HERBAL ESSENCES

Clary sage	Peppermint
Eucalyptus	Rosemary
Lavender	Spearmint
Pennyroyal	Wintergreen

SPICY ESSENCES

Carnation	Clove
Cinnamon	

FIXATIVES

Fixatives are used to preserve the mixture and the fragrance of potpourris and sachets. They can be added after the essential oils, by mixing in about one ounce fixative to two quarts potpourri mix. All of the fixatives listed below are *powders* except for the clary sage oil.

Calamus root—From the sweet flag or sweet sedge, this semiaquatic plant is found in marshy areas. It adds a spicy quality to potpourris.

Clary sage oil—This is a large, bushy aromatic herb with striking pink and purple flowers. Its oil makes a good fixative for flowery and fruity blends.

Gum benzoin—This is the resinous gum from the tree Styrax benzoin growing in Indonesia. Especially good with flowery scents. Called benjamin in perfumery.

Labdanum—This resin is from a Mediterranean rockrose that has a strong, very sweet fragrance. The oil blends well with herbal and flowery mixes.

Myrrh—A resinous gum from a tree native to Arabia, in ancient times this herb was used in medicine, as an incense, and in potpourris and sachets for Oriental scents.

Oakmoss—A lichen that yields a resin that acts as a fixative. This is especially effective with lavender, fruity scents, and flower blends.

Orrisroot—The rootstock of the Florentine iris, it has a violet-like smell that blends with floral mixtures.

POTPOURRI AND SACHET RECIPES

Prepare potpourris and sachets by combining the dried flowers and herbs in a large bowl, then tumble them gently around so that their aromas are blended and their colors distributed. Smell your mixture and add essential oils drop by drop until just the right fragrance is obtained. Finally, put in the powdered fixative and mix well, tossing the petals lightly in the air. For a sachet omit any large whole blossoms such as rosebuds. Crush the mixture with a mortar and pestle and sew into little bags.

I have provided a few recipes indicating specific proportions to give you a general idea of the balance of ingredients. Some of my best potpourris have been spontaneously made without measurements. Let your mixture season in a tightly closed container for a few weeks or months before using. Then find pretty jars, bottles, or baskets for your potpourri creation, or pleasing fabrics and trimmings with which to sew your sachets.

LAVENDER-ROSE-ROSEMARY POTPOURRI OR SACHET

    2 ounces lavender
    2 ounces rose petals
    1 ounce rosemary flowers and leaves
    1 to 5 drops lavender oil
    2 ounces orrisroot

PURE ROSE POTPOURRI OR SACHET

    4 ounces rosebuds
    2 ounces rose petals
    2 ounces rose geranium flowers and leaves
    1 to 5 drops pure rose oil
    3 ounces orrisroot

FLOWERING HERB POTPOURRI OR SACHET

    2 ounces lavender
    1 ounce sweet marjoram flowers and leaves
    1 ounce orange mint flowers and leaves
    2 ounces rosebuds and/or petals
    ½ ounce rosemary flowers and leaves
    1 ounce thyme flowers and leaves
    1 ounce mixed flowers for color, such as borage, violet, calendula,
        and so on
    2 ounces orrisroot or calamus root
    10 to 20 drops lavender and rosemary oil

MOTH AND INSECT REPELLENT SACHET

2 ounces tansy
2 ounces lavender
1 ounce wormwood flowers and leaves
2 ounces santolina flowers and leaves
1 ounce pyrethrum
2 ounces pennyroyal flowers and leaves
1 ounce clary sage flowers and leaves

Store this sachet with woolens.

SWEET GARDEN POTPOURRI OR SACHET

4 ounces rose
2 ounces orange
2 ounces jasmine
2 ounces lavender
2 ounces honeysuckle
1 ounce orrisroot
1 ounce oakmoss

SPICY FRUIT MIX

2 ounces orange blossom
2 ounces lemon verbena
2 ounces lemongrass
2 ounces carnation
3 ounces cloves
1 to 2 teaspoons clary sage oil, to scent
1 to 2 teaspoons carnation oil, to scent
1 to 2 teaspoons cinnamon oil, to scent
1 ounce calamus root

TROPICAL GARDEN POTPOURRI OR SACHET

4 ounces gardenia
4 ounces plumeria
4 ounces ginger
2 ounces hibiscus
2 ounces bougainvillea
½ ounce gum benzoin

POMANDERS

A pomander is a clove-studded orange, lime, lemon, or apple. The word originates from the French *pomme*, meaning apple, and *ambre* for ambergris, the secretion of the intestine of the sperm whale that was used as a fragrance. Apples and ambergris are not commonly employed in making pomanders today. Instead, a firm, medium-sized orange is preferred.

In medieval days pomanders were used like sachets, to help disguise unpleasant smells. They would be worn around the neck, like necklaces, for easy accessibility to the nose, or they would be hung in homes in closets or cupboards. The clove *(Eugenia caryophyllata)* is a large tree native to Indonesia; cloves are the dried, brown, unopened buds that are harvested before the pink to green flowers bloom. The name comes from the French *clou*, meaning nail, referring to the nail-shaped buds.

To make a pomander, press cloves into the skin of an orange, lime, lemon, or apple. If necessary, use an awl, large needle, or skewer to help place them. Space them close together, approximately one quarter inch from center to center, but not so close that the skin of the fruit splits. Hang the finished pomander and let it dry in the air until the fruit has shrunk and dehydrated. The cloves should then be touching and totally covering the fruit. You may then shake it in orrisroot and add an essential oil for heightened fragrance. When the pomander is totally dry, hang it in the closet or put it in a drawer to keep away the moths and to keep in the delicious aroma.

FLOWER DYEING—COLOR FROM NATURE'S FLOWERS

Take a walk on a bright clear day. Gather some flowers, bring them home, simmer them in water with some natural fiber, and discover a beautiful color unlike that of any manufactured dye. As examples, blue lupine creates a soft green dye; dahlias infuse wool with warm rust tones; and iris flowers yield shades of blue and violet. Natural fibers such as silk, linen, and cotton can all be dyed using flowers.

In prehistoric times primitive peoples first accidentally stained themselves or their garments with berries, nuts, and roots; this then led to the deliberate coloring of their bodies, faces, clothes, baskets, pottery, and cave walls. The process of dyeing then evolved to the soaking of fibers with plants and urine, which helped to fix the color in the material. Next came the use of heat, which allowed the dyes to penetrate the fibers more quickly. Natural dyes were used in the manufacturing of fabrics until about 1860 when the first artificial dye was made. The lost art of dyeing with plants is only just beginning to be rediscovered.

Gathering the flowers

Collect flowers for dyeing on a warm, clear day after the dew has dried and choose those that are in full bloom. Always leave more flowers than you take. They can be air-dried by hanging them in a warm place or by putting them on trays or screens. When completely dry, store the flowers in paper bags or glass jars until you are ready to use them. As a general rule, you will need four times the weight of your fiber in plant material. For example, for one ounce of wool you will need four ounces of flowers. If the dye plant cannot be stored, a dye bath can be made up and kept in the refrigerator or even frozen until enough is prepared. Experiment with different flowers and storage techniques. The amount of moisture, the soil, and the time of day or year are some of the variables that can influence the color you obtain from your flowers.

Materials

There are certain materials you will need for dyeing with flowers. First, choose the fiber you wish to dye. Wool and silk take more readily to natural dyeing than cotton or linen. Then find two large pots made of enamel or stainless steel that you will use only for dyeing. If special color effects are desired pots made of copper, which greens the fiber, or iron, which darkens colors, may be used; dyeing in a tin can "blooms" or brightens colors. Have wooden chopsticks or spoons on hand to stir and lift the fiber out of the pot.

You will also need some chemicals, called *mordants,* that aid in bonding the color to the fiber. Mordants prepare the fiber for dyeing; they break down the molecules in the material and allow the color to penetrate it. Cream of tartar is used along with the mordants to soften their effect on the fiber. The most common and safest mordant is alum. Chrome is a mordant that is toxic and must be used with great care; it creates deep, rich colors. Chrome alum gives a bluish tint to the fiber. Tin, copper, or iron may be added as powdered mordanting chemicals, but I prefer obtaining their effects on colors by simply dyeing with pots made of those metals. Mordants may be purchased in most weaving supply stores or by mail from the companies listed in the Appendix of Sources (see page 271).

After dyeing wool, you may rinse it with ammonia to draw colors out or with vinegar to brighten and set colors.

STEPS IN FLOWER DYEING

1. If you are dyeing yarn, prepare skeins that are tied in two or three places. If you are dyeing fabric, cut it into the smallest pieces

possible for your project. If you want to experiment, make small skeins that weigh about one-quarter ounce (fifteen to twenty turns from hand to elbow). Tie them with cotton, silk, linen, wool, or jute to see how different fibers take dye.

2. Soak the material in water overnight. If the fabric seems very machine-processed, add a few tablespoons of baking soda to the water.

3. The next day, wash the fiber well by hand with gentle soap and warm water. Be sure to wash any lanolin out of the wool. Let the fiber soak overnight once again in the same water.

4. The following morning rinse the fiber well with warm water. Avoid extreme hot or cold temperatures that might shock the fiber. Squeeze the fiber gently; do not wring it.

5. Mordant the fiber by first filling a large enamel or stainless steel pot with enough water to cover the fiber. Wear rubber gloves and work in a well-ventilated area. Choose the mordant you wish to use and dissolve the correct amount in a cup of water (see chart below for the correct proportions). Pour this solution into the pot of water and then add the fiber. Simmer for one hour and let it cool in the pot. This mordanted fiber may be used immediately for dyeing, stored in a plastic bag in the refrigerator for a few days, or dried and resoaked when needed.

MORDANTS

Per 8 ounces of fiber:

ALUM	4 tablespoons
with cream of tartar	1 tablespoon
CHROME	1 teaspoon
with cream of tartar	1½ teaspoons
CHROME ALUM	¾ teaspoon
with cream of tartar	1 teaspoon
COPPER	1½ teaspoons
with cream of tartar	1½ teaspoons
IRON	1½ teaspoons
with cream of tartar	4 teaspoons

6. Put the washed, mordanted, wet fiber in an enamel or stainless steel pot or in a tin, iron, or copper pot if that effect is desired. Add the flowers (about four times the weight of the fiber) torn into small pieces and enough water to cover the blossoms and material. If possible use soft water, rainwater, or distilled water, otherwise use tap water.

7. Bring the dye bath slowly to a simmer and cook gently for 1 hour, then leave it to soak overnight.

8. The next day, rinse the fiber carefully, avoiding extreme water temperatures.

9. If a final rinse of ammonia or vinegar is desired, add it by the spoonful to a pot of warm water until strongly scented. Then add the fiber and let it soak 15 minutes. Rinse.
10. Hang the fiber to dry in a warm, shady place out of direct sunlight.
11. If it is not being used immediately, label it, indicating the date, the material, and the flower used.
12. It's helpful to keep a notebook with samples of different fibers and all information about your experiments. Accompanying your swatches with pressed dye flowers turns it into a very special herbarium (see pages 103–104).

Natural dyes wear well, and their colors mellow with age. I have a naturally dyed sixty-year-old Afghan rug that is still rich and vibrant-looking. To test for color fastness, make a card with samples of the dyes, cover half the card, and leave it in a sunny window for a few weeks. Then compare the uncovered material with the covered half to see the difference.

FLOWERS FOR NATURAL DYEING

Following is a list of flowers that are known as good dye flowers; most of them will give soft, clear colors. A range of tones can be obtained from any of these flowers; part of the enjoyment of natural dyeing is accepting whatever subtle shade a flower yields. Test other plants and flowers that are available to you.

Acacia	Daisy	Marigold
African daisy	Dock	Morning glory
Anemone	Farewell-to-spring	Mugwort
Broom	or Godetia	Mullein
Buttercup	Fennel	Pansy
Calendula	Geranium	Penstemon
Camellia	Goldenrod	Petunia
Canterbury bell	Hibiscus	Pincushion flower
Chamomile	Hollyhock	Rosemary
Chrysanthemum	Hyacinth	Rudbeckia
Cineraria	Iris	Saint-John's-wort
Coreopsis	Lilac	Snapdragon
Crocus	Lobelia	Stock
Daffodil	Lupine	Viola
Dahlia	Marguerite	Yarrow

FLOWER DYE EXPERIMENTS

ACACIA
(Acacia spp.)

These tiny yellow flowers are like golden suns, and they transmit their color to the wool. The acacia grows plentifully and fast and it's easy to gather the blossoms by carefully "pruning" several trees. Collect them when they are most full of color and aroma.

Color
Bright acacia yellow
Fiber
1 ounce prewashed alum-mordanted wool
Plant
4 ounces acacia blossoms

In a non-reacting pot (stainless steel or enamel) bring the fiber and acacia blossoms to a simmer in water to cover and simmer mixture for 45 minutes. Remove fiber, add 1 teaspoon salt and 1 pinch of tin. Add fiber and simmer 45 minutes. Steep overnight. Use a tin can instead of the tin crystals, if desired.

YELLOW DAHLIAS
(Dahlia spp.)

Dahlias are one of my favorite garden plants. When I first experimented with them I wasn't deliberately growing them for dyeing, but had simply been tending a neighbor's plants by keeping them pruned.

Color
Deep rust on wool
light orange for second bath
Fiber
1 ounce prewashed chrome-mordanted wool
Plant
4 ounces dahlia petals and heads

In a non-reacting pot bring the wool and the flowers to a simmer in distilled water to cover and simmer mixture for 30 to 60 minutes. Soak overnight. The next day give the wool a tepid ammonia bath (1 teaspoon ammonia to 1 quart water) for a few minutes, rinse, and then hang it to dry out of direct sunlight.

YELLOW DOCK
(Rumex spp.)

Dock is another common weed often found growing in fields and ditches. It is easily recognized in the fall by its tall, dark-brown seed stalks. One flowering top is enough for a small experiment.

Color
Yellow-tan (alum) to rich gold browns (chrome) on wool
Light pinkish-tan on cotton
Brown on silk
Fiber
1 ounce prewashed alum- and chrome-mordanted wool (½ ounce each)
Plant
4 ounces dark-brown dock tops and heart-shaped flowers (no stems)

In a tin can bring the fiber and dock tops and flowers to a simmer in water to cover and simmer for 1 hour. Steep overnight. If using a non-reacting pot (stainless steel or enamel), simmer the fiber and plant for 30 minutes, remove the fiber, and add 1 pinch tin crystals per ounce. Return fiber to pot and simmer 30 minutes more.

LUPINE
(Lupinus spp.)

Lupine blooms plentifully in the spring. Both the blue and the yellow flowers can be used for different colors. Gathering the blossoms is an intoxicating experience; they are so rich in pollen. I like to pick the flowers with the deepest color before the seed pods begin to form. Lupine is a member of the pea family.

Color
Blue lupine: greenish gold (chrome) to bright green (alum) on wool
pale green on silk
Yellow lupine: bright yellow (alum) to deep gold (chrome) on wool
yellow (alum) to greenish yellow (chrome) on silk
Fiber
1 ounce prewashed alum- and chrome-mordanted wool (½ ounce each)
Plant
4 ounces lupine blossoms (no stems)

In a tin can bring the fiber and lupine blossoms to a simmer in water to cover and simmer mixture for 1 hour. Steep fiber and flowers overnight in the dye bath.

DEEP PURPLE IRIS
(Iris spp.)

Iris are very elegant. I always look forward to their graceful flowers and delicate fragrance in my garden. I was happy to discover a way to extract their colorful essence. Gather them during a dry spell for the most potent color.

Color
Shades of blue and violet
Fiber
1 ounce prewashed chrome-mordanted wool
Plant
4 to 6 ounces iris flowers

In a non-reacting pot bring the fiber and iris flowers to a simmer in water to cover and simmer mixture for 45 minutes. Steep overnight.

RUDBECKIA
(Rudbeckia spp.)

Rudbeckia is a cultivated black-eyed Susan with large dark centers and vibrant yellow-to-orange petals. They grow easily as short-lived perennials in most gardens and flourish with little care in full sun.

Color
Shades of green
Fiber
1 ounce prewashed chrome-mordanted wool
Plant
4 to 6 ounces rudbeckia flowers

In a non-reacting pot bring the fiber and rudbeckia to a simmer in water to cover and simmer mixture for 30 to 45 minutes. Steep overnight.

FLOWER PILLOWS

Create flower pillows to gently lull you to sleep, induce dreams, awaken love, or stimulate the senses. There is mention in ancient literature that the Greeks dried fragrant flowers to fill pillows. The English continued this custom with scented herbs—sweet woodruff was a favorite because of the new-mown-hay scent it develops when dried. This aroma is due to the chemical constituent in woodruff, coumarin, that is used in perfumery for its pleasant vanilla-like smell and as a fixative. King George was said to have slept on a pillow of the calming herb hops.

When making flower pillows, take the time to create beautiful covers using velvet, silk, or other soft, natural materials. You might dye your own fabric with blossoms from your garden. Hand-embroidered flowers add a special charm.

It takes many dried flowers to make a pillow; so sew them small enough to fill easily. I've created fluffy, little two- by four-inch baby pillows and larger, elegant ones that measure eight inches by twelve inches. Make an inner lining of muslin to hold the flowers and keep little bits of them from leaking out. Experiment with proportions of dried flowers for the scent you want and add a few drops of essential oils for extra aroma. Refer to the potpourri and sachet section of this chapter for guidelines in creating mixtures for your flower pillows.

SWEET DREAMS—A LOVE PILLOW

These floral scents inspire visions of flowering spring and warm days, a time for love.

Lavender
Lemon balm, flowers and leaves
Rosemary, flowers and leaves
Rose petals
Spearmint, flowers and leaves
Violets

BABY PILLOW

This pillow combines the sleep-inducing properties of chamomile and hops with fennel. It is known to relieve gas and help a colicky baby.

Chamomile
Fennel, flowers and leaves
Hops
Fennel oil

STIMULATING PILLOW

This pillow may be more appropriate in your living room than on your bed. The spicy aromas of the herbs will help to awaken the senses and stimulate conversation.

> Carnation
> Cloves
> Orange
> Peppermint, flowers and leaves
> Sage, flowers and leaves

SOOTHING SLEEP PILLOW

All the flowers and herbs used in this pillow are known to help calm and relax. Lay your head on it, breathe in the aroma, and enjoy a serene rest.

> Chamomile
> Elder flower
> Hops
> Linden
> Passionflower
> Rose geranium
> Rose oil

Have a fragrant sleep, and pleasant flower-dreams!

4

NATURAL
FLOWER FOODS

Nibble a nasturtium flower. Enjoy its smooth petals and spicy, sweet taste. Nasturtiums were my first flower food. They grow wild with almost jungle-like growth where I live, and I walk by meadows of their large, round leaves and striking orange and yellow flowers. I knew from my studies of herbal medicine of the nasturtium's healing properties and high vitamin C content. I also learned that in Victorian times they were very popular and often used in foods; this intrigued me.

One old recipe from that era describes dainty tea sandwiches made with nasturtium flowers pressed between thin pieces of buttered bread, the petals forming a colorful fringe. Another recipe describes how to make pickled nasturtium seed pods, a good substitute for capers, by gathering the young, plump seed pods after the flowers wither and covering them with vinegar and spices. I found that the brilliant color and pungent taste of nasturtiums were a natural complement to salads; they became an important ingredient in my Flowering Circle Salad (see page 150). Their shape makes them ideal for stuffing as a savory appetizer or as a honeyed dessert. Sometimes I eat them directly off the plant for a delicious "flower snack." Nasturtiums introduced a whole new world of flavor and color into my food.

Flower recipes were popular in earlier times when flowers were prized for their medicinal qualities, fragrance, and flavor. Many of these recipes date from the seventeenth through the nineteenth centuries. Several are mentioned in the early herbals of Culpeper and Gerard. Some were kept by families in handwritten books and passed down from generation to generation. Other recipes were printed in small volumes with engaging titles such as, *Delights for Ladies, The Compleat Housewife,* and *The Queen's Closet Opened.*[1]

Borage, rose, violet, gillyflower (pinks), elder flower, and cowslip were among the favorite flowers of those times. They were made into a variety of foods, many of them sweet. Sugary syrups (water, sugar, and flowers) and conserves (ground flowers and sugar) were especially popular. Culpeper wrote of the star-like blue borage flowers:

> The flowers candied or made into a conserve are helpful . . . . used as a cordial . . . For those that are weak in long sickness, and to comfort the heart and spirits.

These candied crystallized flowers, as well as violets, gillyflowers, or rose petals, appeared in many old recipes. They were made by coating the flower in beaten egg white, covering it with sugar, and allowing it to dry in the sun. Flower honeys were another sweet delight and were usually made with violets or roses.

Clove pinks or gillyflowers have a distinct, spicy fragrance and taste. The word gillyflower was derived from the French, *giroflier*, for clove tree, referring to the flower's clove-like scent. The blossoms were used to flavor wine, a custom that originated in ancient Rome, and were sometimes called sops-in-wine, referring to the flowers soaked in wine.

Flower petals and herbs were also used to create flavorful vinegars. Culpeper gives a recipe:

> Take of elder flower half a pound, the flowers of red roses, rosemary and lavender, each four ounces, of nutmeg and cloves two drams, of cinnamon three drams, pour upon them five pints of the sharpest white wine vinegar, let all infuse a month or six weeks, and after having pressed it out well, and the liquor is settled, put it into bottles and keep it well stopped for use.

Cowslip was another popular flower food of our ancestors who used it in syrups, salads, conserves, and wines. Employed in herbal tradition as a healing herb for coughs, the bright yellow bell-shaped blossoms are related to the primrose. Cowslip is a wild flower in England and may be cultivated in most gardens.

There were other blossoms used in early flower fare. I've read recipes for orange flower water, honeysuckle syrup, hawthorn honey, rosemary conserve, pot marigold (calendula) cheese, acacia liqueur, and dill and cauliflower pickles. The flowers that delighted our forebears are the same as those used in the flower food recipes in this chapter.

Remember when you were a child and sucked the sweet end of the petunia or honeysuckle to enjoy the drop of nectar stored there? In my garden I grow Mexican tree sage with long red flowers that have the most plentiful and honeyed nectar I've ever tasted. Some mornings I sip this naturally sweet syrup with breakfast.

Flowers are rich in nectar and pollen. Studies have revealed that pollen is a nutritious food filled with vitamins and minerals. It has been used to treat allergies and digestive and intestinal disorders. Aromatic flowers also contain fragrant essential oils. Nectar, pollen, and essential oils help make flowers a sweet and appealing food.

EDIBLE FLOWERS

There are many edible flowers and flowering herbs to grow and gather. Most of them can be easily raised in a small garden space or in pots and planter boxes. They may also be found in the wild. Start with those that are simplest to grow or collect. Avoid chemically treated flowers and those growing next to dusty or busy roadways. Experiment with different flowers to get a sense of how to use them. I love to stroll through my garden, see what flowers are available, and then plan special meals with them.

Select the most healthy, vibrant flowers and cut them carefully to encourage the new buds left on the plant to open. If possible, gather the blossoms just before using and spray them lightly with water. If they are to be stored in the refrigerator, put them in an open plastic or waxed bag, or a woven basket, and keep them moist. Once they are on salads, cakes, or other foods, mist them occasionally with a fine spray of water.

Each flower has its own flavor, aroma, and quality. The orange nasturtiums and yellow mustard flowers have a hot and spicy sweetness and add brightness to foods. The pink and purple onion and chive blossoms, with their distinctly strong taste, can be divided into florets and mixed with salads, grains, or other dishes. The gentle taste and soft blue and violet tones of borage, Johnny-jump-ups, violas, pansies, and forget-me-nots are especially suited for lighter dishes such as salads, drinks, desserts, and fruits. Roses, pinks, honeysuckle, jasmine, and violets all have their delicious aroma in their taste. They can be used either alone, in flower-flavored butter, or together, as in mixed flower teas. Calendulas and chrysanthemums are flowers of the sun and add their color and flavor to main dishes, soups, or salads. Use them by removing their petals from the center of the flower. Rosemary, thyme, dill, fennel, sage, lavender, and other herb flowers are rich in the scent and flavor of the herb.

Following are lists of the edible flowers divided according to their flavors—savory herb, mild herb, sweetly floral, and mild floral. *Always identify a flower accurately as one of those I've listed to be certain it is edible. Include flowers with foods for their beauty and flavor; consume them in small amounts. Some people are particularly susceptible to allergic reactions. If you are, try rubbing an edible flower or herb that you have not eaten before on your wrist. If your skin reacts badly to it, do not eat it.*

SAVORY HERB

These herb flowers have a taste rich in the pleasantly strong aroma of the herb. They enliven foods with their distinct aromatic essential oils. Use the leaves, removed from their stems, with flowers of herbs, such as basil, dill, fennel, hyssop, lemon balm, lemon verbena, sweet marjoram, oregano, sage, sweet woodruff, and thyme.

Basil *(Ocimum basilicum)*
Bee balm *(Monarda didyma)*
Chamomile *(Matricaria recutita)*
Chives *(Allium schoenoprasum)*
Coriander *(Coriandrum sativum)*
Dill *(Anethum graveolens)*
Fennel *(Foeniculum vulgare)*
Garlic chives *(Allium tuberosum)*
Hyssop *(Hyssopus officinalis)*

Lavender *(Lavandula officinalis)*
Lemon balm *(Melissa officinalis)*
Lemon verbena *(Aloysia triphylla)*
Mustard *(Brassica* spp.)
Nasturtium *(Tropaeolum majus)*
Oregano *(Origanum vulgare)*
Rosemary *(Rosmarinus officinalis)*
Saffron crocus *(Crocus sativus)*—Do not confuse this crocus with
   the poisonous Autumn crocus *(Colchicum autumnale)*
Sage *(Salvia* spp.)
Sweet marjoram *(Origanum majorana)*
Sweet woodruff *(Galium odoratum)*
Thyme *(Thymus* spp.)

MILD HERB

I think of mild herbs as those which have a sweet rather than a
pungent flavor. They lack the fragrant essential oils that savory herbs
contain. Some of these flowers tend to be slightly bitter, including
chicory, dandelion, and yarrow. Borage and calendula have a pleasing
taste and brighten foods with their rich blue and orange colors. Use the
leaves with the flowers of chickweed, mallow, or salad burnet.

Borage *(Borago officinalis)*
Calendula *(Calendula officinalis)*
Cattail *(Typha latifolia)*
Chickweed *(Stellaria media)*
Chicory *(Cichorium intybus)*
Clover, red *(Trifolium pratense)*
Dandelion *(Taraxacum officinale)*
Elder flower *(Sambucus canadensis* or *S. caerulea)*
Hawthorn *(Crataegus* spp.)
Hibiscus *(Hibiscus* spp.)
Mallow *(Malva* spp.)
Mullein *(Verbascum* spp.)
Passionflower *(Passiflora* spp.)
Safflower *(Carthamus tinctorius)*
Salad burnet *(Poterium sanguisorba)*
Yarrow *(Achillea millefolium)*
Yucca *(Yucca* spp.)

SWEETLY FLORAL

Sweetly floral flowers impart the perfume of their fragrant oils to
foods. One simple way to experience these flower flavors is to put a few

violets, rose geranium, jasmine, or honeysuckle in a glass of water for ten minutes. You will be able to taste their delectable scent!

Acacia *(Acacia* spp.)
Apple blossom *(Malus* spp.)
Carnation or pink *(Dianthus* spp.)—Use smaller, fragrant clove
   pinks *(D. caryophyllus)* or cottage pinks *(D. plumarius)* instead of
   hothouse carnations.
Day lily *(Hemerocallis* spp.)
Geranium *(Pelargonium* spp.)
Honeysuckle *(Lonicera japonica)*
Jasmine *(Jasminum* spp.)—Do not confuse edible jasmine with the
   poisonous Carolina Jessamine *(Gelsemium sempervirens).*
Lemon blossom *(Citrus limon)*
Lemon geranium *(Pelargonium crispum)*
Lilac *(Syringa vulgaris)*
Orange blossom *(Citrus sinensis)*
Peppermint geranium *(Pelargonium tomentosum)*
Petunia *(Petunia hybrida)*
Plum blossom *(Prunus domestica)*
Rose *(Rosa* spp.)
Rose geranium *(Pelargonium graveolens)*
Violet *(Viola odorata)*

MILD FLORAL

Mild floral flavors are subtle, but delicately sweet. They lack the distinct aromatic overtones of the sweetly floral tastes. Chrysanthemum and daisy petals often have a slightly bitter flavor. The other mild flowers add color, texture, and their delicious nectar to flower foods.

Chrysanthemum *(Chrysanthemum morifolium)*
Cowslip *(Primula veris)*
Daisy *(Bellis perennis)*
Gladiolus *(Gladiolus* spp.)
Hollyhock *(Alcea rosea)*
Johnny-jump-up *(Viola tricolor)*
Pansy *(Viola wittrockiana)*
Peony *(Paeonia* spp.)
Poppy *(Papaver* spp.)—Use only poppy petals; avoid opium poppy
   (Papaver somniferum).
Primrose *(Primula vulgaris)*
Sunflower *(Helianthus annuus)*
Squash blossom *(Cucurbita* spp.)
Thistle *(Cirsium* spp.)
Tulip *(Tulipa* spp.)
Viola *(Viola cornuta)*

A WORD ABOUT SPECIAL INGREDIENTS

There are several foods that I use in the following recipes that may be unfamiliar to you—*miso,* soy sauce, *tofu,* agar-agar, arrowroot, lecithin, carob, tahini, nutritional yeast, protein powder, and sprouts. They are common ingredients in my vegetarian diet, and can be found in your local health food store, if not at the nearest supermarket.

Miso, soy sauce, and *tofu* all originated in Japan. Soy sauce is made from fermented beans, sea salt, and wheat. *Miso* is made from a fermented bean or grain paste that is usually aged for up to three years. Both are very salty and concentrated; use them in small amounts. *Tofu,* often called bean curd, is made from soy beans and is a power-packed food high in protein, phosphorous, and potassium.

Agar-agar and arrowroot are both excellent thickeners. Agar-agar, a seaweed high in trace minerals, has the ability to absorb and hold moisture. I use it to gel jams, desserts, and jellies. Arrowroot is a white, powdery starch made from the young rhizomes of the arrowroot plant— a native of tropical America. It thickens soups, jams, and sauces.

Lecithin, a food derived from soy beans, acts as an emulsifier in foods. It may be used to thicken mayonnaise instead of egg yolk. Lecithin helps to break up fat particles in the body and emulsifies cholesterol.

Carob, known as St. John's Bread, is a tree native to the eastern Mediterranean with flat, dark brown pods up to one foot long. Powdered, it makes a sweet and tasty chocolate substitute. Carob is high in trace minerals, calcium, and potassium and is low in fat and starch. The pectin content in it makes it toning to the bowels. Use carob in drinks and desserts.

Tahini, a butter made from ground sesame seeds, is a source of calcium, protein, and vitamin E. Use it in salad dressings, sauces, pie crusts, soups, and sandwiches.

Nutritional yeast is a non-leavening yeast that is used as a food supplement. It provides B vitamins, protein, and minerals. Protein powder is a concentrated source of protein usually derived from soybeans. Add it to "smoothies," baked goods and sauces.

Sprouts, young growing beans or seeds, make a nutrition-packed addition to soups, salads, main dishes, and sandwiches. You can often find sprouts in produce markets or grow them yourself. First soak about two tablespoons of the smaller seeds or three quarters cup of the larger beans overnight in a quart of water. Cover the jar with a muslin or wire mesh. Drain them the next day and put them in a warm, dark place to sprout. Keep the jars upside down, but at a slight angle so that the sprouts receive air and drain easily. Rinse the sprouts well three or four times a day. When they are one to one-and-a-half inches long, they may be put into indirect light for several hours in order to turn their leaves green. Store them in the refrigerator, continuing to rinse them once a day. Alfalfa, red clover, and radish are all small seeds that may be sprouted alone or combined. Lentil, mung, and aduki beans are larger in size and also make a good combination.

I use cayenne (ground red chili pepper), kelp (a powdered sea-weed), and garlic, as well as soy sauce and *miso,* regularly for their flavor and nutritional value. It's fine to omit these from my recipes and substitute other seasonings that you enjoy.

It's also possible to use grains other than wheat when making flour, such as rye, millet, buckwheat, and rice. These can be purchased as flour or ground at home in a grain grinder or small electric coffee grinder. I use a coffee grinder or a blender to grind nuts and seeds.

Most of these recipes call for fresh flowers. Some kinds of flowers, such as calendula petals, rose petals, thyme, rosemary, and dill may be dried and mixed into wet ingredients. But dried blossoms don't work well to decorate the top of foods. When using dried rather than fresh ones, double the amount called for in the recipe.

New recipes come to me spontaneously as I live with the flowers and discover new ways to use them. The recipes that follow are a few of my favorite foods—both with and without flowers. Let them inspire culinary creations of your own, using all of the edible flowers in your garden.

APPETIZERS, SOUPS, SANDWICHES

STUFFED NASTURTIUMS

Stimulate your appetite with these bright, plump nasturtiums served on a platter lined with round nasturtium leaves.

    ½ cup ricotta cheese
    ¼ cup walnuts, chopped fine
    2 tablespoons basil, ground fine
    Soy sauce to taste
    15 to 20 nasturtiums

Mix all the ingredients together well and form into small balls to fit inside the nasturtium flowers. Top each one with a forget-me-not, Johnny-jump-up, or other small edible flower. Serves 6 to 8.

BASIL MUSHROOM PUFFS

In India, basil is a holy plant. With a strong, aromatic scent, it was said to be worthy of a king's palace. Basil is known in herbal tradition to soothe the stomach and digestive system. Gerard wrote:

> The smell of Basil is good for the heart . . . it taketh away sorrowfulness, which cometh of melancholy and maketh a man merry and glad.

½ pound cream cheese or ricotta cheese
½ cup plain yogurt
1 cup walnuts, chopped medium to fine
2 teaspoons basil flowers and leaves, dried
20 to 30 medium to large mushrooms, stems removed
Flowers of the season

Preheat oven to 325°. Mix together the cream cheese or ricotta cheese, yogurt, walnuts, and basil flowers and leaves. Stuff the mushrooms with a generous amount of the mixture. Put in a pan with a little water, cover it and bake for 15 minutes or until juicy. Top the mushrooms with a flower of the season. Serves 4 to 6.

FLOWERED VEGETABLE DIP

This recipe shows you how to use flowers and vegetables to transform a dip into a lovely and nutritious appetizer.

½ cup water, as needed for consistency
1 pound *tofu*
¼ to ½ cup tahini
1 tablespoon *miso* or soy sauce, or to taste
Garlic, cayenne, and kelp (seaweed) to taste
¼ to ½ teaspoon cumin seed, ground
¼ cup sesame seeds, ground
Sliced vegetables, such as cauliflower, broccoli, cucumber, carrots, celery, mushrooms, jicama, zucchini
1 head leaf lettuce
Edible flowers of the season, especially nasturtiums

Put the water in the blender or food processor, add the *tofu*, tahini, *miso*, garlic, cayenne, kelp (seaweed), cumin, and sesame seeds, and blend to make a thick dip. Add more *tofu* if too thin; more water if too thick. Pour into a bowl and place in the middle of a 12- to 16-inch platter. Lay the lettuce leaves on the platter and arrange the sliced vegetables decoratively around the bowl. Top with edible flowers. Serves 4 to 6.

SUMMER COOL CUCUMBER SOUP
WITH DILL FLOWERS

Dill is a light, feathery aromatic herb with umbels of bright yellow flowers. Its smell always reminds me of my Mother's Dill Pickles (see recipe page 156). Dill has been used in herbal tradition for its soothing effect on the digestive system, relieving upset stomachs and flatulence. It has been known to comfort babies suffering from colic and the name, dill, comes from the Norse word *dilla,* meaning to lull. Use the flowers, leaves, and seeds, fresh or dried, for their flavor.

> 2 cucumbers, peeled and chopped
> 1 cup water
> 1 cup plain yogurt
> ½ avocado
> 2 to 4 tablespoons dill flowers and leaves
> Lemon juice, garlic, cayenne, and soy sauce to taste

Put all the ingredients in the blender or food processor and mix well. The soup should be of a fairly thick consistency. Thin it with water or more cucumber; thicken it with more avocado. Chill all day or overnight. To serve, float a slice of cucumber in each bowl with a dill flower or other flower on it. Delicious for a warm summer evening. Serves 4.

THYME FLOWER SOUP

My favorite thyme is the ground cover called mother-of-thyme. It has small pink flowering tops that are easy to gather and use in foods. There are many varieties of this herb, including lemon, caraway, silver, garden, and woolly thyme.

> 1 pound ripe tomatoes
> 2 cups milk
> ½ cup sesame seeds, ground
> 2 cloves garlic
> 1 tablespoon olive oil
> 2 to 3 tablespoons *miso* or soy sauce, or to taste
> 2 tablespoons thyme flowers and leaves
> ¾ cup water
> ½ onion, chopped
> ¾ pound *tofu,* chopped into small pieces
> 1 tablespoon powdered vegetable broth
> Thyme flowers

Fill the food processor or blender three quarters full with ripe tomatoes. Add 1 cup milk, the sesame seeds, garlic, oil, *miso,* and the thyme flowers and leaves. In a sauce pan gently heat the remaining cup of milk and the water with the onion, *tofu,* and vegetable broth for 8 to 10 minutes or until the onion is cooked. Pour in the tomato mixture and heat at the lowest temperature until just warm. Serve with thyme flowers. Serves 4.

FRUIT BLOSSOM STRAWBERRY SOUP

The ideal setting for enjoying this soup is under a blossoming fruit tree where an occasional petal will fall into your bowl.

  2 cups water
  ¾ cup almonds, ground fine
  1 pint strawberries
  2 peaches
  4 apricots or other seasonal fruit
  ½ lemon, juiced
  1 tablespoon honey
  3 to 4 sprigs fresh mint leaves
  Apple, lemon, or other flower blossoms
  Plain yogurt

Put the water, almonds, strawberries, peaches, and apricots in the blender and mix well. Add lemon juice, honey, and mint to taste. Refrigerate for several hours until well chilled. Serve topped with a spoonful of yogurt and floating blossoms. Serves 3 or 4.

HOLLYHOCK "SANDWICHES"

There is a certain child-like magic about hollyhocks. Here is my favorite fanciful description of that flower:

> She sometimes thought of the hollyhock as a rocket that had taken off from earth, but had become transformed into a plant before it could reach the sky.[2]

Hollyhocks belong to the mallow family whose members are known for their soothing and softening effect on irritated tissue; they are very gentle plants.

  10 large hollyhock blossoms
  2 avocados, sliced thin
  10 pieces mild cheese, sliced thin
  2 cups alfalfa sprouts (see page 136)

Layer slices of the avocado and cheese over the hollyhock blossoms. Top with sprouts and serve with your favorite dressing, sprouts, and edible flowers of the season. Serves 4.

NASTURTIUM LEAF "SANDWICHES"

Nasturtium leaves are as tasty as the flowers. Their pungent flavor complements the other ingredients in this recipe.

¾ pound *tofu,* cut into 6 thin slices
¼ cup water
6 tablespoons nutritional yeast (optional)
¼ cup sesame seeds, ground
2 avocados, mashed
Soy sauce, garlic, and cayenne to taste
¼ cup chopped parsley
6 large nasturtium leaves
6 nasturtium blossoms
½ quart alfalfa sprouts (see pages 136–137)

Place the *tofu* slices in a frying pan with ¼ inch of water and heat gently. Sprinkle 1 tablespoon of the nutritional yeast, if used, or 1 tablespoon ground sesame seeds on each slice of *tofu* and sprinkle lightly with soy sauce. Combine the avocados with garlic, cayenne, and soy sauce to taste and the parsley. Spread this mixture over the full, round nasturtium leaves, add the cooked *tofu* and alfalfa sprouts, and top with a nasturtium flower. Serves 3.

FLOWER ENTRÉES

SAUCY GRAINS WITH MUSTARD FLOWERS

Mustard flowers are hot to the taste, and the entire plant is known for its stimulating effect on the body. Because they are very strong, use them with moderation.

    1½ cups dry millet or brown rice
    ¾ to 1 pound spinach
    ½ pound *tofu*

½ cup olive oil
1 cup water
2 cloves garlic
½ cup sunflower seeds
1 bunch parsley
Soy sauce and cayenne to taste
2 cups mixed bean sprouts (see page 136)
2 to 4 tablespoons mustard flowers or other spicy edible flowers of
    the season

Rinse the millet or rice and add to 2 cups boiling water. When it just begins to simmer, cover, turn to the lowest temperature, and cook millet for 30 minutes and rice for 45 minutes to 1 hour or until the water is absorbed and the grain is tender. Steam the spinach until just wilted, about 2 minutes. In a blender blend the spinach with the *tofu,* olive oil, water, garlic, sunflower seeds, parsley, and soy sauce and cayenne to taste. Pour the sauce over the hot millet or rice and top with bean sprouts and mustard flowers or other spicy edible flowers of the season. Serves 3 or 4.

HEARTY RICE, BEAN, AND FLOWER CASSEROLE

Garlic chives, an interesting relative of chives, have a distinct garlic taste. I have a border of them in my herb garden. The purple flowers are bell-shaped and dangle from long stalks. They make a tasty addition to flower foods.

1 cup dry brown rice
½ cup dry wild rice
1 cup dry lentils
5 to 6 cups water
½ cup olive oil
¼ cup plain yogurt
¼ cup sesame seeds, ground
2 tablespoons tahini
½ cup water
Garlic, cayenne, kelp, and soy sauce to taste
3 to 4 tablespoons herbs, such as sweet marjoram, oregano,
    tarragon
¼ to ½ cup chive flowers, broken into florets
Grated Cheddar or Swiss cheese

Soak the brown rice, wild rice, and lentils overnight in the water. The next day drain them, add fresh water to cover them by ½ inch and bring them slowly to a simmer, reduce the heat to low, and cook for 45 minutes to 1 hour or until the liquid is absorbed and the rice and beans are tender. If you have a crock pot, soak overnight and slow-cook for 6 to 8 hours or until done. In the blender mix together the oil, yogurt, sesame seeds, tahini, water, garlic, cayenne, kelp, soy sauce, and herbs and stir into the rice and beans. Adjust flavor to taste. Fold in the chive flowers, reserving some for the top. Sprinkle with grated cheese and serve with steamed vegetables. Serves 6.

SPICY FLOWER TOSTADAS

I find this an easy meal to prepare for company by just putting all the ingredients on the table and allowing everyone to make their own tostadas. It makes an attractive and nourishing lunch or dinner.

> 2 cups raw pinto beans
> 4 to 5 cups water
> 1 tablespoon oregano and sweet marjoram
> ¼ cup chopped parsley
> Garlic, cayenne, soy sauce to taste
> 1 cup grated carrots
> 1 cup grated zucchini
> 1 cup grated Cheddar cheese
> 1 head leaf lettuce
> 1 cup olives
> 1 cup hot sauce
> 1 cup alfalfa sprouts (see pages 136–137)
> Nasturtiums, mustard flowers, broccoli flowers, bok choy flowers,
>   cress flowers, or other spicy flowers
> 3 to 4 avocados
> 10 tortillas, heated

Rinse the pinto beans and soak them in the water overnight. Drain the beans the next morning and cover the beans by ½ inch fresh water. Bring to a boil, reduce heat, and simmer, covered, for about 2½ to 3 hours or until very soft. This will make about 4 cups of beans. Mash the beans and season them to taste with oregano, sweet marjoram, parsley, garlic, cayenne, and soy sauce. Keep them warm until ready to eat. Put the carrots, zucchini, and cheese into serving bowls. Put the leaf lettuce, olives, hot sauce, sprouts, and flowers into bowls. Mash the avocados with lemon juice, garlic, cayenne, and soy sauce to taste. Heat the tortillas one by one in a dry frying pan on the stove and keep warm, covered, in the oven until ready to serve. Or cover with a damp towel and warm in the oven.

You can prepare each tostada ahead of time, starting with the tortillas, beans, avocados, cheese, carrots, zucchini, lettuce, sprouts and ending with the flowers. Olives and hot sauce can be served separately. Serves 4 or 5.

CALENDULA QUICHE

Culpeper wrote of calendulas, which were called marigolds in his time, and are called pot marigolds today:

> The flowers, either green or dried, are much used in possets, broths, and drink, as a comforter of the heart and spirits. . . .

CRUST:
1 cup whole-wheat flour
½ cup butter
1 tablespoon grated Parmesan cheese
¼ cup cold water

FILLING:
½ pound mushrooms, sliced
1 medium onion, sliced
1 tablespoon butter
4 to 5 eggs
1½ cups milk
Garlic and soy sauce to taste
1 bunch parsley, chopped
8 to 10 calendulas, petals only
1½ cups grated Swiss or Cheddar cheese

Preheat oven to 425°. In a mixing bowl combine the flour, butter, and cheese and cut these ingredients with table knives until they are in pea-sized pieces. Add enough of the water until the mixture is a good pliable dough, sticking together without sticking to you. Roll out on floured waxed paper and turn into a buttered and floured 9- to 10-inch pie dish. Bake for 10 to 15 minutes.

Reduce oven to 350°.

Sauté the mushrooms and onion in the butter. Mix together the eggs, milk, garlic, and soy sauce, beating until frothy. Add the parsley and calendula petals. When crust is done, put drained mushrooms and onions on the bottom, pour in the egg mixture, and sprinkle the cheese on top. Bake for 50 minutes or until a knife comes out clean when inserted 1 inch from the edge of the pie. Let stand 10 minutes to cool. Sprinkle the top with calendula petals. Serves 4 to 6.

ONICA'S VEGETABLE CASSEROLE WITH SAVORY BLOSSOMS

My friend Onica first created this casserole for a vegetarian Thanksgiving feast. The licorice and cashews make a distinctly sweet sauce blending with the flavors of the savory herbs.

3 avocados, mashed and seasoned with soy sauce and garlic
4 to 5 stalks celery, chopped fine
20 to 30 medium mushrooms, sliced
1 onion, chopped fine
30 medium olives, pitted and halved
¾ to 1-quart jar mixed bean and seed sprouts—pea, mung, lentil,
    sunflower, pumpkin, radish (see page 136)

SAUCE:
2 cups cashews, ground
1 cup water
1 tablespoon ground licorice root
1 bunch parsley
2 to 4 tablespoons sweet marjoram flowers and leaves, or dill, basil,
    thyme, rosemary, oregano, chive
2 cloves garlic
Soy sauce and cayenne to taste

In a blender or food processor blend cashews, water, licorice root, parsley, herb flowers and leaves, garlic, cayenne, and soy sauce into a thick sauce. (If too thin, add more cashews; if too thick, add more water.) In a 9-inch pie dish arrange from the bottom up: avocado, celery, mushrooms, a layer of sauce, onion, olives, another layer of sauce, and put the sprouts on the top. Garnish with edible flowers. Serves 4 or 5.

CHRYSANTHEMUM VEGETABLES

The word chrysanthemum comes from the Greek, *chrysos,* meaning gold, and *anthos,* meaning flower. In the Orient, they have been cultivated for over two thousand years and were revered by nobility. In China there's a traditional dish called the chrysanthemum bowl, a rich soup on which chrysanthemum petals are elegantly floated before serving. The Chinese also use one or two blossoms to make a fragrant chrysanthemum tea.

This dish was inspired by my stepson, Matthew, who serves it over a mound of steaming rice with cheese melted on top.

2 potatoes, sliced
2 carrots, sliced diagonally
25 button mushrooms, sliced
3 large bunches broccoli, in florets
½ cup olive oil
¼ cup water
1 tablespoon *miso*
1 tablespoon fresh ginger, grated
¼ cup plain yogurt
¼ cup sesame seeds, ground
Cayenne and garlic to taste
5 chrysanthemums, petals only

Steam the potatoes. When they're nearly done, add the carrots, mushrooms, and broccoli and steam for 5 to 7 minutes more. In the blender mix together the oil, water, *miso*, ginger, yogurt, sesame seeds, cayenne and garlic to taste; pour into a saucepan and heat very gently until just warm. Pour over the steamed vegetables and top with fresh chrysanthemum petals. Serves 4.

SQUASH BLOSSOM FEAST

Squash have been cultivated for thousands of years and their blossoms are especially relished in Mexico and Italy. I've seen the fresh golden flowers in market places and tasted them fried, sautéed, and stuffed.

    1½ cups dry brown rice or millet
    20 mushrooms, sliced
    1 carrot, grated
    1 onion, chopped fine
    1 pound *tofu*, chopped
    ½ cup sesame seeds, ground
    ½ cup cashews
    1 bunch parsley, chopped
    ¼ cup olive oil
    Curry powder, kelp, and cayenne to taste
    10 squash blossoms

Rinse 1 cup rice or millet and add to 3 cups boiling water. When the water begins to simmer again, turn heat to the lowest temperature, cover the pot, and cook millet for 30 minutes and rice for 45 minutes to 1 hour, or until the water is absorbed and the grain is tender. This will make about 3 cups. Mix in the mushrooms, carrot, chopped onion, *tofu*, ground sesame seeds, and cashews. Continue to heat for 10 to 15 minutes or until vegetables are lightly cooked. Add the parsley and olive oil and season to taste with curry powder, kelp, and cayenne. Stuff into squash blossoms; top with another edible flower of the season. Serves 4 to 5.

CURRIED FRUIT FLOWER

When I visited Hawaii, a beautiful woman named Lily served a tropical curry made with freshly picked bananas and papayas from her backyard. We ate it by candlelight in the soft trade breezes of a perfect Maui evening. You can use whatever fruit you have available.

    ¼ cup water
    ½ cup apple juice
    1 cup plain yogurt
    1 to 2 tablespoons curry powder, or to taste
    1 tablespoon grated fresh ginger
    1 teaspoon cardamom seeds, whole (optional)
    5 bananas, sliced
    ½ pineapple, sliced and cubed
    4 apples, chopped
    ½ cup raisins
    ½ cup fresh coconut, grated in large pieces
    ¾ cup cashews
    Nasturtiums or other edible flowers of the season

Mix together the water, apple juice, yogurt, curry powder, ginger, and cardamom seeds, if used, and pour over the fruit and nuts in a large saucepan. Cover and heat very slowly for 20 minutes. Serve over rice, topped with edible flowers of the season. Nasturtiums especially enhance the spiciness of this dish. Serves 4 to 6.

SALADS
AND
VEGETABLES

HERB GARDEN POTATO SALAD

The golden flower umbels and light, lacy foliage of fennel have a distinct anise taste and aroma. It has been used in herbal medicine to help the digestive system and relieve flatulence.

> 5 medium potatoes, sliced and steamed
> 3 ripe avocados
> 1 bunch parsley, chopped fine
> 1 carrot, grated
> 3 to 4 tablespoons fennel flowers and leaves, or dill, sweet marjoram, oregano, thyme flowers and leaves
> 2 cloves garlic, pressed
> Cayenne and soy sauce to taste
> 4 to 6 tablespoons mayonnaise or plain yogurt

Cut cooked potatoes and avocados into small chunks, add the parsley, carrot, herb flowers and leaves, garlic, and cayenne and soy sauce to taste. Mix in the mayonnaise or yogurt by the spoonful until the mixture is just moistened. Chill and serve topped with flowers on lettuce leaf bowls. Serves 4.

GREEK FLOWER SALAD

Mix bright petals into this salad, such as rich orange calendulas and nasturtiums or clear yellow mustard and bok choy. These colors create a striking contrast to the deep green spinach leaves.

> 1 to 2 pounds spinach
> ½ pound Feta cheese, crumbled or chopped
> ¼ pound Greek black olives
> 15 medium mushrooms, sliced
> 10 cherry tomatoes, halved
> ¼ cup chopped parsley
> ¼ cup olive oil
> ½ lemon, juiced
> 2 to 4 cloves garlic, pressed
> Kelp and cayenne to taste
> 2 tablespoons oregano flowers and leaves or sweet marjoram flowers and leaves
> Edible flowers of the season, especially spicy mustard, bok choy, or nasturtium flowers

Break the spinach into small pieces, add the Feta, black olives, mushrooms, cherry tomatoes, and parsley. In a separate bowl mix together the olive oil, lemon juice, garlic, kelp and cayenne, and oregano or sweet marjoram flowers and leaves. Pour over the salad and toss well. Top with edible flowers. Serves 4 to 6.

FLOWERING CIRCLE SALAD

Guests always feel honored to be served this special salad. Its vibrant circles of color make a vivid visual impression; its mingling of flower and vegetable flavors delight the palate. You can adapt it to fit on a dinner plate or a large round tray. Other vegetables and flowers may be substituted for the ones included; try different combinations of them, making each salad a unique creation.

Red or green leaf lettuce or red chard leaves
Calendula Petal Mixture (see page 166)
2 beets, or 1 small red cabbage, grated
1-quart jar mixed bean sprouts—mung, lentil, aduki, radish (see page 136)

2 to 3 carrots, grated
2-quart jar alfalfa sprouts (see page 136)
Edible flowers in season
Dill Flower Dressing (see page 158)

On a 12-inch round tray or plate arrange the lettuce or chard leaves in a circle, leaving a few inches of the leaf tip extending over the edge. Place a large mound of the Calendula Petal Mixture in the center; circle this with a border of grated beet or red cabbage, encircled by mixed bean sprouts, grated carrots, and finally a ring of alfalfa sprouts. Surround this arrangement with the orange and yellow of sun-warmed flowers, such as nasturtiums or calendulas. Then gather other edible flowers of the season—roses, chives, Johnny-jump-ups, carnations, violas, or borage—put a large blossom, such as calendula, in the middle, and arrange the others over the vegetables and sprouts, maintaining the circular design, the flower motif. Serve with Dill Flower Dressing. Serves 6 to 8.

WILD SPRING-GREEN SALAD

Early spring is a time of fresh green energy. Mother Nature renews herself and wild edible plants abound. I love to take long walks in the undisturbed countryside and gather young growing greens and flowers for salads. Many of these often find their way into my garden; it helps the garden when I pick them and the weeds are transformed into delicious food. Gather any of the following:

Chickweed, leaves and flowers—A delicious tender herb with white star-like flowers, known to soothe the digestive system.
Dandelion, leaves and flowers—Young, very tender leaves, they are high in vitamins and minerals. In herbal tradition they are known to be cleansing to the blood and liver. The flowers have a mildly bitter taste.
Dock leaves—These have a slightly tart taste; they are traditionally used as a drying astringent. Eat only young leaves.
Mallow, leaves and flowers—The leaves are roundish with pink flowers; this is a gentle herb that softens and soothes.
Miner's lettuce—The plant has succulent round leaves with tiny white flowers. It's high in vitamin C.
Mustard flowers—These are hot, spicy, and stimulating. Use them moderately.
Plantain, young leaves and flowering tops—An important plant in herbal medicine, the leaves can be used as "nature's Band-Aid" for cuts and minor wounds. Eat young leaves only; older ones are too strong. The flowering tops have tasty little seeds which American Indians dried, then ground for bread flour.

Radish flowers—These are similar to mustard flowers and have a pungent flavor.

Sheep sorrel leaves—Slightly sour in taste, these should be used in moderation.

Sweet woodruff, leaves and flowers—Called Muge-de-boys, "musk of the woods," in old French, this is a subtle tasting, aromatic plant.

Wild onion flowers—These recall the strong taste of onion and have white bell-shaped flowers. They are very strong; use moderately.

Tear the leaves of these salad plants into small pieces and use the flowers whole, with the exceptions of the wild onion, mustard, and radish flowers, which should be broken into florets. Mix well and top with Chickweed Dressing (see page 157).

TABOULEH ONION FLOWER SALAD

Make this salad for a summer picnic or a light supper on a warm evening. Its flavor is enhanced by pungent onion or chive flowers.

    1 cup bulgur (cracked wheat)
    2 cups water
    1 cucumber, chopped
    1 large carrot, grated
    1 bunch green onions, chopped
    10 cherry tomatoes, quartered
    ¼ cup olive oil
    1 lemon, juiced
    1 bunch parsley, chopped
    Garlic, soy sauce, and cayenne to taste
    5 to 10 onion or chive flowers, broken into florets

Bring the bulgur and water to a boil, covered, in a pot, then turn heat to low, and cook until water is absorbed, 10 to 20 minutes. When cool, mix with cucumber, carrot, green onions, tomatoes, olive oil, lemon juice, and parsley and season with garlic, soy sauce, and cayenne to taste. Chill and serve topped with onion or chive florets. Serves 3 to 4.

HERBED BEAN SALAD

This is one bean dish that pleases everyone in my family. Use the herb-flavored beans alone as a salad or mix them with greens or cottage cheese.

½ cup dry garbanzo beans
½ cup dry kidney beans
½ cup dry pinto beans
1 small onion, chopped
1 bunch parsley, chopped
½ cup olive oil
1 to 2 lemons, juiced
4 tablespoons apple cider vinegar
½ cup water
Soy sauce, garlic, and cayenne to taste
3 to 4 tablespoons herb flowers and leaves, such as sweet marjoram, sage, rosemary, thyme, oregano, chives, calendula, or others (a mixture is best)

Rinse all the beans and soak them overnight in 3 to 4 cups water. Drain the beans the next day and cover them with fresh water by 1 inch. Simmer the beans, covered, adding more water if necessary, until very tender, 2 to 3 hours. Drain the beans. (This will make about 3 cups of beans.) Combine the beans, onion, and parsley together in a bowl. In a blender mix the olive oil, lemon juice, apple cider vinegar, water, seasonings, and 1 handful of the herb flowers and leaves. Pour over the beans and mix in the remaining handful of herb flowers and leaves. Allow to marinate several hours or overnight.

CHIVE FLOWER SALAD BOWL

The combination of *tofu*, bean sprouts, and sesame seeds makes for a tasty and especially nutritious salad.

1 pound *tofu*, cut into small pieces
5 celery stalks, chopped
1 onion, chopped fine
1 cucumber, chopped
2 carrots, grated
1 cup mixed bean sprouts (see page 136)
½ cup sesame seeds, ground
1 bunch parsley, chopped
¼ cup chive flowers, broken into florets
¼ cup olive oil
1 lemon, juiced
2 cloves garlic, pressed
Miso or soy sauce and cayenne to taste

Put the *tofu*, celery, onion, cucumber, and carrots in a large bowl with the bean sprouts, sesame seeds, parsley, and chive flowers. In a bowl mix the olive oil, lemon juice, garlic, *miso* or soy sauce, and cayenne and pour over the salad. Toss well and serve with a sprinkling of chive florets. Serves 4 to 6.

NUTTY CUCUMBER SALAD WITH DILL FLOWERS

Golden dill flowers and their green leaves season this cool and crunchy salad.

  2 large cucumbers, sliced
  20 to 30 olives, sliced
  ½ cup walnuts, chopped
  1 cup plain yogurt
  2 to 4 tablespoons dill flowers and leaves
  1 clove garlic
  Soy sauce to taste

Mix together the cucumbers, olives, walnuts, yogurt, dill flowers and leaves (save a few for the top), garlic, and soy sauce. Chill the salad a few hours or overnight so that the flavors blend nicely. Serve garnished with dill flowers. Serves 3 or 4.

FLOWERED FRUIT SALAD

This salad makes an elegant breakfast, light lunch, or dessert and can also be served with a bowl of yogurt.

  12 large leaves of an edible plant
  1 cup cherries, stemmed
  5 to 6 peaches, sliced

2 large bunches green grapes
3 bananas, sliced diagonally
Lemon juice
Borage, Johnny-jump-ups, calendulas, poppy, or other edible
    flowers

Lay the leaves on a 10- to 12-inch round platter so that the tips extend over the edge. Place the cherries in the center and surround them with the peach slices arranged alternately with the pit side up and the skin side up. Surround these with grapes, taken off the bunch, and encircle them with a ring of banana slices. Squeeze fresh lemon juice over the peaches and bananas. Begin to add the flowers by placing a large one in the center over the cherries and continue arranging the smaller flowers in concentric circles, alternating colors for contrast. Use as few or as many flowers as you wish. Spray the flowers lightly with water and refrigerate the fruit salad until served. Serves 6 to 8.

ARTICHOKES WITH LEMON SAUCE AND LEMONY FLOWERS

Artichokes belong to the thistle family. They blossom with large purple thistle-like flowers and the part you eat is the unopened flower head. A lemony flavor goes well with the mild-tasting artichoke. This sauce is especially good with the tender heart.

1 tablespoon lemon juice
1 tablespoon liquid lecithin or 1 egg yolk
1 cup olive oil
2 tablespoons chopped parsley
1 tablespoon lemony flowers from the lemon geranium, lemon
    thyme, lemon balm, or a lemon tree
4 artichokes, cooked

In the blender combine the lemon juice with the liquid lecithin or the egg yolk, blend well, with the blender set at low, and slowly add the olive oil. When thick, add the parsley and lemony flowers, reserving a few. Serve with the artichokes and top with the rest of the lemony flowers. The artichokes are delicious warm or chilled. Serves 4.

MARINATED VEGETABLE MIX WITH HERBS AND HERB FLOWERS

This dish makes a wonderful salad to accompany a meal. The flowers add their colors and flavors to the marinade.

    1 large bunch broccoli, cut into florets
    1 head cauliflower, cut into florets
    3 carrots, sliced
    1 onion, sliced
    3 cloves garlic, chopped
    Edible flowers, such as borage, Johnny-jump-ups, violas, calendulas, or available herb flowers

    MARINADE:
    1 cup olive oil
    1½ cups water
    2 lemons, juiced
    4 to 6 tablespoons apple cider vinegar
    Cayenne and soy sauce to taste
    4 tablespoons parsley, thyme, sweet marjoram leaves and flowers

Steam the broccoli and cauliflower for 5 to 6 minutes. Make the marinade and place it in a bowl or jar with all the vegetables. Mix well, cover, and leave overnight, shaking and stirring frequently. Add the edible flowers a few hours before serving. Serves 6.

MOTHER'S DILL PICKLES

This recipe is in its third generation and hopefully will continue to be passed down through the family. I have fond memories of our dill-scented pantry, where my mother made these pickles every summer, and even better recollections of eating them!

    4 quarts cucumbers
    1 gallon water
    ¾ cup sea salt
    1 cup apple cider vinegar
    ¼ cup pickling spices
    3 to 4 cloves garlic, sliced
    6 dill stalks with flowering heads
    1 slice rye bread

Scrub the cucumbers thoroughly. Bring to a boil the water, salt, vinegar, and pickling spices. Let cool. Layer cucumbers in a 2-gallon crock with slices of the garlic and sprigs of dill until all ingredients are used. Cover with liquid and put a slice of rye bread on top of the liquid. Cover the crock with a dish weighted with a heavy stone to hold the dish in place. Cover with a cloth to keep dirt out. Place in an out-of-the-way spot for 1 week to 10 days. Pickles should be put into sterilized jars, covered tightly and refrigerated, and eaten within a month or so.

DRESSINGS AND SAUCES

CHICKWEED DRESSING

The rich green color of this dressing reflects the vibrant tones of early spring. Chickweed is a mild-tasting herb that is a storehouse of vitamins, minerals, and chlorophyll.

> ¾ to 1 cup chickweed, flowers and leaves
> 1 cup olive oil
> 1 lemon, juiced
> ½ cup water
> 1 clove garlic
> Soy sauce, kelp, and cayenne to taste

Mix the chickweed and olive oil in the blender. Add lemon juice, water, garlic, and soy sauce, kelp, and cayenne to taste. Serve with fresh green salad, avocado, or wild spring-green salad. Serves 4.

CREAMY HERB FLOWER DRESSING

Cashews sweeten this herb-flavored dressing, which may also be used on steamed vegetables.

>½ cup cashews
>¾ cup water
>1 tablespoon *miso*
>½ cup olive oil
>¼ cup plain yogurt
>2 cloves garlic
>2 to 4 tablespoons herb flowers and leaves, such as thyme, dill, rosemary, oregano, or others

Put the cashews in the blender and chop them fine, add water, and blend well. Add the remaining ingredients and adjust the flavor and consistency: add more water if too thick; more cashews if too thin. Serve the dressing over mixed salad greens and top it with herb flowers. Serves 4 to 6.

DILL FLOWER DRESSING

Avocado gives this dressing a thick consistency and lovely color; dill adds a savory flavor.

>½ cup olive oil
>½ cup water
>½ cup plain yogurt
>½ lemon, juiced
>½ avocado
>¼ cup sunflower seeds
>¼ cup dill flowers and leaves
>Soy sauce, garlic, and cayenne to taste

Put the olive oil and water in the blender, add the yogurt, lemon juice, avocado, and sunflower seds, and blend well. Add half of the dill flowers and leaves and soy sauce, garlic, and cayenne to taste. If too thick, add more water or yogurt; if too thin, add more avocado. Top with the remaining dill flowers. You may also use forget-me-nots, roses, calendulas, or other seasonal flowers as a garnish. Serve with Flowering Circle Salad or other salads. Serves 6.

MARTHA'S PLANTATION GREEN DRESSING

This is a sweet, spicy dressing for vegetable or fruit salads.

    1 orange, juiced
    2 limes, juiced
    1 tablespoon olive oil
    3 to 5 tablespoons water
    1 avocado
    2 tablespoons tahini
    2 to 3 cloves garlic
    1 teaspoon soy sauce
    ½ teaspoon curry powder
    ½ to 1 teaspoon ginger
    1 teaspoon honey or maple syrup
    1 tablespoon mint or other flowering herbs
    Edible flowers of the season

Put the orange juice, lime juice, olive oil, water, and avocado in the blender and mix together. Add the tahini, garlic, soy sauce, curry powder, ginger, honey or maple syrup, and herbs and blend. If a thicker sauce is desired, use less water. Serve in a bowl and garnish with edible flowers. Serves 6.

FRAGRANT FLOWER VINEGAR

These vinegars make lovely gifts when you bottle them decoratively.

Place sprigs of aromatic flowering herbs—dill, rose, oregano, thyme, basil, sweet marjoram, violet, fennel, chives, and so on—in a bottle or pint jar of apple cider vinegar. Use the vinegar in salad dressings, leaving the flowers in the bottles or jars. Experiment with different flowers for different flavors.

CARNATION SAUCE

The best flower to use for carnation flavor is the clove pink or gillyflower. Cut off the bottoms of the petals which are often bitter. Serve this delicious spicy sauce over waffles or pancakes.

1 cup plain yogurt
6 to 10 pinks, petals only
¼ cup apple juice
½ cup almonds, ground
½ teaspoon cinnamon

In the blender mix half of the yogurt with half of the petals and add the apple juice, almonds, and cinnamon. Fold in the remaining yogurt and petals. Makes 1½ to 2 cups.

DATE NUT DRESSING

This is a sauce to stimulate your sweetest taste buds. Pour it over fruit salads, yogurt, frozen fruit, or other desserts.

1 cup apple juice
15 to 20 small pitted dates
½ cup walnuts, chopped fine
Violas or other flowers of the season

Put the apple juice in the blender, add the chopped walnuts and the dates, and blend until thick. Serve and top with walnuts and flowers. Makes 1¾ to 2 cups.

ROSE GERANIUM SYRUP

Scented geraniums are particularly good in flower foods; a few blossoms and leaves will quickly yield their potent flavor. Choose from a variety of scents, including rose, apple, peppermint, nutmeg, coconut, and lemon.

1 cup water
2 tablespoons arrowroot
2 tablespoons honey
½ lemon, juiced
1 quart strawberries, sliced
2 to 4 tablespoons of rose geranium flowers and 2 rose geranium
    leaves

Mix together the water and the arrowroot and heat slowly, stirring often, until thick. Add the honey, lemon juice, and strawberries and heat until berries soften. Mash the berries with a fork, leaving some large pieces. Stir in the rose geranium flower petals, removed from the calyx. Put a rose geranium leaf in the bottom of a jar, pour in the syrup, and put another leaf on top with several blossoms. Makes 1 quart. Serve on yogurt, waffles, or pancakes.

VIOLET HONEY

Violets have a delicate perfume that is superb to the taste. There is a wonderful myth in Greek and Roman mythology that relates how the violet came to be. Jupiter, king of the gods, had a lover named Io, whom he turned into a heifer when his wife, Juno, became jealous. Io was so unhappy eating coarse grasses that Zeus transformed her tears into violets. She then had the sweetest food to eat.

Half fill a jar or crock with violets. Other aromatic edible blossoms may also be used such as roses, pinks, or honeysuckle. Then fill the jar with honey. Leave at least 10 days in a warm place, and strain, if desired. The flowers may also be left in. Honey is a natural preservative. Use the honey to sweeten herb tea, yogurt, or desserts.

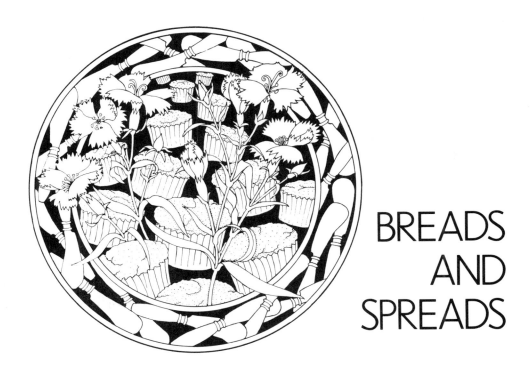

BREADS
AND
SPREADS

CARNATION SPICE MUFFINS

Serve these muffins warm from the oven with Carnation Blossom Butter and Carnation Honey for a spicy breakfast that is totally delectable.

- 2 cups whole-wheat flour (or substitute a mixture of millet, rice, buckwheat, or oat flour)
- 5 to 10 pinks, petals only, with the bitter white petal-bottoms cut off. (Use the small, fragrant pinks, not hothouse carnations.)

¼ cup whole sunflower seeds
1 teaspoon cinnamon
⅛ teaspoon cloves
¼ teaspoon ginger
¼ teaspoon nutmeg
2 teaspoons baking powder (optional)
¼ cup butter, softened or melted
¼ cup honey
1 teaspoon vanilla
1 egg, separated or 1 teaspoon liquid lecithin
½ cup plain yogurt or milk

Preheat oven to 350°. Mix together the flour, petals, sunflower seeds, cinnamon, cloves, ginger, nutmeg, and baking powder, if desired. In a separate bowl stir the butter with the honey and vanilla until well blended, add the egg yolk or lecithin and yogurt or milk. Pour this mixture into the dry ingredients and stir just enough to moisten. Beat the egg white and gently fold it in. Fill lightly oiled muffin tins three quarters full and bake about 20 minutes or until golden brown. Makes 8 muffins.

ELIZABETH'S HERB FLOWER BREAD

Make this dense, whole-grain bread with a mixture of herb flowers and leaves so that each bite offers a subtle blend of flavors. Use it for open-faced sandwiches or to accompany dinner.

2 cups whole-wheat flour
2 teaspoons baking powder (optional)
½ cup sunflower seeds, chopped lightly
2 tablespoons sesame seeds, ground
1 tablespoon whole caraway seeds
1 to 2 tablespoons rosemary flowers and leaves, or dill, thyme, basil, sweet marjoram, or other herb flowers and leaves
2 eggs, separated
¼ cup honey
¼ to ½ cup milk or water

Preheat oven to 350°. In a bowl combine the flour, the baking powder, if used, the seeds, and the herb flowers and leaves. Beat the egg yolks and honey and add them to this mixture. Stir in enough milk or water to moisten the batter completely. Beat the egg whites until stiff and fold them in. Continue mixing until the dough leaves the sides of the bowl; it will be slightly sticky. Pour into an oiled 9×5×3-inch loaf pan and bake 40 to 60 minutes or until a toothpick inserted in the center comes out dry. Turn out of the pan and cool on a wire rack. Makes 1 loaf.

ROBERTA'S GOLDEN
  PUMPKIN-CALENDULA BREAD

Calendulas give their golden hues to food and have been used as a substitute for expensive saffron. Chopping or crushing the petals before using in cooked foods helps to release the color.

    1½ cups pumpkin purée
    2½ cups whole-wheat flour
    2 teaspoons baking powder (optional)
    6 to 8 calendulas, petals only, chopped
    1 teaspoon cinnamon
    ¼ teaspoon cloves
    ½ cup butter, softened
    ¼ cup honey
    3 eggs, separated
    3 tablespoons lemon juice
    1 cup milk

Preheat oven to 350°. Cut a small pumpkin into 1- to 2-inch pieces, remove the seeds, and steam it for 15 to 20 minutes or until tender. Remove the pulp from the skin and put it in the blender or processor with enough water (use water from steaming) to form a thick purée.

Stir the dry ingredients together. In another bowl blend the butter with the honey, egg yolks, and lemon juice, beating until smooth. Mix in the pumpkin purée and continue beating, adding the flour mixture and milk, until well blended. Beat the egg whites until stiff, fold them in, and pour the mixture into two 9 × 5 × 3-inch buttered and floured loaf pans. Bake for 1 hour or until a knife comes out clean and dry. Makes 2 loaves.

SPROUTED WHEAT HERB FLOWER BREAD

This is a long-lasting and nourishing bread. It is perfect with avocado and sprouts.

    1 quart wheat or rye berries
    2 quarts water
    ½ cup herb flowers and leaves, such as dill, thyme, rosemary,
        oregano, or others
    1 cup sesame seeds, ground

Soak the wheat or rye berries in the water overnight. Pour off the water the next day (you can use it to water house plants) and sprout the berries in a warm, darkish place. Rinse 2 or 3 times a day. When just sprouted, no more than ½ inch long, run them through a hand mill, meat grinder, Champion juicer (with water), or food processor. Mix in the herb flowers and leaves and the ground sesame seeds. Stir well so that the mixture has an elastic texture. If too thin, add more ground sesame seeds; if too dense, add some water. Form into ½-inch-thick round cakes about 3 inches in diameter and put in an oiled Pyrex or stainless steel pan. Bake in the slowest preheated oven possible, not over 140 degrees in order to retain the nutrients in the sprouts, for 16 to 24 hours, or put in a food dehydrator or in the hot sun until crusty and fairly dry inside. Turn them every few hours and break one open to test it if you think they're almost done. Makes 10 to 12.

TOFU WAFFLES WITH CARNATION SAUCE

This recipe was given to me by my friend Judy, who accurately described the waffles as "light, fluffy, and full of protein."

> 1¼ cups water or milk
> 1 pound *tofu*
> 2 tablespoons honey
> 1 teaspoon vanilla
> ¼ cup sesame seeds, ground
> 1 teaspoon liquid lecithin (optional)
> ¾ cup whole-wheat, buckwheat, or millet flour
> 1 teaspoon baking powder (optional)
> Carnation Sauce (see page 159)

Put the water or milk in the blender with the *tofu* and blend well. Add the honey, vanilla, sesame seeds, and lecithin. Stir this mixture into the flour and baking powder, if used. Pour into a preheated waffle iron. Cook the waffles until lightly browned; they will usually stop steaming when ready. The batter may also be made into pancakes. Serve with Carnation Sauce. Makes 2 large waffles.

AROMATIC BLOSSOM BUTTER

Butter easily absorbs the strong flavors of aromatic flowers. You can create a butter to complement other foods: for example, Carnation Butter with Carnation Spice Muffins.

> ¼ pound sweet butter, softened
> ¼ cup aromatic petals, such as those of rose, violet, pinks, herb
>   flowers, and other seasonal flowers

Mix the butter and the petals together until well combined. Cut with a cookie cutter into shapes or mold into a small serving container or in butter molds. You might also sculpt your butter into fanciful flower shapes. Leave it in a cool place overnight. The fragrance will permeate the butter. Other aromatic petals such as lilac or scented geranium may be used. Savory herb flowers such as thyme, sweet marjoram, oregano, and dill also make wonderful butters. Another method of making flower butter is to wrap the petals in cheesecloth and layer them between slices of butter. After a few days remove the petals.

ROSE PETAL JAM

The best roses to use in flower food are the fragrant, old-fashioned ones such as the damask, cabbage, or moss rose. The wild rugosa rose is also good. If the petals are red with white ends, clip off the white part before using because it is bitter.

> 2½ cups water
> 1½ cups fresh rose petals or ¾ cup dried
> 1 to 2 teaspoons rose water (optional)
> 1 small lemon, juiced
> 2 to 4 tablespoons honey or to taste
> 1⅔ tablespoons agar-agar flakes

In a blender mix together 1½ cups water, the rose petals, rose water, if used, lemon juice, and honey. In a small saucepan heat the remaining 1 cup water and add the agar-agar flakes. Soak for 1 minute, bring to a boil, and simmer 4 minutes, stirring occasionally. Blend this with the rose mixture. A layer of ground rose petals and frothy liquid may separate on top of the jam; remove this before the jam sets. Pour into jars and refrigerate for immediate use. For long-term storage, the mixture must be heated and poured into hot canning jars and sealed airtight. Follow the instructions that come with your jars. Place a rose bud on the top of each container. Delicious in yogurt or on toast. Makes 2½ cups.

CURRIED NASTURTIUM SPREAD

The curry powder in this recipe will turn the *tofu* a bright golden yellow. It makes a striking combination with orange nasturtiums.

> ½ pound *tofu*
> 2 tablespoons plain yogurt
> ¼ cup tahini

1 to 2 tablespoons *miso*
1 tablespoon curry powder
Garlic to taste
2 stalks celery, chopped fine
1 carrot, grated
¼ cup finely chopped chives or green onions
½ lemon, juiced
20 nasturtiums

Mix the *tofu*, yogurt, tahini, *miso*, curry powder, and garlic together. Add the celery, carrot, and chives or green onions. Adjust the seasoning to taste. Serve in a bowl surrounded by nasturtiums or stuff them with the curried *tofu* mixture. Use the spread on bread or as a vegetable dip. Serves 4.

CALENDULA PETAL MIXTURE

Gerard wrote in his *Herbal* about calendulas:

> The yellow leaves of the flowers are dried and kept throughout Dutchland against winter, to put into broths, in physicall potions, and for diverse other purposes, in such quantity, that in some grocers or spice-sellers houses are to be found barrels filled with them, and retailed by the penny more or less, insomuch that no broths are well made without dried marigolds.

¾ pound *tofu*
2 avocados
½ cup sesame seeds, ground
Garlic, soy sauce or *miso*, cayenne, and kelp to taste
6 to 10 calendula flowers, petals only
2 to 3 stalks celery, chopped
1 small onion, chopped
½ cup whole sunflower seeds

Using a fork, spoon, or pastry cutter, mix together the *tofu* and avocados until well blended and fairly smooth. Add the ground sesame seeds to the mixture with garlic, soy sauce or *miso*, cayenne, and kelp to taste and add the calendula petals. Put in the celery and onion with the sunflower seeds. Mix well and serve in the center of a Flowering Circle Salad (see page 150), as a spread, or as a dip with carrots, celery, cauliflower, or other vegetables. Serves 6 to 8.

DRINKS

LEMON BLOSSOM LEMONADE

Lemon trees usually produce ripe lemons, fragrant blossoms, and immature fruits at the same time. This makes it possible to use both the lemons and the flowers for their refreshing flavor.

> 6 lemons, juiced
> 1 quart water
> Honey to taste
> ¼ to ½ cup lemon blossoms

Add the lemon juice to the water with a little honey, if desired. Stir in the lemon blossoms and leave the mixture in the sun for a few hours. Chill and serve with fresh blossoms floating in each glass. Orange blossoms and oranges or lime blossoms and limes can be substituted.

FLOWER HERB TEAS

Traditionally many flowers have been made into teas for their healing effects. Because flowers contain volatile oils that may easily evaporate from too much heat, it is usually best to prepare them as infusions. First boil the water, then turn it off, add the flowers, and let them steep for twenty to thirty minutes. The usual proportion is one teaspoon to one tablespoon of dried flowers per cup of water. Double this amount for fresh flowers. I have briefly noted the traditional herbal uses of the following flowers when enjoyed as teas. Use all of these with moderation and respect.

Borage—An herb with blue star-shaped blossoms that is known to reduce fevers and calm and tone the body.

Calendula—A flower of the composite family with clear orange or yellow petals. It is warming and stimulating to the body, has astringent properties, and is used to induce sweating.

Chamomile—These white-petaled, yellow-centered daisy-like flowers are known to calm and relax.

Chicory—The blue composite-type flowers of this herb make a soothing eyewash. The roots may be roasted as a coffee substitute.

Clover, red—The reddish-pink blossoms of this clover are used to strengthen, tone, and cleanse the entire system.

Elder flower—These small cream-white flowers make a traditionally favorite tea combined with peppermint to induce sweating and break fevers.

Fennel—Its feathery leaves, golden blossoms, and flavorful seeds are all known to soothe the digestive system, relieve flatulence, and increase milk in nursing mothers. Fennel is also used as a gentle diuretic.

Hibiscus—Jamaica, which grows in Mexico, is my favorite type of hibiscus. The flowers are deep red and make a tart, pink astringent tea high in vitamin C.

Hyssop—Its leaves and bluish-purple blossoms are used for the respiratory system, for coughs and congestion. *Use hyssop in moderation.*

Lavender—These long spikes of purple flowers are known to calm upset stomachs and the entire digestive system. They have a stimulating aroma for headaches and feelings of dullness.

Orange—The white blossoms of the orange are gently stimulating with a calming, fragrant aroma.

Passionflower—These large, four-inch white and purple-blue flowers are known to soothe and calm the nervous system.

Rose—The lovely rose is used to cleanse the system and tone the nerves and the heart.

Rosemary—The small purple-blue flowers, as well as its leaves, are stimulating, with a very strong oil. *Use even the flowers with moderation internally.*

Sage—Garden sage has bluish-purple flowers and gray-green leaves. It is a very powerful herb, best used as a cold infusion or extract. Sage is known as an herb for colds, sore throats, and other respiratory complaints. It also helps to wean babies from mother's milk. *Use sage moderately.*

Thyme—There are many varieties of thyme with whorls of pink to purple blossoms. It contains thymol, an antiseptic, also used in respiratory problems. *Use thyme moderately.*

Yarrow—This herb has white, sweet-smelling flowers that grow in umbels. It is used to break fevers, regulate the liver, and help curb excessive menstruation. Yarrow is a bitter-tasting herb.

FLOWER NECTAR SUN OR MOON TEA

I've noticed how a glass of this tea makes almost everyone feel especially refreshed and revitalized.

Gerard wrote:

> The leaves and flowers of Borage, put into wine make men and women glad and merry, and drive away all sadness, dullness and melancholy. . . .

This sun tea is made without wine and uses many flowers, but its effects are the same as those Gerard describes.

> Handfuls of freshly gathered: honeysuckle, borage, rose petals, calendula petals, jasmine, poppy petals, Johnny-jump-ups, violas, forget-me-nots, or other edible flowers, sweet in nectar
>
> 2 quarts water

Fill a half-gallon jar one third full of edible flowers that have been gathered just before the last of the dew dries on a sunny day. Fill the jar immediately with water and cover. Place in the sun several hours or in the full moonlight overnight. Serve strained and topped with a fresh flower. The pollen and oils from the flowers will flavor the water with their rich natural essence.

WOODRUFF JUICE

It is traditional in Germany to celebrate May Day with a drink made by steeping sweet woodruff in white wine; they call it May wine. This makes a pleasant vanilla-flavored drink. For a nonalcoholic version try this variation.

> 5 to 10 sprigs sweet woodruff in flower
> 1 quart fruit juice

Leave the sweet woodruff in the juice overnight. Serve topped with a sprig of the leaves and flowers.

HOLLYHOCK PUNCH

This is lovely served in a large bowl on a festive occasion.

> 2 quarts apple or grape juice
> 2 quarts carbonated mineral water
> 2 lemons, juiced
> 1 pint strawberries, sliced
> 5 to 10 large hollyhock blossoms

Mix together the apple or grape juice, water, and lemon juice. Stir in the strawberries and float hollyhocks on top.

STRAWBERRY BORAGE COOLER

The intense blue of the borage flowers complements this reddish-pink drink. Try it on a hot summer day.

> 1 quart carbonated mineral water
> 2 lemons, juiced
> ½ teaspoon fresh ginger, grated
> 1 pint strawberries
> 20 borage flowers

Combine all the ingredients (except the borage flowers) in the blender, add a little ice, and mix well. To serve, float the borage flowers on top. Raspberries, blackberries, or loganberries may also be used instead of strawberries.

BLOSSOMING SUMMER "SMOOTHIE"

I relish the sweet, juicy fruits of summer. Plump, deep-red cherries are my favorites and they will color this smoothie—a wholesome breakfast on a warm day—a pleasant shade of pink.

    15 to 20 cherries, pitted
    2 plums, skinned and pitted
    Seedless grapes, small bunch
    2 apricots, pitted
    ½ cup apple-papaya or apple juice
    ½ cup water
    ½ cup plain yogurt
    2 teaspoons protein powder (optional)
    ¼ cup sunflower seeds
    Edible flowers of the season, such as Johnny-jump-up, calendula,
        viola, borage, or rose

In a blender mix the fruit, apple juice, and water. Add the yogurt, protein powder, if used, and sunflower seeds and blend until smooth. Serve with assorted edible flowers floating on top. Serves 2.

HIBISCUS TROPICAL FRUIT TEA

This drink was inspired by my friend Serena who serves it full of glorious seasonal fruits. If using dried flowers and herbs, remember to double the amounts.

    2 quarts water
    2 to 4 tablespoons hibiscus blossoms, dried or fresh
    2 to 4 tablespoons mint leaves, dried or fresh
    2 to 4 tablespoons lemon grass, dried or fresh
    ½ cup pineapple, chopped
    2 oranges, sliced
    1 papaya, sliced
    Mango or other tropical fruit (optional)

Bring the water to a boil, turn off the heat, and add the hibiscus, mint, and lemon grass. Let steep 20 to 30 minutes and strain. Put the pineapple, oranges, papaya, mango, or other tropical fruit into a 2-quart jar and pour the liquid over the fruit. Refrigerate overnight. Serve the next day with a hibiscus blossom floating on top. Serves 4.

FLOWER ICE CUBES

Put your favorite edible flower in the ice tray, fill the tray with water, and freeze. Use for drinks, punch, or just for fun.

DESSERTS

FLOWER NUT TORTE

This is a special treat for a celebration—a very rich uncooked nut torte—best served in small slices. To make it into a valentine, form it into a heart, add a little fresh beet juice to make a pink frosting, and decorate with rosebuds!

    3 large bananas
    12 soft dates, pitted
    ¼ to ½ cup apple juice
    1 cup sesame seeds, ground
    1½ cups cashews, ground
    1 cup almonds, ground
    5 to 7 tablespoons carob powder
    1 tablespoon grated organic orange peel
    ¼ cup grated coconut
    Edible flowers and leaves of the season, such as Johnny-jump-ups,
        pansies, violas, honeysuckle, roses, petunias, or calendulas

FROSTING:
½ pound softened cream cheese or ricotta cheese
1 banana
2 tablespoons honey or maple syrup
1 tablespoon grated organic orange peel
1 teaspoon vanilla

Mix in the blender the bananas, dates, and apple juice until the mixture is thick and smooth. (Add more apple juice as needed.) Pour the mixture into a bowl and stir in the ground seeds and nuts until the batter is thick. If needed, add more nuts. Add the carob powder, orange peel, and coconut, then form into a round or heart-shaped cake.

For the frosting, mix together all the ingredients until mixture has a smooth, creamy consistency. Line a platter with edible flower leaves, frost the cake, put it on the platter. Refrigerate for a few hours. Then surround it with large edible flowers and use other edible flowers to imaginatively decorate the top of the torte. Serves 8 to 10.

SWEET NASTURTIUMS

This dessert offers an intriguing blend of sweet and pungent flavors.

½ cup cream cheese
4 tablespoons plain yogurt
2 to 3 teaspoons honey or maple syrup
¼ cup walnuts, almonds, or cashews, chopped
¼ cup dried black currants
1 teaspoon vanilla
15 to 20 nasturtiums

Mix all the ingredients, except the flowers, together well and form into small balls to fit inside the nasturtiums. Top each one with a small edible flower. Arrange on a plate that is covered with round nasturtium leaves. Serves 6 to 8.

APPLE PETAL CRISP

When the first apples of late summer are ripe I enjoy making this crisp. The rose petals add a subtle flavor that goes well with the fruit. Enjoy it for dessert or warm for breakfast.

8 to 10 apples, cored and sliced
5 large roses, petals only (see page 165)
¼ cup rose water (optional)
½ cup water or apple juice

CRISP TOPPING:
¾ cup butter, softened
1 cup whole-wheat flour or buckwheat or millet flour
½ cup old-fashioned rolled oats
2 tablespoons maple syrup or honey
1 cup walnuts, chopped

Preheat oven to 350°. Mix the apples, rose petals, and waters or juice and pour into a 9-inch pie dish. For the topping, mix together the butter, flour, oats, maple syrup or honey, and walnuts until slightly crumbly. Press lightly over the apples and bake for 40 minutes to 1 hour or until the topping is brown and the fruit is bubbling. Cool, garnish with rose buds or petals, and serve with yogurt. This crisp is delicious made with a mixture of apples, berries, bananas, or other fruits. Serves 8.

PERISSA'S CAROB SILK PIE

"Fantastic," "smooth," and "rich" are just a few of the appreciative comments I've received after serving this pie. Once I made it topped with sliced kiwi fruit and blue borage flowers—a good combination of textures, flavors, and colors.

1 cup butter, melted
¼ to ½ cup honey
1 pound ricotta cheese
¾ cup carob powder
2 teaspoons vanilla
2 eggs, beaten, or 2 teaspoons liquid lecithin
1 teaspoon cinnamon
Edible flowers, especially borage or Johnny-jump-up

CRUST:
¾ cup butter, softened
1 cup whole-wheat flour
½ cup sesame seeds, ground
1 cup walnuts, chopped
1 teaspoon honey

Preheat oven to 350°. For the pie filling, combine the butter and honey, blending well. In the food processor or blender or with a mixer purée the ricotta until smooth. Add the carob powder, vanilla, eggs or lecithin, honey-butter, and cinnamon and blend until light and well mixed. For the crust, mix together all the ingredients and press into a buttered and floured 9-inch pie dish. Bake for 15 to 20 minutes. Cool, add the filling, top with edible flowers, and refrigerate. Serves 8.

FROZEN GLADIOLUS DESSERT

The following frozen fruit blends make a healthy substitute for ice cream. I first tasted this dessert in Hawaii, where it was made from papaya, mango, and banana put through an expeller-type juicer that processed them into a creamy consistency. I make it often for a light and satisfying dessert.

Method I:
4 bananas
4 peaches, pitted
15 cherries, pitted
2 cups apple juice
1 cup plain yogurt
1 teaspoon vanilla
2 tablespoons almonds, ground
Gladiolus and edible flowers
¼ cup walnuts, chopped

Blend in a food processor or blender the bananas, peaches, cherries, apple juice, yogurt, vanilla, and almonds. Pour into a bowl and put in the freezer. Just before it is totally hard, spoon it into the gladiolus blossoms and sprinkle the tops with chopped walnuts and a lovely edible flower. Day lilies or petunias may also be used.

Method II:
For those with a Champion expeller-type electric juicer.
4 bananas, halved
4 peaches, pitted and quartered
15 cherries, pitted

Freeze the fruit until solid, then put through a Champion or similar expeller-type juicer. Mix in a little yogurt or cream, if desired, and serve in gladiolus as above. This dessert is also superb served in a bowl and topped with edible flowers. Serves 4 to 6.

MARTIN'S FLOWERED FRUIT WHIP

My husband, Martin, originally made this elegant-looking dessert with ripe persimmons, which turned the yogurt a soft shade of orange. You can make it with other fruits, but our favorite every fall is flowered persimmon whip.

3 to 4 oranges, halved and hollowed out
1½ cups plain yogurt
3 bananas, sliced small, or 1 cup berries or other fruit
1 teaspoon vanilla
2 tablespoons honey (optional)

Mix together in a blender the yogurt and 2 of the bananas with the vanilla and honey. Pour in a bowl and fold in the remaining banana. Divide among the orange shells. Place in the freezer until just barely hard and serve topped with borage flowers and other seasonal flowers. Cherries, peaches, strawberries, raspberries, and persimmons are all excellent substitutes for the bananas and look beautiful in the orange halves. Serves 3 to 6.

ROSE TREATS

Gerard wrote:

> The distilled water of roses is good for strengthening of the heart and refreshing of the spirits and likewise for all things that require a gentle cooling. The same being put into . . . dishes, cakes, sauces and other pleasant things, giveth a fine and delectable taste.

10 soft, dried figs or prunes, pitted
10 soft dates, pitted
¼ to ½ cup rose water (optional) or water
½ cup almonds, ground
5 to 7 roses, petals only (see page 165)
½ cup coconut, shredded or whole sesame seeds
Edible flowers

Mix the figs or prunes and dates in the blender with the rose water or plain water to make a thick paste; some small pieces of fruit remaining in the mixture are fine. Pour into a bowl and stir in the ground almonds. If it's not thick enough, add more almonds. Mix in the rose petals, form into balls, and roll in coconut or sesame seeds. Top with a rosebud and refrigerate until ready to eat. Serves 4.

MIA'S BLUEBERRY DAY LILIES

Day lilies are one of the most carefree plants to grow in your garden. They spread easily, providing an abundance of flowers from spring through early fall, in a rich variety of reds, oranges, and yellows. Their name refers to the short day-long bloom of each flower. In the Orient the flowers, buds, and tubers are used either raw or cooked in vegetables or salads.

Gather the flowers fresh or just withered at the end of the day. Dry your own blossoms on wicker or wire trays in a warm place out of the sun. Dried day lilies are usually available in Chinese markets. The young flowering stalks can be eaten like asparagus.

    1 cup plain yogurt
    1 quart blueberries or other berries of the season
    2 tablespoons honey or to taste
    Day lilies and other edible flowers

Blend half of the yogurt, 1 cup of the blueberries, and the honey in the blender. Fold in the rest of the yogurt and blueberries and fill the day lilies with the mixture. If it's too thin, add more yogurt. Top with a beautiful edible blossom of the season. You can also serve this blueberry-yogurt dessert in a bowl with the day lilies surrounding it. Serves 6 to 8.

BLOSSOM BERRY PIE

This is a tasty pie to enjoy during strawberry season. Rose petals add the finishing touch, enhancing the pie with their beauty and delicate flavor.

    2 cups cottage cheese
    1 cup plain yogurt
    ¼ to ½ cup honey or to taste
    ¼ cup rose water (optional)
    2 pints strawberries
    1 cup water
    5 tablespoons agar-agar flakes
    5 roses, petals only (see page 165)

    CRUST:
    ½ cup walnuts, ground
    ½ cup almonds, ground
    ½ cup sesame seeds, ground
    ½ cup tahini
    3 tablespoons butter, softened
    5 dates or 2 to 3 tablespoons honey or to taste
    1 teaspoon vanilla
    1 cup walnuts or cashews, large pieces

For the filling, in the food processor or blender blend the cottage cheese, yogurt, honey, and rose water. Add 1 pint of the strawberries. Boil the water with the agar-agar for 1 minute and simmer 4 minutes, stirring to dissolve it. Blend with strawberry mixture.

For making the crust, combine the walnuts, almonds, sesame seeds, tahini, and butter. Add the dates or honey, vanilla, and chopped walnuts or cashews. Mix well. Press into a 9-inch pie dish and add the filling. Chill 3 to 4 hours or overnight. Top with rose petals and the remaining pint of strawberries, sliced. Serves 8.

CINDRA JOY'S PANSY PARFAIT

Cindra Joy is a friend who serves this dessert in pottery bowls that she makes and then decorates with pictures of flowers and hummingbirds. She experiments continually with different fruit and nut blends such as bananas and cashews or peaches and walnuts. Combine other fruits, nuts, and juices to create your own unique desserts.

    1 cup apple juice
    2 bananas
    ½ small pineapple, sliced
    1 teaspoon vanilla
    4 tablespoons grated coconut
    ½ cup almonds, ground
    5 dates or ¼ cup raisins
    1 cup water
    4 tablespoons agar-agar flakes
    ½ to 1 pint whipping cream, whipped
    10 to 20 violas
    5 to 6 large pansies

In a blender blend together the apple juice, bananas, pineapple, vanilla, coconut, almonds, and dates or raisins; this will make about 4 cups. In a saucepan bring the water to a boil, add the agar-agar, boil 1 minute and simmer 4 minutes. Let cool and add to the blender, mixing well. Pour into a bowl and chill until thick. Then either fold in 1 pint whipped cream or serve layered with whipped cream and violas in parfait glasses. Top with pansies and violas. Serves 6.

A FLOWER FEAST WEEKEND

When your garden is overflowing with blossoms you can enhance many of your meals with flower foods in flowery settings. You might have breakfast on a balcony overlooking the sea, a picnic lunch by a stream under the lush shade of a weeping willow, or a candle-lit dinner on the veranda with the sweet music of violins and the aroma of night-blooming jasmine carried on the breeze. I have envisioned a luxurious imaginary weekend where every meal would be created with flowers. Of course, it's not likely that you would eat such an abundance of flower foods in such a short time, but you can choose from the menus below in planning blossoming meals for any day of the year.

Saturday Flower Feast

CARNATION BREAKFAST

Hibiscus Tropical Fruit Tea
Carnation Spice Muffins
Aromatic Blossom Butter
Flowered Fruit Salad
Flower Fruit Cream

PLACE SETTING AND TABLE DECORATION

Carnation flower arrangement.
Pink on each plate.

NASTURTIUM LUNCH

Stuffed Nasturtium
Nasturtium Leaf
   "Sandwiches"
Curried Nasturtium Spread
Water with Nasturtium
   Flower Ice Cubes
Sweet Nasturtiums

Nasturtium flower arrangement.
Served on large nasturtium leaf
   "plates"—to be eaten when
   finished.

FLOWER SNACK

Eat a borage, nasturtium,
   Johnny-jump-up, or
   other edible flower right
   from the plant.

CALENDULA DINNER

Summer Cool Cucumber
   Soup
Calendula Quiche
Green Salad with Edible
   Flowers
Creamy Herb Flower
   Dressing
Blossom Berry Pie
Borage-Mint Tea

Calendula flower arrangement.
Menu written on card decorated
   with pressed calendula petal
   arrangement.
Napkins dyed with calendula
   flowers.
Calendula on each plate.
Sprinkle calendula petals over
   food.

Sunday Flower Feast

ROSE GERANIUM BREAKFAST

Flowering Summer
  Smoothie
Tofu Waffles
Rose Geranium Syrup
Water with Rose Geranium
  Blossoms

Rose geranium bouquet.
Basket of potpourri to enjoy the
  scent.

ROSE LUNCH

Flowering Circle Salad
Dill Flower Dressing
Elizabeth's Herb Flower
  Bread
Rose Treats
Lemon Blossom Lemonade

Rose flower arrangement.
Rose water for finger bowls.
Rose oil on the napkins.
Sprinkle rose petals over food.
Rose on each plate.

MIDAFTERNOON FLOWER DRINK

Strawberry Borage Cooler

GLADIOLUS DINNER

Basil Mushroom Puffs
Squash Blossom Feast
Marinated Vegetable Mix
Sprouted Wheat Herb
  Flower Bread
Frozen Gladiolus Dessert
Hibiscus, Rose, Lavender
  Tea

Gladiolus flower arrangement.
Sprinkle gladiolus petals over
  food.
Floral scented candles.

SWEET DREAMS

Flower Nectar Moon Tea

5
FLOWER
ALCHEMY

It's a fine, clear summer morning, the dew has just barely dried on the blossoms. It's a perfect time for some flower alchemy—the art of transmuting flowers into beautifying and healthful substances that capture their essences. The sun illuminates a garden of rainbow colors—bright reds, oranges, yellows, soft blues, and violets. A gentle breeze spreads their aromas—sweet jasmine, spicy pinks, pungent rosemary, and thyme. Herbs and flowers are at their peak. Bees are pollinating the blossoms; butterflies and hummingbirds fly gracefully among the plants.

Today I've come to my garden to gather blossoms to make a garden flower salve from specially chosen plants. Silently I tell the flowers of my purpose. Then, carefully, I go from plant to plant cutting the fullest, ripest flowers, leaving many buds to open in the day's sunshine. My basket fills with mullein, borage, calendula, bergamot, and comfrey.

When I have enough, I bring them to my kitchen, put them in a double boiler, cover them with oil, and heat them gently for thirty minutes. Then I leave the mixture to steep overnight, and by the next morning the alchemy will have taken place; the flowers and leaves will have released their essence into the oil, turning it a deep, aromatic green. The salve is completed by slowly heating the flowers and herbs again, straining the oil and adding beeswax to it. The entire process of making this salve, from gathering the flowers to the finished salve itself, exemplifies the art of flower alchemy.

I recall walking on many warm scented nights and wishing I could somehow preserve the delicious fragrances of jasmine, mock orange, or honeysuckle. Sometimes they would all blend in the darkness into a unique aroma. The memory of these fragrance-laden nighttime walks led me to learn the many-faceted secrets of flower alchemy so that I might make my own perfumed preparations.

From earliest times, fragrant and healing herbs and flowers have been utilized for many purposes. Tutankhamen was king of Egypt during the eighteenth dynasty in fourteenth century B.C. His tomb was discovered intact in 1922. A minor pharaoh, his tomb was not as elaborate as those of more important rulers, yet it was filled with gilded works of art, fine carvings, and other treasures. Among the resplendent pieces were several carved stone containers filled with unguents made with frankincense and spikenard. These were over three thousand years old and yet when they were opened a faint aroma still lingered.

The herb alchemist's art evolved over the ages with the creation of scented oils, perfumes, powders, and salves. The Romans were known for their lavish use of rich oils. The Bible speaks of how Jesus was annointed with costly ointments and oils. From the fourth through the fifteenth centuries Constantinople became a busy center for commerce in spices and aromatics. Distillation was discovered in the tenth century, bringing with it fragrant waters and oils. In the sixteenth and seventeenth centuries in England remedies, called "simples," made with aromatic flowers and herbs were used for daily life.

Early Americans also had basic herbal medicine—a salve would be made on the stove from little more than herbs and lard cooked together. All of these were the forerunners of today's natural body care products.

FLOWER PREPARATIONS

It's exciting to learn how to make these preparations. All you need are blossoms, natural ingredients, and the recipes that follow. Your first lavender water, honeysuckle oil, spring salve, and fragrant, creamy lotion will delight you. Hair rinses, vinegars, and flower facials are all enjoyable to make and use. You will discover a variety of steams, saunas, and baths that are beneficial and relaxing. You'll soon be supplying yourself and friends with luxurious, homemade skin care creations.

FLOWERS AND HOW THEY AFFECT THE SKIN

Below is a list that will help you find the best flowers and flowering herbs to use for different skin conditions. Herbal terms are defined, such as emollient and astringent, and specific flowers are given for each category. Use this list when creating recipes to pamper and nourish your particular skin type. When flowering herbs are used, such as rosemary and thyme, include the leafy tops with the flowers. *Some people may be allergic to particular flowers or herbs. If you think you might be, test the preparations by putting some on a small area of your skin and leaving it there for twenty-four hours. If you have an unfavorable reaction such as itching or inflammation, do not use the product or the flower on your skin.*

EMOLLIENT

This term refers to the ability of a flower or herb to soothe, soften, and heal dry or irritated skin. Usually, the plants used contain a thick, mucilaginous substance slippery to the touch, which actually coats and protects the skin. Some emollient flowers also act as astringents, drying as they relieve irritation; these include mullein, pansy, violet, and comfrey.

Acacia   Lily
Borage   Mallow, flowers and leaves
Chickweed, flowers and leaves   Melilot
Comfrey, flowers and leaves   Mullein
Hibiscus (Rose of China)   Pansy
Hollyhock   Violet

ASTRINGENT

Flowers and herbs that have an astringent effect promote a drying, tightening, cleansing, and firming of the tissue through contraction of the skin cells. Use astringents to dry out oily skin and to help check excessive discharge of fluid from sores or wounds.

Calendula   Miner's lettuce
Cleavers, flowers and leaves   Mint, flowers and leaves
Clove   Mullein
Clover, red   Nasturtium
Columbine   Pansy
Comfrey, flowers and leaves   Periwinkle
Cowslip   Plantain
Daisy   Primrose
Dock   Rose
Fuchsia   Rose geranium, flowers and leaves
Geranium   Rosemary, flowers and leaves
Goldenrod   Sage, flowers and leaves
Hibiscus (Jamaica)   Saint-John's-wort
Lavender   Violet
Lemon   Yarrow
Lemon balm, flowers and leaves

TONING

Flowers and herbs that I refer to as "toning" invigorate the skin; they restore tone to healthy tissue. For dry skin combine toning flowers with emollient flowers and herbs. For an oily complexion use them with astringent flowers. Toning flowers help to beautify normal skin.

Calendula   Honeysuckle
Chamomile   Lavender
Clover, red   Mint, flowers and leaves
Comfrey, flowers and leaves   Orange
Cowslip   Rose
Dandelion, flowers and leaves   Rosemary, flowers and leaves
Elder flower   Thyme, flowers and leaves
Fennel, flowers and leaves   Violet

STIMULATING

These are flowers and herbs that are energizing and activating to the tissue, that increase circulation. The skin will usually become red as the action of the flowers or herbs stimulates and dilates the blood vessels and blood is drawn to the surface. This helps relieve inflamed and sore tissue and muscles.

Calendula
Carnation
Eucalyptus, flowers and leaves
Ginger
Goldenrod
Hyssop, flowers and leaves

Lavender
Mint, flowers and leaves
Mustard
Rosemary, flowers and leaves
Sage, flowers and leaves
Thyme, flowers and leaves

ANTISEPTIC

Flowers and herbs that prevent and inhibit growth of harmful bacteria and infection are called antiseptic. They are used in facial steams and saunas for congestion and for minor cuts and sores.

Clove
Eucalyptus, flowers and leaves
Lavender
Nasturtium
Thyme, flowers and leaves

CLEANSING

These are flowers that help clear the skin of blemishes, eruptions, and dirt. Use them in steams, baths, or as facial waters.

Burdock, flowers and leaves
Chamomile
Cleavers, flowers and leaves
Clover, red
Elder flower

Hyssop, flowers and leaves
Rose
Tansy
Thyme, flowers and leaves
Yarrow

AROMATIC

These flowers are prized for their pleasant-smelling essential oils that perfume many kinds of cosmetic preparations. Many affect the skin in various ways; look for them in other sections of this list. Their aromas can also have specific healthful effects. (See Chapter 6, page 228.)

Acacia
Bee balm, flowers and leaves
Carnation
Chamomile
Clove
Elder flower
Fennel, flowers and leaves
Frangipani or Plumeria
Gardenia
Ginger
Heliotrope
Honeysuckle
Jasmine
Lavender
Lemon balm, flowers and leaves
Lemon verbena, flowers and leaves
Lilac

Lotus
Melilot
Mint, flowers and leaves
Orange
Rose
Rosemary, flowers and leaves
Scented geraniums, flowers
    and leaves
Sweet pea
Thyme, flowers and leaves
Tuberose
Violet
Wallflower
Woodruff (dried), flowers
    and leaves
Ilang-ilang
Yucca

GATHERING AND DRYING FLOWERS

Gather flowers and flowering herbs for waters, oils, salves, and other preparations in the morning after the sun has dried the dew from their petals. The maximum amount of essential oils will be drawn into the blossoms at this time. Use the flowers that look most vital, and be sure you leave buds on the plants. As a general rule, use twice as many fresh flowers as dried flowers in any given recipe.

To dry blossoms that you gather, lay them out on a wicker or screen tray so that they don't touch each other. Put the trays in a warm, dry spot out of direct light and shake them daily. When the blossoms are totally dehydrated, store them in tightly sealed glass jars until needed. Dried flowers and flowering herbs remain potent enough to use as long as they retain their aroma and/or color.

AROMATIC FLOWER WATERS

The fragrance of flower waters is refreshing and reminds me of a lightly perfumed cooling breeze on a hot summer afternoon. They can be made from a variety of aromatic blossoms and added to foods, baths, or simply splashed on the face or body.

The creation of flower waters most often involves the distillation of the flower essence. The process of distillation was discovered by an Arabian physician, Avicenna, in the late tenth century. He was the first to make rose water and later went on to distill other essences. This simple process involves using heat and water to extract the essence and the oil from the flowers. If just the oil is wanted, a few drops can be collected floating on top of the distilled water.

It's quite easy to set up a simple home distillation unit with the following materials:

One 6- to 8-quart pot with a domed lid
1 small bowl with a raised bottom that can withstand high
    temperatures
Ice cubes and cool water
Flowers—1 pint to 1 quart of fresh, 1 cup to 1 pint of dried,
    depending upon the strength of the aroma, the more the better
½ quart hot water

Place the bowl inside the empty pot. Then put the flowers inside the pot, around but not inside the bowl. Pour the hot water over the flowers, being careful not to let any get into the bowl. Keep the heat low so that the water simmers. Invert the domed lid, put it on the pot, and fill it with ice cubes and cold water.

Be sure the water doesn't boil; if it bubbles up over the top of the

bowl, your flower water will be diluted. As the water simmers, the steam touches the cold lid, condenses, and drops into the bowl. An ice cube in the bowl will prevent the water from re-evaporating. Empty the bowl as it fills. This distilled water contains the aromatic essential oil of the flowers. Pour some into an attractive bottle for daily use and store what remains in a sterilized dark container in the refrigerator. To sterilize the bottles or other containers, put them in a large pot of cold water so that they are totally covered, inside and out. Turn the heat on to medium, bring to a boil, and simmer gently ten to twenty minutes.

Another way to make flower water is to put several drops of essential flower oil into pure water and shake it up. This is an easy way to create rose, lavender, orange, violet, or other water without the distillation process. (These waters may be used in Aromatherapy, Chapter 6, page 228.)

The following are some of the flower waters you can make. When using flowering herbs, such as mint and rosemary, include some leaves. Flower waters may be made from one flower or several combined, such as rose and lavender; rose, elder flower, and lavender; elder flower and orange.

Elder flower water was very common in earlier days and prized for its ability to cleanse the complexion of blemishes. It has a subtle fragrance and is known for its mild astringent and softening abilities. This water has been used to help irritated eyes.

Honeysuckle flower water has a delicate aroma that captures the sweet essence of the flowers. It is nurturing to the skin and helps to improve tone and vitality.

Lavender flower water is reviving and stimulating; it cleanses and tightens the pores. It's also useful as an antiseptic wash for bruises, stings, scrapes, and other minor injuries. Lavender water leaves your skin feeling clean and fresh.

Mint water has an invigorating fragrance and effect on the skin. Peppermint contains menthol, which leaves the skin feeling cool. Mint water also acts as an astringent-tonic, resulting in a radiant complexion.

Orange flower water is restoring and moisturizing to dry skin. This water has a subtle fragrance; it is not as true to the aroma of the fresh flowers as the concentrated oil of orange flowers.

Rosemary water has a pungent, pine-like fragrance that awakens the skin and the senses. It gently dries and renews oily complexions.

FLOWER OILS

Flower oils preserve the delicious scent of flowers and extract the healing qualities of many flowering herbs. Oils made at home are different from the essential oils made by commercial distillation that require a large quantity of plant material for a small amount of oil. (It takes about two hundred pounds of roses to make one ounce of pure commercially distilled rose oil.) Fragrant oils are wonderful for soothing the skin and can be used for massage and for the bath. Some herb flower oils, such as mullein and pennyroyal oils, are used for specific purposes as indicated below.

It's best to use the mild oils of apricot and almond as a base to which flowers are added; olive and sesame oils may smell too strong for delicately scented blossoms. As you are making your flower oil preparations, some flowers, such as honeysuckle and gardenia, may need to be changed frequently. If they show signs of browning or molding, strain them with a kitchen sieve immediately. Be sure to squeeze all the oil out of the blossoms. Honeysuckle sometimes needs straining after several hours in a warm place. The more times flowers are added, the stronger and more fragrant the oil will be. Store flower oils in a sterilized dark bottle in the refrigerator. Be sure to label them with the ingredients and the date.

Nicholas Culpeper wrote in his seventeenth-century *Herbal:*

Of Oils.

The way of making them is this; having bruised the herbs or flowers you make your oil of, put them into an earthen pot, and to two or three handfuls of them pour a pint of oil, cover the pot with a paper, set it in the sun about a fortnight or so, according as the sun is in hotness: then having warmed it very well by fire, press out the herb, &c. very hard in a press, and add as many more herbs to the same oil; bruise the herbs (I mean not the oil) in like manner, set them in the sun as before; the oftener you repeat this, the stronger your oil will be . . .

This was the basic precedent for the methods used today.

When making oils, experiment with your favorite scented flowers. Also choose flowers for specific needs, such as astringent and toning flowers for oily skin, emollient flowers for dry skin, and toning flowers for normal skin (see pages 184–187). The following flowers have strong aromas which are particularly good for oils.

Acacia	Lilac
Carnation	Lily
Elder	Orange
Frangipani or Plumeria	Rose
Ginger	Rosemary
Honeysuckle	Scented geranium
Jasmine	Sweet pea
Lavender	Violet
Lemon	

FIVE METHODS FOR EXTRACTING FLOWER OILS

1. Water Method

This is a good way to make your own rose oil, which is very expensive to buy. Fill a glazed ceramic crock with flower petals, using the most fragrant, fresh, and undamaged flowers. Press them down gently with your hand or a wooden spoon and add pure water (rain, spring, or distilled) until they are covered by one quarter inch of liquid. Put a light piece of cheesecloth over the top of the crock and put the crock in a very sunny place. Each day remove the cheesecloth and add a few fresh blossoms. After about six days a film will begin to form on the water—this is the oil. It can be carefully absorbed with a piece of cotton and squeezed into a small sterilized bottle. Because some water will also drop into the bottle, cover the top of the bottle with cheesecloth for a few days so that the water will evaporate, then store the oil in the refrigerator.

2. Oil Method

This method uses oil as an extracting medium so that the essential oils of the flowers merge with a pure vegetable oil. Fill a quart jar with flowers and cover them with almond, apricot, or avocado oil for delicate flower oils. Use olive or sesame oil for stronger scented medicinal oils. Set the jar, covered, in a warm place for a few hours to a week, depending on the flowers. Shake the jar frequently. Continue to add fresh flowers to the oil, strain and squeeze out the old flowers until the aroma is as strong as you want. Then strain the oil for the final time and bottle it. Jasmine, honeysuckle, and violet oil, as well as the herb flower oils (see page 193) are best prepared with this method. Try mixing different flowers for a potpourri-scented oil.

3. Gently Heated Oil Method

This is the same process as the oil method except that the oil and flowers are placed in a sealed jar in a pot of just boiling water. Keep the water over gentle heat for an hour, just simmering, so that the oil inside the bottle is warmed but not boiled. Then strain the flowers out and add more; repeat until the scent is to your liking.

4. Cotton Ball Oil Method

Place a cotton ball saturated with almond or apricot oil in a jar and cover with petals, filling the jar. Then place the jar, covered with cheesecloth, in the sun. Change the petals daily and when the oil in the cotton ball has absorbed enough of the aroma, squeeze the fragrant oil into a sterilized dark glass bottle and store it in the refrigerator.

5. Essence Method

Add a few drops of commercially prepared essence to a mild oil, such as almond, apricot, or avocado. This type of oil can be used in Aromatherapy (see page 228).

HERB FLOWER OILS

Several flowering herbs have been traditionally used for making medicinal oils. Prepare them by following the oil method (see page 192). They are:

Mullein *(Verbascum thapsus)*—This plant has silver leaves and bright yellow blossoms. The flowers are used to make an oil that is an emollient for irritated tissue, a mild astringent, and an antiseptic for earaches.

Pennyroyal *(Mentha pulegium)*—This member of the mint family is a wild or cultivated herb with whorls of light purple flowers. It has a strong, minty scent that repels mosquitoes, fleas, and other insects. To make a natural insect repellent oil for external use, infuse the flowering tops in olive oil. I gather pennyroyal flowers by a lake where large "families" of them bloom in late summer; the whole lakeside becomes a meadow of purple blossoms. Some of the flowers I hang upside down to dry as well as to decorate my house. Pennyroyal should not be used by pregnant women as it brings on menstruation. In any case it is a very strong herb and should only be used externally.

Saint-John's-wort *(Hypericum perforatum)*—This is an attractive herb growing about two or three feet tall with bright yellow blossoms that have black dots on them. The leaves have oil glands that are visible when held to the light. The juice of the plant is red, which colors the oil made from it. Saint-John's-wort oil is a preparation that has been known from earlier times for its astringent properties—healing cuts, scrapes, inflammations, bruises, and burns. Only this variety of Saint-John's-wort will produce the medicinal red oil. Use it externally.

TINCTURE OF BENZOIN

A tincture is an herbal preparation made with pure alcohol or strong, pure vinegar that extracts and preserves the medicinal properties of an herb.

Tincture of benzoin may be used to preserve oils—a few drops per quart. It may slightly alter the scent of a delicate flower oil. Benzoin is a gum from a tree native to Indonesia. It is used as a fixative for sachets, perfumes, potpourris, and oils. The powdered gum is readily available at most herb or health food stores. Tincture of benzoin may be made by mixing:

> ½ cup powdered gum benzoin
> 1 cup vodka or rubbing alcohol

Combine the ingredients in a glass jar and let the mixture sit, covered, shaking it daily, in a sunny place for 7 to 10 days. Strain out the benzoin and use.

FLOWER OIL RECIPES

SUPER FLOWER SKIN OIL

I use this oil on my skin daily. It combines the revitalizing and toning properties of chamomile, elder flower, and honeysuckle; astringent-toning qualities of rose, and the nurturing, emollient effects of comfrey. Comfrey contains allantoin, a cell proliferant, used in many cosmetics for its ability to rejuvenate tissue.

> Several handfuls elder flower, rose petals, chamomile, honeysuckle, comfrey, flowers and leaves (one handful equals about ½ ounce)
> 1 cup apricot oil
> 1 cup almond oil
> ½ cup avocado oil
> ½ cup olive oil
> ½ cup sesame oil
> ½ ounce vitamin E oil

Using the oil method, place the flowers in a half-gallon jar and cover with the combined oils. Let sit in a warm place, shaking daily, for a few days to one week. Strain out the flowers and store in a sterilized bottle in the refrigerator. Scent the preparation with fragrant essential oils, such as rose, orange, lavender, or lemon.

FLOWER BALM OIL

This is a simple oil using the essence method. The oil is effective as a heating and warming balm for sore muscles, for clearing the sinuses of congestion, and for relief of headaches. The oils of wintergreen, lavender, peppermint, and rosemary stimulate circulation and warm the skin. Eucalyptus and clove penetrate and are antiseptic. Only use this oil externally and *keep it away from eyes and mucous membranes.* Some people are allergic to the methyl salicylate in wintergreen oil. If you think you might be, test a small amount on your wrist before adding it.

> ¾ cup apricot, almond, sesame, or olive oil
> ½ ounce peppermint oil
> ½ ounce eucalyptus oil
> 2 teaspoons lavender oil
> 2 teaspoons clove oil
> 2 teaspoons wintergreen oil
> 1 teaspoon rosemary oil

Mix the above ingredients together and bottle; store in a cool place.

FLOWER SALVES

Originally salves were made from herbs and animal fat cooked together in a big pot. This was one of the traditional forms for preserving the fragrant and healing properties of flowers and herbs. Today the more refined cold-pressed oils such as olive, apricot, almond, or sesame, as well as coconut oil, cocoa butter, or lanolin, are available as natural bases. Salves are easy to create in your kitchen with a minimum of ingredients.

BASIC SALVE RECIPE

This recipe will provide the guidelines for making any type of salve. Vary the flowers and the herbs with the season and for particular needs. Experimenting and creating unique potions is part of the enjoyment of flower alchemy.

> 2 ounces fresh flowers and flowering herbs, or 1 ounce dried flowers and flowering herbs
> 1 cup vegetable oil, such as olive, apricot, almond, sesame, and so on
> 2 ounces beeswax

1. Chop or tear the flowers and herbs into small pieces, or put them through a grinder or an expeller-type of juicer, or in a food processor.
2. Gently heat the oil and flowers and herbs in a double boiler for 45 minutes to 1 hour; stir frequently and do not allow to boil. (A few spoonfuls of alcohol, vodka or wine, can help dispel the smell caused by overheating the oil.) If you have the time, let the mixture sit overnight to extract more of the essence.
3. Reheat the mixture the next day. Strain the mixture through a sieve or a piece of cheesecloth or muslin into the double boiler, pressing the oil from the flowers and leaves.
4. Add the beeswax to the strained oil and melt slowly. Beat together when melted.
5. Put a spoonful of this mixture in the freezer to see what its consistency will be when it cools. If it is excessively hard, then add more oil. If too thin, add more beeswax.
6. Add a few drops of tincture of benzoin as a preservative (see page 193) and a few drops of fragrant essential oil, if desired.
7. Pour into sterilized jars. This recipe will make about 1¼ cups of salve. Label with the ingredients and date, and store in the refrigerator or other cool place.

FLOWER SALVE RECIPES

I've discovered various combinations of flowers and flowering herbs that are especially effective in salves. You can make the following flower salves using the preceding recipe as a guide for the correct proportions of oil, beeswax, flowers, and herbs. For example, if you have 6 ounces of fresh plant material, you will need 3 cups of oil and about 6 ounces of beeswax. You can create your own salves using your favorite flowers and herbs.

SPRING WILD FLOWER HERB SALVE

This salve will both dry and relieve irritated tissue. It contains astringent plantain, dock, and miner's lettuce; cleansing cleavers, and emollient chickweed and mallow.

Chickweed, flowers and leaves
Cleavers, flowers and leaves
Dock, leaves
Mallow, flowers and leaves
Miner's lettuce, flowers and leaves
Plantain, leaves

GARDEN FLOWER SALVE

These flowers have toning, astringent, and emollient properties. Use them for irritations, rashes, and other minor skin problems. Refer to the Lists of Flowers (see pages 184–187) to see how each of these flowers affects the skin.

Calendula
Chamomile
Comfrey, flowers and leaves
Honeysuckle
Mullein
Nasturtium
Rose
Rose geranium, flowers and leaves
Thyme, flowers and leaves
Violet, flowers and leaves

GENTLE SALVE

Hollyhock, comfrey, and chickweed are nurturing; elder flower is softly revitalizing; jasmine is aromatic and calming; orange flower helps to moisturize. This is a mild salve for dry skin.

Chickweed, flowers and leaves
Comfrey, flowers and leaves
Elder flower
Hollyhock
Jasmine
Orange flower

FLOWER LOTIONS

A lotion is made by using less beeswax than in a salve and by emulsifying the oil and water together into a creamy consistency. In making lotions, fragrant flower waters can be used. Thickening agents such as liquid lecithin, coconut oil, or lanolin can replace the need for beeswax. After making the lotion, pour a small amount into a container for daily use and store the rest in the refrigerator.

The following two lotions make aromatic creams that nourish your skin.

ROSE-LAVENDER FLOWER LOTION

Lavender and rose water make a perfumed lotion that will tighten and beautify your skin. The oil and vitamin E help to smooth and nurture.

>   1 cup almond or apricot oil
>   1 cup rose-lavender flower water (or pure water with rose and lavender oil added)
>   2 teaspoons liquid lecithin
>   1 tablespoon vitamin E oil
>   Rose or lavender essential oil, to scent

Warm the oil and the flower water separately. Pour the oil slowly into the water with the liquid lecithin, beating continuously with an electric beater until it has a creamy consistency. Beat in the vitamin E oil and add a few drops of rose oil, if desired. Pour into sterilized bottles and store in the refrigerator. If a hand cream consistency is desired, add more lecithin and beat well. If the lotion separates, shake before using. Yield 2⅛ cups.

ROSE-CHAMOMILE-LAVENDER LOTION

This recipe was created by a friend who spent many years perfecting it.

>   2 cups water
>   4 to 6 ounces mixed rose, chamomile, and lavender flowers
>   2 cups vegetable oil, such as olive, apricot, almond, sesame, and so on
>   ½ ounce beeswax
>   Rose or orange essential oil, to scent

Bring the water to a boil, turn off the heat, and add the flowers. Let the flowers steep 30 to 40 minutes, as in making a tea. Warm the oil in a double boiler, add the beeswax, and heat until melted. Strain the flowers out of the water and pour the water into a mixing bowl. Float the bowl of flower water in a larger bowl filled with ice water. Add about half the oil-beeswax mixture to the water slowly, beating at a medium speed with an electric mixer. When well mixed, add the rest of the oil slowly, beating at a lower speed. The mixture will turn into a wonderful thick lotion. Add essential oil, if desired. Other flowers may be substituted, such as elder, fennel, calendula, or comfrey. There is no preservative in this lotion, so keep it in sterilized bottles, refrigerated. Use a small amount in a jar for your daily needs. Yield 4⅛ cups.

To make a longer lasting lotion, extract the essence of the flowers in vinegar (see page 205), and use one tablespoon of each flower vinegar instead of the flower "tea" water. Use the two cups of plain water as in the above recipe. The vinegar will help preserve this preparation. Your skin will feel deliciously well cared for from the oils and toning flowers.

FLOWER BALMS

A balm is a salve that soothes; these two are specifically for chapped or dry lips and sore muscles.

CARNATION LIP BALM

½ cup carnation petals, or a few drops pure carnation oil
1 cup olive, almond, or apricot oil
1½ ounces beeswax
2 tablespoons vitamin E oil
1 tablespoon honey (optional)

Heat the carnation petals gently in the oil for 30 to 35 minutes, or add the carnation oil to the oil. Strain out the petals and add the beeswax, vitamin E oil, and honey. When the beeswax is melted, beat well. Pour into small sterilized containers, label, and refrigerate. Yield 1¼ cups.

Other flowers may be used in lip balms for their fragrance and/or mild, restorative properties. Try comfrey, elder flower, honeysuckle, melilot, orange, rose, or violet.

WARMING BALM

This balm should be used specifically for sore muscles, headaches, and sinus congestion. Because the oils are so strong and penetrating, *they should be kept from eyes and mucous membranes and only used externally.* Made from the essential oils of flowers and herbs that are stimulating, it creates a pleasant warmth in the tissues.

½ cup apricot, almond, or olive oil
1½ ounces camphor oil
½ teaspoon lavender oil
¼ teaspoon clove oil
1 tablespoon peppermint oil
1½ tablespoons eucalyptus oil
½ to 1 ounce beeswax

Heat all the ingredients very gently in a double boiler until the wax is just melted. Beat well for a few minutes and put a spoonful of the balm in the freezer to check consistency. If it is too thin, add more beeswax. Pour into sterilized containers and label with ingredients and the date. Yield ¾ to 1 cup.

FLOWER FACIALS

Have you ever watched children playfully smear mud or food on their faces? They are unwittingly creating facials for themselves. I too enjoy covering my face with preparations made from food, clays, and flowers. Almonds, honey, avocado, yogurt, cucumber, and papaya are all nutrient-rich foods excellent for external application as well as internal digestion. These ingredients nourish, tone, and cleanse the skin. Make your own facials with different foods and flowers that are suited to your particular needs. Last night's soup or salad dressing may easily become today's facial!

ELDER FLOWER-HONEY-YOGURT FACIAL

Honey is a softener and moisturizer, yogurt feeds the skin with protein and calcium, and elder flowers are toning.

> ¼ cup elder flowers
> ¼ cup plain thick yogurt
> 2 tablespoons honey

Mix together the flowers, thick yogurt, and honey. Spread on face with cotton balls. Relax for 15 to 30 minutes and rinse off.

CUCUMBER-ROSE PETAL FACIAL

Cucumber is refining, cooling, and tightening to oily skin. Rose petals are revitalizing and slightly astringent.

> 1 cucumber
> 2 handfuls rose petals

Blend the cucumber and rose petals in the blender. Apply to face and neck with cotton balls, leave on for 10 to 20 minutes while you relax.

ROSE GERANIUM-ALMOND MASK

The rose geranium flowers and the rose water are astringent and firming, creating a good balance with the emollient qualities of the oil-rich almonds.

½ cup almonds, ground medium fine
1 handful rose geranium flowers, dried and powdered
Rose water or pure water

Mix together the almonds and the powdered rose geraniums or rose petals. Add enough rose water or pure water to make a paste and apply to face and neck. Relax for 15 to 20 minutes, then wash off, rubbing slightly, so that the almond granules cleanse the pores.

AVOCADO-CHAMOMILE MASK

Avocado is rich in vitamin E and will, like chamomile, improve and nourish tired, dry skin.

1 avocado
1 handful chamomile flowers, fresh or dried

Mix the avocado and chamomile flowers together and rub over the face and neck. Relax for at least 10 minutes.

SALAD DRESSING FACIAL

One day my favorite herbalist friend came to lunch and after enjoying a delicious garden fresh flower salad demonstrated to me how good the dressing was for the skin. He first used it as a hand lotion; later, I carried it a step farther and used it on my face.

As a facial, this recipe offers the nurturing effects of the oil, avocado, and sunflower seeds, the reviving chlorophyll of the parsley, and the toning benefits of the calendulas.

¼ cup olive oil
¼ cup water
1 avocado
1 bunch parsley
¼ cup sunflower seeds
1 handful calendula petals

Mix all the ingredients together in the blender, reserving some of the calendula petals to fold in later. The mixture should be very thick. For a salad dressing we double the amount of oil and water and add garlic, cayenne, and soy sauce.

GARDENIA-PAPAYA-BANANA MASK

Living in Hawaii, in the middle of a papaya and banana orchard with fragrant gardenias blooming prolifically, gave me the opportunity to use the fruit both internally and externally. The banana and papaya are both nourishing and gentle to the skin; the papaya is also slightly astringent.

> 1 ripe banana
> 1 ripe papaya
> 1 small gardenia, petals only

Mash together the banana, papaya, and gardenia petals and apply to the face and neck. After 20 minutes it will dry and begin to tighten the skin. Wash off with warm water and splash with cool water or Flower Facial Vinegar (see page 205).

FULLY FLOWERING FACIAL

This mixture is a good balance of emollient, astringent, and toning flowers. Adding fennel flowers will help remove wrinkles.

> 2 handfuls each, petals only, of rose, chamomile, calendula, hollyhock

Crush all together gently with your fingers until their juices are released and they stick together. Then apply directly to your face and let dry for 15 to 20 minutes.

HONEY-ROSEMARY-ROSE PETAL FACIAL

The honey both preserves and extracts the essence of the flowers. They, therefore, may be left in or strained out. As a skin food, honey revitalizes, moisturizes, and softens. The rose petals and rosemary act as astringents.

I have a small brown crock of this honey mixture always ready for an instant facial.

1 cup honey
1 handful rose petals
1 handful rosemary flowers

Simply mix the honey and flower petals together and leave them in a warm place for a few weeks, then store, covered, in the refrigerator.

Apply this facial by the fingerful, allowing it to pull and massage the face gently. It will become tacky and patting the face will stimulate circulation. Be careful around the delicate areas of the eyes. Leave on for 15 to 20 minutes and rinse off with warm water. Your skin will have a pink glow and feel very smooth. If the refrigerated honey becomes hard, put the container in a saucepan of water and heat gently. See Flowering Facial Ritual (page 217).

FLOWER CLAYS

Earth contains many fine deposits of powdered clays in an array of colors—green, white, rose, yellow, blue—that can be used as skin cleansers and toners. Clay has been recognized since earliest times for its healing properties. It is rich in minerals, such as iron, calcium, magnesium, and silica, and is able to absorb toxins and impurities from the body. Skin problems such as pimples, clogged pores, and minor irritations respond well to clay treatments.

Clay is the first thing I reach for if I'm stung by a bee. After I remove the stinger, the clay helps to draw the poisons out and reduces the swelling. This is helpful to remember in the woods! A little clay by the stream and some water or saliva can quickly tend to a scrape or sting.

Many health spas provide clay baths in which the whole body is submerged in warm mud. I was once led, salamander fashion, right into the mud and slimy green algae in a lake—it was a very sensual, if slippery, experience. My resistance soon gave way to a child-like abandonment of playing in the mud and getting totally "messy." After rinsing, my skin felt exceptionally good. Clay can also be used dry as a baby powder or deodorant. Or, it can be added to bath water for the beneficial effects of its minerals.

For a facial mask, clay may be prepared with ground aromatic flowers selected for their scent and their effect on the skin. When clay is used in this way, it stimulates the circulation and tones and rejuvenates facial tissue. There are many colors of clay for particular skin types and needs:

Green clay—This is used for first-aid, external applications and is very strong, tightening, and cleansing.
White clay—This very mild clay, good for delicate skin, can also be used as a deodorant or powder.
Red or rose clay—This substance is good for oily skin and rough areas.
Yellow clay—This is best on very oily or blemished skin.
Blue clay—This stimulates, balances, and tones all types of skin.

Add the following dried ground flowers for their respective specific effects:

Elder flower	Rose
Chamomile	Rose geranium
Lavender	Thyme

To prepare a facial mask, mix one handful dried and powdered flowers to one cup clay and mix well. Place the clay in a deep bowl, earthenware crock, or nonmetallic container and cover by ½ inch water. Mix together gently with a wooden spoon. Let sit for a few hours or days so that the clay absorbs all the water it needs and becomes ready for immediate use. If the clay dries out, add more water. The clay can also be combined with pure vegetable oils, such as olive, almond, or safflower, rather than water for dry skin. It should be a smooth paste.

To apply the clay, simply coat the face and neck with a thin layer. Let dry well, then wash it off with warm water; a washcloth or *loofah* sponge may be needed to cleanse the skin well.

For a quick application, mix the clay in the palm of your hand or in a small bowl with a little water until it's a creamy consistency. To treat problem areas or pimples, apply a thick coat of clay and leave on overnight. Clays are available in many natural food stores. It has been said that the clay nearest you is the best to use—perhaps you can find some in your own back yard!

FLOWER FACIAL VINEGARS

Flower vinegars are good for firming and invigorating the skin after bathing, shaving, or a facial sauna. Apple cider vinegar helps to restore the proper pH to the skin. The pH of the skin refers to its acid-alkaline balance. There is an "acid mantle" on the skin that is important to maintain because it resists harmful bacteria.

    1 cup apple cider vinegar
    1 cup rose, rose-lavender, or rose-elder flower water
    1 handful chamomile flowers
    1 handful elder flowers

Put all of the ingredients in a quart jar in a warm place, shaking daily, for 10 days to 2 weeks. Then strain out the flowers and store the vinegar in the refrigerator. Because apple cider vinegar is raw, a "mother" or dark mass may form in the bottle; this will not hurt the vinegar and may be used to start new vinegar.

The same recipe may be used with clover, rosemary, violet, or other flowers depending on your particular skin type.

FLOWER HAIR RINSES

Flower hair rinses leave the pleasing aromas of the flowers in your hair as they remove unwanted soap residues. They also condition and nourish the hair.

    1 quart pure water
    1 handful each chamomile, lavender, rosemary, flowers and leaves,
        calendula, nettle leaves (handle nettles with care as they may
        "sting" your skin)
    2 tablespoons agar-agar flakes
    1 cup water
    ½ cup apple cider vinegar

Boil the water, turn off the heat, and add the flowers and herbs. Steep 30 minutes or leave overnight. The longer it is left, the stronger it will be. Bring the cup of water to a boil with the agar-agar, boil 4 minutes, stirring frequently, and add the strained flower tea. Pour in the

apple cider vinegar and stir the mixture well. Store in sterilized jars in the refrigerator. Use 1 to 2 tablespoons on washed hair. Either leave on or rinse out, as desired.

For a simpler way to make a flowering hair rinse, omit the agar-agar and just add the vinegar to the flower tea. You may also omit the tea, simply add the herbs directly to the vinegar, and let the mixture steep in a warm place for several weeks. Strain and bottle and use the rinse by the tablespoonful diluted in one cup water. If your hair is dry, one ounce jojoba or one quarter cup olive oil may be added to the above recipe; if your hair is oily, add more vinegar.

Following is a list of flowers and flowering herbs that may be substituted in the above recipe for a particular type of hair:

DRY HAIR

Chamomile	Elder flower
Clover	Nettle
Comfrey	Rosemary

OILY HAIR

Calendula	Mullein
Fennel	Nettle
Lavender	Rose

NORMAL HAIR

Chamomile	Rose
Clover	Rosemary
Nettle	

Chamomile, calendula, and mullein lighten or brighten blonde hair. Sage darkens brunette or auburn hair.

FLOWER POWDERS

Facial and body powders have been in and out of fashion over the years. When I was young, I used to visit the cosmetic lady at my father's department store and watch her mix them to match the skin color of her clients. She had jars full of brown- to rose- to white-toned powders and big fluffy powder puffs.

The following natural ingredient flower powders are good to use after baths, as deodorants, and on a baby's delicate skin. Some people are allergic to orrisroot. Be sure to test the powder on your skin for possible reactions.

> 2 ounces flowers, dried and powdered flowers, such as chamomile, elder flower, honeysuckle, lavender, lilac, orange, rose, thyme, violet
> 2 ounces arrowroot
> 1 ounce orrisroot

Combine the ingredients, put into jars, and label.

FLOWER STEAMS, BATHS, AND SAUNAS

Facial steams, baths, and saunas are used to open the pores, to stimulate sweating, and to help your body receive the beneficial properties of the flowers. Different flowers can be added for their effect on the skin (see pages 184–187), or they can be helpful in the relief of congestion, headache, and tension.

Sweating helps to cleanse toxins from the system and to improve circulation in the body. The skin, which normally releases about thirty percent of the body's wastes through perspiration, is the largest eliminative organ. For good health it is important to encourage the cleansing action of the skin by inducing sweating with a bath or sauna. These are also relaxing to the muscles, effective in dissolving tension and in improving skin tone.

FLOWER FACIAL STEAMS

To prepare a flower steam, first gather the necessary fresh or dried flowers or flowering herbs. One or two handfuls of each per four quarts of water are sufficient. *Use half the amount of flowers if they are dried.* Bring the water to a boil, turn off the heat, and add the flowers. Steep, covered, for 10 to 20 minutes.

Prepare a comfortable place for steaming, a table or desk. Place towels under the pot. Remove the lid, put face over pot, and place a towel over your head and the pot, adjusting it to allow some of the heat and steam to escape if it is too hot. Carefully inhale the delicious aroma.

The scent of the flowers will perfume the room. When a few drops of sweat fall into the pot, take it as a signal to stop. The cleansing process has occurred and the flower steam has been deeply inhaled. Steam your face more than once, if desired, then rinse with cool water to close the pores. Afterwards you'll have a bright, glowing face and soft, clean skin. Now step outside; the day will often seem fresher and clearer than before. A few drops of essential oil may be used instead of the flowers, but be *careful* because some of them are *very strong*.

The following are some combinations of flowers and flowering herbs to use for specific facial steams.

CONGESTION STEAM

The aromas of these flowers are stimulating and penetrating and will open the sinuses. Eucalyptus and lavender are known for their antiseptic properties that deter disease-promoting bacteria present in colds and congestion. Sage and eucalyptus are known in herbal medicine for their use as expectorants.

Eucalyptus, flowers and leaves
Lavender
Peppermint, flowers and leaves
Sage, flowers and leaves

ENERGIZER STEAM

The strong, bracing aromas of these flowering herbs will help awaken your senses. This steam is good for feelings of dullness and oily skin.

Lavender
Lemon
Mint, flowers and leaves
Rosemary, flowers and leaves
Sage, flowers and leaves
Thyme, flowers and leaves

TENSION STEAM

These flowers and herbs are known to be calming and relaxing. Each breath of this fragrant steam will help ease your tension while refreshing your skin.

Catnip, flowers and leaves
Chamomile, flowers and leaves
Hops
Jasmine
Linden

PORE-CLEANSING STEAM

This steam will open your pores. The flowers in it help pull impurities out as you perspire, healing blemishes and leaving the skin cleansed.

Burdock, flowers and leaves
Calendula
Chamomile
Clover, red
Elder flower

See Facial Ritual (page 217) and Headache Ritual (page 217) for other steams and the Lists of Flowers (pages 184–187) to create facial steams for your particular needs.

FLOWER BATHS

Nature's own flower baths are the pools in rivers where aromatic blossoms fall and scent the water. One of my richest memories is of hiking through the Hawaiian jungle to a waterfall and pool with lovely African tulip blossoms floating luxuriously on the surface.

Throughout history bathing has gone in and out of style. The Greeks saw water as a direct link with the gods, to be used for healing purposes. Homer, in his epics, wrote about the custom of honoring guests with baths and aromatic oils. Steam baths, sulfur baths, and mineral baths were all known for their therapeutic properties. The Grecian baths were often associated with the athletes and the gymnasium. They were taken cold for stimulation before games and hot for relaxation after performing.

The Romans, with their advanced system of aquaducts to carry water, created public baths that were among their finest architectural and artistic achievements. They were huge complexes adorned with elaborately sculpted marble, gilded and painted ceilings, and splendid works of art. They included theaters, galleries, libraries, and meeting rooms along with the baths. A typical visit to a bath could take up to five hours, beginning with an application of oil, then on to exercise, steam baths, cold and hot rinses, and ending with a massage using aromatic oils. These baths became important social gathering places.

During the Middle Ages there was very little bathing for cleanliness or for pleasure. Primitive living conditions made it very difficult to even prepare a bath. However, when the knights returned from the Crusades in the East, they brought the idea of Turkish baths with them. The Europeans called these baths "stews" and they were common in the twelfth century. These public baths began to degenerate in the fourteenth and fifteenth centuries; they became havens for illicit behavior and were eventually closed down.

Elizabethans of the sixteenth century rarely bathed, relying largely on perfumes and powders to mask odors. During the late seventeenth century there was a renewed interest in bathing, especially in England, where it was quite fashionable to entertain while bathing. All this came to a self-conscious end in the eighteenth century, when the prevailing

sense of morality discouraged nudity. Even in early nineteenth century Europe, bathing was a rare luxury.

Early American Puritans disapproved of baths, and the amount of bathing and sale of tubs were regulated by law. This jurisdiction gradually relaxed, but on a practical level it was still a major event to prepare a bath. Wood and water had to be carried into the house, the fire built, the water heated, the area prepared, and when it was all over the water had to be taken out again. It wasn't until the late nineteenth century that bathrooms with hot and cold running water first became a household standard. By the turn of the present century the bathroom was much as we know it now.

Today there's a renaissance of pleasurable and therapeutic bathing utilizing hot tubs, saunas, steam baths, and all the necessary embellishments. Baths are both relaxing and nurturing. By adding flowers to the tub it is possible to create specific effects for specific needs. Taking the time to prepare special flower baths can do much to promote continued well-being.

Each year I grow, gather, and dry flowers—chamomile, rose petals, lavender, thyme, lemon balm, comfrey, and calendula—for my own baths and to give to friends. Prepare a flower bath by gathering together a handful (about one half ounce) of each dried flower or two handfuls of each fresh flower. Bring to a boil two to three quarts of water, turn off the heat, add the flowers. Steep twenty minutes. Then strain this strong flower infusion into the filled tub. Another method is to put the herbs into a muslin bag and allow the hot bath water to run through it, then float it in the tub.

One of the sweetest baths I've ever taken was made for me by a beautiful little girl we visited in Florida. She floated handfuls of freshly picked orange blossoms in the bath. This is a wonderful luxury but can also clog the drain, so be careful of floating blossoms unless they are large.

To make a hand or foot bath, follow the same directions for the bath above and strain the flowers into a container of warm water large enough for the hands or feet. Concentrated *mint oil,* because of the cooling effect of the menthol, is not good in the bath. However fresh mint leaves are fine to use. Other fragrant essential oils may be added by the dropful directly to the bath.

SORE MUSCLE BATH

The lavender and rosemary in this bath stimulate circulation, easing sore muscles. Comfrey, hollyhock, elder flower and chamomile comfort and calm your aching body.

> Chamomile
> Comfrey, flowers and leaves
> Elder flowers
> Hollyhock
> Lavender
> Rosemary, flowers and leaves

RELAXING BATH

Lie back and allow the restful properties of all these flowers to ease your tension. A perfect bath to enjoy before bedtime for a sweet repose.

    Chamomile
    Lemon balm, flowers and leaves
    Linden flowers
    Jasmine
    Passionflower (large enough to float whole)
    Rose

FRAGRANT BATH

Choose any of these aromatic flowers and use singly or in combination.

    Acacia
    Elder flower
    Gardenia
    Honeysuckle
    Jasmine
    Lavender
    Lemon verbena
    Rose petals
    Scented geranium
    Violet

ITCH AND INFLAMMATION BATH

These flowers and herbs are all emollients, easing the discomfort of irritated tissue.

    Chickweed, flowers and leaves
    Borage
    Comfrey, flowers and leaves
    Mallow, flowers and leaves

ASTRINGENT BATH

The flowers in this bath firm, tighten, and dry. They are good for oily skin conditions or minor scratches.

    Lemon flowers
    Orange flowers
    Rose geranium
    Rosemary, flowers and leaves
    Thyme, flowers and leaves

SKIN-SOFTENING BATH

A bath to leave your skin glowing, silky, and youthful. Elder flowers revive and soften, while the rest of the flowers are gentle emollients.

Comfrey, flowers and leaves
Elder flower
Hollyhock
Mallow, flowers and leaves

FLOWER SAUNAS

The word sauna comes from the Finnish word referring to the bathhouse. Most saunas as we know them today originated in the early Finnish culture and first came to America in the seventeenth century with Finnish immigrants.

A sauna is a small wooden room or building that is heated by a wood stove or a gas or electric unit on which river bed rocks are placed. There are wooden benches for seating, and the room is usually heated to 160 to 210 degrees. *(People with heart problems or sensitive systems should sauna only with a doctor's approval.)* The idea of inducing sweat as a form of bathing is a very old one. Ancient Romans took regular steam baths in the *calidarium* and the Turkish were known for their indulgent sweat-inducing baths.

American Indians had sweat lodges that were small stick-frame huts covered with a mixture of mud, pine needles, and grass or with buffalo hides, rugs, and blankets. Heated rocks were put into a pot in the center and water was thrown onto them, creating a hot vapor. They were almost always located by a stream which the bathers would jump into afterward. These were a place for communal bathing and social gathering. Indian traditions suggested that steam baths chased unwanted spirits from the body.

Taking a sauna is a pleasant event to enjoy with friends or alone for its cleansing, relaxing, and rejuvenating effects. It's best not to eat before sweating, since the digestive process is inhibited by excessive heat. A hot cup of Flower Sauna Tea facilitates sweating. Combine:

Calendula
Elder flower
Peppermint, flowers and leaves

Use 1 tablespoon of the mixture of dried herbs for 1 cup of boiled water. Steep 20 minutes. Yarrow blossoms may also be used, but include only a few because they are bitter. These herbs are diaphoretic, which means they have a relaxing action on the sweat glands; this results in increased perspiration and improved blood circulation.

A dry brush massage is excellent before taking a sauna. This is done with a natural bristle, long-handled brush. Rub all over the body in a vigorous, circular motion, brushing off any dead skin. In Finland they rub themselves with birch twigs before and during the sauna. This promotes sweating and cleanses the skin.

While in the sauna, the different beneficial effects of Flower Teas can be enjoyed in ways other than by drinking them. Make these teas by using a handful of each flower or flowering herb (about ½ ounce) per 2 quarts of water, boil the water, turn off the heat, and add the flowers. Steep 20 minutes and strain; it is now ready to be sprinkled *over the rocks.*

SINUS FLOWER SAUNA

These flower aromas help promote decongestion of the sinuses—terrific for a cold.

Eucalyptus, flowers and leaves
Mint, flowers and leaves
Sage, flowers and leaves

STIMULATING FLOWER SAUNA

These aromas refresh your body and mind. You'll probably feel alert and fully awake after the sauna.

Bee balm, flowers and leaves
Carnation
Lavender
Rosemary, flowers and leaves
Thyme, flowers and leaves

CALMING FLOWER SAUNA

All three of these flowers are known in herbal medicine as calmatives. They help to ease an overwrought nervous system.

Chamomile
Linden
Violet

SWEET SCENT FLOWER SAUNA

This is a way to bring your garden into the sauna and luxuriate in rich aromas.

Honeysuckle
Jasmine
Rose

After a sauna you can take a cool to warm shower; some people like to come back to normal temperature slowly, while others like the shock of immediately closing their pores by dipping into a pool, stream, or cold shower. Then RELAX. I like to lie down in my chamomile lawn and do some deep breathing or a Flower Visualization (see page 245) for at least fifteen minutes. It's a good time for yoga, stretching, or massage. Treat the skin to some Super Flower Skin Oil (see page 194) or a little Flower Balm Oil (see page 195) if you have any sore muscles. Remember that it's important to replenish the water that your body has lost. Drink a light Flower Nectar Sun Tea (see page 169) or some pure water. It's been said that everyone looks most beautiful an hour after a sauna.

FLOWERING HEADACHE RITUAL

This ritual almost always brings some relief. Begin by gathering flowers and flowering herbs from the garden. Going outside to be among the plants helps me to feel better immediately. If fresh herbs are not available, use half as many dried herbs. The invigorating aromas of rosemary and thyme will clear your head; chamomile, lemon balm, and rose provide calming scents. Gather large handfuls of:

Chamomile flowers
Comfrey, flowers and leaves
Lemon balm, flowers and leaves
Peppermint, flowers and leaves
Rose petals
Rosemary, flowers and leaves
Thyme, flowers and leaves

Put the flowering herbs into 3 to 4 quarts of boiling water, turn off the heat, and steep, covered, for 20 minutes. Then lift the lid, cover the head with a towel, and carefully breathe in the steam (as explained in Flower Facial Steams, see page 207). Enjoy the refreshing fragrance, then cool off with a splash of water.

I also prepare Chamomile Tea (2 teaspoons per cup of hot water), let it steep for 20 minutes, and when it is ready and the steaming is over strain the potful of flowering herbs into a filled bathtub. Then I lie back and sip my chamomile tea. The flowers leave my skin feeling renewed, firm, and smooth. Then I crawl into bed and sleep for an hour or so. When I wake up I usually feel rejuvenated and thankful for the aromatic flowers.

FLOWERING FACIAL RITUAL

This ritual requires at least an hour of relaxing and caring for yourself. Doing this facial a few times a month will make your skin shine with renewed vitality. Invite a few friends over and enjoy indulging in skin care together.

Flower Steam

Gather together such ingredients as:

Chamomile
Comfrey, flowers and leaves
Elder flower
Lavender
Mint, flowers and leaves
Rosemary, flowers and leaves

Boil 3 to 4 quarts of water, turn off the heat, and add 1 handful of each flowering herb if fresh, ½ handful each if dried. Steep, covered, for 10 to 20 minutes, remove the lid, and cover your head with a towel over the pot. (See Flower Facial Steams, page 207.) Breathe deeply and adjust the intensity of the steam. The combination of astringent, toning, cleansing, and emollient flowers will open and cleanse your pores while gently strengthening the tissue. When you are sweating sufficiently, take a break, rinse your face in cool water and go on to—

Flower Clay Pack

Using a toning, light white or blue clay mixed with dried, ground elder and rose petals, cover the face and neck with the moistened mixture. For dry skin, moisten the clay with oil. For oily skin, moisten with fragrant flower water (such as rose-lavender) or just pure water. Normal skin can take either the oil or the water method. (See Flower Clays, page 203.) Lie down and relax. It's a good time for a guided Flower Visualization described in Chapter 7 (see page 245). After the clay is dry, 10 to 20 minutes, rinse your face with warm water and continue with—

Rose-Rosemary Honey Facial

Honey is a natural moisturizer and emollient that leaves the skin very soft and silky. The rose petals and rosemary flowers are both toning to the skin. (See page 202 for the recipe.) Using your fingertips, cover your face with the honey and flower petals. When it becomes tacky, pat your face with your fingertips; this will cleanse the pores, increase circulation, and tone the skin. Try doing it cheek to cheek with a friend and don't forget to lick your lips. Leave on 10 to 15 minutes and rinse off with warm water.

Super Flower Oil or Flower Skin Toner

If, after all this, your skin feels dry, apply just a touch of Super Flower Skin Oil (see page 194). If your skin feels very oily or even just right, you might want to use some Flower Facial Vinegar (see page 205). The vinegar restores the proper pH while the flowers rejuvenate the skin.

Relax and enjoy a cup of flower tea.

THE SENSUAL FLOWERS

The Tantric love ritual, which devotes much time to preparing for love—sharing baths, massage, yoga, and breathing—has inspired the Sensual Flower Ritual. Flower fragrances can be wonderfully seductive; their soft, gentle enveloping aromas can lead to relaxation and to love. Begin by gathering and preparing the sensual flowers with your lover.

Flower Petal Bath

Gather handfuls of rose petals, honeysuckle blossoms, and jasmine flowers; heat a pot of water until just hot, add the flowers, and steep for 30 minutes; strain it into the tub. Float roses, rosebuds, and one gardenia in the water. Luxuriate in the healing aromas; allow them to relieve your deepest tension.

Moonlight Flower Tea

To be made in moonlight and shared in moonlight. Gather fresh blossoms of edible sweet flowers, such as honeysuckle, Johnny-jump-up, rose, borage, orange blossoms, rosemary, or lavender. Fill a quart jar half full of them, fill with pure water, and let sit in the moonlit night. Full-moon flower tea is best when set out just as the sun sets and the moon rises. Serve with a fresh flower floating on top and drink it in beautiful glasses while bathing.

Jasmine or Carnation Massage Oil

Massage is the next step in this sensual flower experience. It is meant to ease any persistent tension or inhibition and delight you with flower aromas. Carnation oil has been known to heighten sensual desire. It is spicy and stimulating. Jasmine smells rich and full bodied; it hints at an earthy sweetness. Pure essential flower oils are expensive, but a few drops can be put into a carrier oil, such as almond or apricot, and used for massage.

After sharing the warmth of a flowering bath, some sweetly perfumed tea under a gently moonlit sky, and a relaxing fragrant massage, luxuriate in love-making amidst sweet-smelling sheets and pillows. Make your bed placing small bags filled with lavender blossoms and rose petals between the sheets and in the pillow cases.

Later, enjoy some exquisite flower food, such as nasturtiums stuffed with cream cheese, walnuts, and currants and topped with borage blossoms. Prepare a beautiful flower salad or a blossom berry pie; food that nourishes the spirit as well as the body.

There are so many ways of sharing flowers sensually!

6
AROMATHERAPY
AND FLOWER
ESSENCES

In the middle of the afternoon on a deliciously warm day stroll through a garden that is perfumed with the fragrance of jasmine, honeysuckle, rose, or carnation. Take a deep breath and experience the voluptuousness of their aromas. Do they make you feel stimulated, or do they calm you? Do pleasant images fill your mind because of these flowers and their unique scents? Sometimes I think of a particular flower and its fragrance just to evoke a pleasant memory or feeling.

The aromas of hyacinth and lily of the valley remind me of some of the best moments of my childhood. Each spring my father would put a large container of my favorite deep purple hyacinths in my bedroom so that I could fall asleep enveloped in their spicy fragrance. Lily of the valley grew as a border to a flower bed in our garden. I eagerly awaited their return each spring and was thrilled when I found the first tiny white bells with their delicate scent. Over the years these flowers have made me remember the security and contentment I knew as a child.

When I first visited Hawaii many years ago I recall walking down the road and being fragrantly greeted by the potent bouquet of night-blooming jasmine. Gardenia and plumeria, with their full-bodied sweetness, send me instantly back to the garden I helped tend there. Their aroma is thick and lush, like a tropical evening.

In Northern California near my home there is a picturesque spot on a cliff overlooking the ocean. There a tree house has been carefully set on the branches of a eucalyptus tree. I enjoy sitting in it, especially when the tree is in full flower, breathing in the clean, pure eucalyptus scent.

Fragrances have affected me in many different ways throughout my life. Aromatherapy is the art of using the aromas of flowers and plants, as well as the essential oils obtained from them, to elicit a particular response in an individual. This therapy is based on years of observation by European doctors, as well as on an understanding of the traditional uses of herbs.

Bring aromatherapy into your personal life in the simplest way possible—just open up your nostrils, take a deep breath, and notice how the different aromas you meet on a daily basis affect you. Pay close attention to the images, ideas, physical feelings, emotions, and associations different smells awaken in you. Enjoy this exploration as you learn more about the world of scent and aromatherapy.

A BRIEF HISTORY OF AROMATICS

The aroma of flowers in perfumes and scented oils has been used since earliest times. The word perfume comes from the Latin, *per* (through) and *fumum* (smoke) and refers to the ancients' use of scented smoke in many of their holy rites. This usually involved burning wood, tree sap, or the dried leaves of aromatic plants. Today similar types of incense are still used in the religious ceremonies of many cultures.

The Egyptians used aromatics in their mummification process, including myrrh, frankincense, cedarwood, and cassia oils. Cleopatra was renowned for her lavish use of perfume and fine oils. It is said that the power of fragrance helped her in winning over Mark Antony. Shakespeare wrote in *Antony and Cleopatra:*

> The barge she sat in, like a burnished throne
> Burn'd on the water; the poop was beaten gold;
> Purple the sails, and so perfumed that
> The winds were love-sick with them.

Fragrant oils were used by the Hebrews for special purification rituals. In the Bible the Song of Solomon is filled with lyrical references to aromatics and spices, such as spikenard, saffron, calamus, cinnamon, frankincense, myrrh, aloes, lily, and camphire (henna).

> His cheeks are as a bed of spices, as sweet flowers: his lips like lilies, dropping sweet smelling myrrh.
>
> (Song of Solomon 5:13)

There are references to Jesus being anointed with fragrant oils:

> Then took Mary a pound of ointment of spikenard, very costly, and anointed the feet of Jesus, and wiped his feet with her hair: and the house was filled with the odour of the ointment.
>
> (John 12:3)

For the Greeks, perfumes and aromatic plants were gifts from the gods. Homer, in the *Iliad* and *Odyssey,* makes several references to perfumes. He describes Juno bathing and anointing herself with "soft oils of fragrance and ambrosial showers."

Romans indulged themselves luxuriously in scented oils and perfumes. These were an important addition to their famous baths. Nero was said to have entertained his guests in banquet halls with fragrant petals falling from the ceiling, showers of rose water, and rose-covered floors. Many small and finely worked perfume bottles have been unearthed which date from that era.

Avicenna, an Arabian doctor and mystic living during the tenth century, discovered the process of essential oil distillation. Before this time whole flowers were used for scenting rooms, clothes, or hair and for flavoring drinks and foods. This required many blossoms and was limited to the flowering seasons. The new concentrated flower oils brought about even more indulgence in the use of scents and an even more strongly perfumed civilization.

In the Middle Ages small bags of strong-smelling herbs and pomanders were commonly carried or worn to mask odors caused by the lack of bathing and poor sanitation. Aromatics, such as frankincense, myrrh, and angelica were burned so that their smoke would purify the air.

Culpeper, Gerard, and other herbalists of the seventeenth century made use of many preparations with aromatic oils, distilled waters, vinegars, and other odiferous extracts for medicinal and cosmetic purposes.

Use of aromatics for their therapeutic properties has continued in more recent times with the work of the twentieth-century pioneers of aromatherapy, Rene-Maurice Gattefossé and Dr. Jean Valnet.[1] Gattefossé was involved in the perfumery business in Grasse, France. His work as a chemist led him to experiment with various flower essences. He explored their uses as powerful antiseptics. Badly burned, he was impressed by the speed with which oil of lavender healed the skin. It was he who created the word *aromatherapy* and wrote a book on the subject in 1938. His research was carried on by Valnet who used natural essences to heal wartime injuries during World War II. These were so effective he was encouraged to experiment with many other ways to use aromas for curative purposes. It was said of Valnet that

> It is almost entirely due to his work that aromatherapy is now recognized as a therapy in its own right.[2]

FINE PERFUMES

For many centuries essential oils have been carefully extracted from flowers and plants for use in creating the world's best perfumes. This is the most common way that people experience the effects of different aromas. You might find that certain individual scents complement your different moods. Often the fragrance you choose to reflect your mood of the moment will be just the one you need to promote your well-being.

The legendary French perfume industry has thrived for centuries providing expensive perfumes to those who can afford them. Since the nineteenth century, one of its main production centers has been in Grasse, in the south of France. Here the jasmine, roses, violets, lilies, lavender, and other fragrant blossoms flourish and are as prized as any farmer's crop. In earlier days these flowers were used to scent leather, and there was a successful glove-making business in Grasse. Over the years it became evident that the flowers could best be used for fine perfumes and not just to perfume fine leather.

Many years ago when I lived in France, I learned about the fascinating art of making perfume. First, an abundance of flowers must be grown outdoors; the fragrance of those cultivated in greenhouses is not potent enough for the finest essences. The flowers are picked at the height of their bloom, early in the morning, when their scent is the strongest. Once gathered, they must be processed within several hours, before they wilt and lose their peak fragrance.

It takes enormous amounts of flowers to make perfume; a thousand pounds of fresh blossoms are usually needed to create only one pound of essential oil, sometimes even less. Most oils are extracted by steam distillation. Others, such as jasmine, are very delicate and cannot endure intense heat; their essence is obtained by oil extraction.

A flower may yield different scents as a result of the conditions in which it is grown, including soil and weather, the method of extraction, and other variables. To most of our noses this may not be evident, but to "THE NOSE" of the perfume industry the slightest difference is obvious. A professional "nose" is skilled in discerning the slightest variations in aroma. With thousands of different natural and synthetic fragrances to choose from, perfumers attempt to find a balanced and full fragrance. They work at a table called an "organ" with rows and rows of bottles on shelves surrounding them, and their skill is indeed like that of a musical composer. They look for what is known as a top or high note, which is the first or immediate scent; a middle or modifier note, which blends the aromas and is the scent you smell after a few moments; and a base or long-lasting note, which is essentially a fixative that makes the perfume linger for a long time. The creation of a uniquely blended fragrance, which begins as an idea in the perfumer's mind, can take months or even years to perfect.

The final perfumed products are made by diluting the essential oils and any other ingredients with water or alcohol. The strongest and most costly product is the perfume itself; it contains a maximum amount of essential oils. Toilet waters and colognes contain more alcohol and less oil.

Perfume reacts differently on each person's skin. A scent that smells terrific on your friend may not suit you at all. Individual chemistry accounts for this and makes it important to wait a few moments before deciding on a perfume. (I like to use the essential flower oils for a totally natural perfume. Try blending a few drops of different scents together to create your own fragrance.) Whenever possible buy oils that are pure and natural.

It's interesting to note that some aromas, such as violet, can only be enjoyed for a short while. When I first experienced the phenomenon of this flower's ephemeral scent I thought I had somehow sniffed all the fragrance from the flower. Later, I learned that it had temporarily exhausted my sense of smell.

ESSENTIAL OIL AROMATHERAPY

Natural essential oils that are used in the world's finest perfumes are also used in aromatherapy. Synthetic oils won't work as well; they lack the vitality and potency of the natural ones. Essential oils are very strong: they concentrate the entire essence of the plant into drops. *USE ALL ESSENTIAL OILS WITH EXTREME CARE, BOTH EXTERNALLY AND INTERNALLY.* A drop or two will usually be all that is needed for any given application.

Essential flower oils are used in many ways for aromatherapy. Several drops in water, vinegar, oil, or honey create aromatic products that benefit the skin, as discussed in the previous chapter. Massage oils prepared with essences help release tension. Use a few drops of the undiluted essential oils in facial steams, baths, and saunas (described in detail using fresh flowers in Chapter 5.) Sometimes I just smell a fragrant oil directly from the bottle or put a drop on a handkerchief to enjoy.

EFFECTS OF FLOWER AROMAS

I'm very sensitive to certain aromas, especially when I'm not feeling well. For example, the heavier floral smells of jasmine, gardenia, or honeysuckle might be much too strong for me when I have a headache and yet seem just right at other times. By having a number of fragrances available, you can try using your own sense of smell to determine the aroma that will make you feel better. Sniff them and see which one works. Then use that one for a facial steam, massage oil, bath, or other treatment.

When I have a headache I enjoy the stimulating aromas of lavender, mint, or rosemary. If I'm tense, I use chamomile, violet, or orange oils, which are known for their relaxing effects. Jasmine, carnation, or rose oils can elicit a rejuvenating, yet calming feeling.

It's possible to fill a whole room with an aroma by adding drops of an essential oil to a pot of boiled water. Since these oils evaporate rapidly their aromas will spread quickly. This is helpful for purifying and freshening the room while receiving the specific benefits of the oils. Once when I was traveling on a long and rough airplane journey I felt a little ill and decided to use some mint oil. I ordered a glass of hot water, put a few drops in it, and breathed in the aroma. So did the rest of the plane. "Smells sort of minty in here," I heard one passenger say. I hope it was as helpful in settling their stomachs as it was mine.

Lavender oil will make the air seem very clean and invigorating. Orange oil will both relax and refresh. Lemon is a very clean and pure fragrance that makes me feel revitalized. I have also noticed that the sweet aromatics extracted from delicate flowers such as rose, jasmine, carnation, gardenia, and honeysuckle help raise my spirits. Stronger scents, such as lavender, mint, and thyme, are extracted from whole herbs, including the flowers. They seem to affect my body more directly.

SPECIFIC ESSENTIAL FLOWER OILS

What follows is a detailed look at a few of the most commonly known flower essential oils: rose, jasmine, lavender, rosemary, and chamomile. An understanding of their history and applications through the ages can be helpful as a guide to their present-day use. It is from the rich storehouse of tradition that much of our herbal knowledge is gleaned. John Gerard, Nicholas Culpeper, and John Parkinson were among the earliest herbalists whose work, in the seventeenth century, was influenced by Pliny's *Historia Naturalis* and Dioscorides' *De Materia Medica,* written in the first century.

Rose Oil

Pure rose oil is rare and very expensive; it takes nearly one hundred pounds of petals to extract one half ounce of oil. Most of the rose oils available today are either synthetic or have a few drops of pure rose essence in a carrier oil.

Rose oil is produced in several areas of the world. Bulgarian rose otto is extracted from the damask rose *(Rosa damascena).* Essence from the cabbage rose *(R. centifolia)* comes from Grasse, France, and oil from the Provence rose *(R. gallica)* is imported from Morocco.

There is a legend from the late sixteenth century that describes how the first rose oil was discovered in the extravagant festivities of a marriage ceremony. A princess and emperor of Persia were to be wed and the grounds were prepared with a watercourse filled with rose water. Can you imagine going for a swim or even dangling your feet in it! During the heat of the day a film appeared on the top of the water; the rose oil had separated and floated to the surface. It was found to be a fine perfume and became the basis of attar of roses.

Oil of rose has a light, yellowish-green color, a contrast to the vivid tones of the petals. Its two major chemical ingredients are cintronellol, which can comprise up to thirty-five percent of the oil, and geraniol, which can comprise up to seventy-five percent of the oil. These are the substances that give the essence its sweet odor.[3]

The rose has a long history of medicinal applications. Herbal tradition has recorded its usage as a nervine for headaches, to stimulate the digestion, and to purify the blood. Culpeper wrote:

> Red roses strengthen the heart, the stomach, the liver, and the retentive faculty; they mitigate the pains that arise from heat, cool inflammations, procure rest and sleep. . . .
> . . . Oil of roses is used by itself to cool hot inflammations or swellings, and to bind and stay the fluxes of humours to sores. . . .

Rose water is known to tone the skin; it is cleansing and revitalizing. Gerard wrote:

> . . . The distilled water of roses . . . bringeth sleep, which also the fresh roses themselves provoke through their sweet and pleasant smell.

Since pure rose oil is so expensive, make your own rose extractions in the form of water, oil, vinegar, or honey as described in the previous chapter. These preparations can then be used for aromatherapy in massages, baths, facials, or food. Or use the most basic form of aromatherapy—simply smell a rose!

Jasmine Oil

Jasmine oil is very expensive, precious, and exotically aromatic. It is primarily extracted from the flowers of Spanish jasmine (*Jasminum grandiflorum*) that flourish in Grasse, France. This jasmine is grown grafted onto stock of *J. officinale*. Arabian jasmine (*J. sambac*) is called pikake in Hawaii and is used for perfumes; in the Orient it is made into jasmine tea.

The jasmine flowers are gathered after the morning dew has dried and are then processed by enfleurage, a means of extraction whereby the blossoms are placed on a fatty base, such as lard or olive oil. The flowers will continue to produce additional essential oil as the fat absorbs it from them. After all the essence is extracted they are replaced by freshly gathered blossoms. Later the essence is extracted with alcohol from the fatty base. Jasmine oil is reddish brown in color and extremely fragrant.

Culpeper wrote of jasmine's use for coughs and the female organs:

> Jessamine is a warm, cordial plant, governed by Jupiter in the sign of Cancer. . . . It warms the womb . . . and facilitates the birth; it is useful for cough, difficulty of breathing, &c. The oil made by infusion of the flowers, is used for perfumes. It disperses crude humours, and is good for cold and catarrhous constitutions, but not for the hot. The oil is good also for hard and contracted limbs, it opens, warms, and softens the nerves and tendons, if used as a liniment to the parts. . . . It removes diseases of the uterus. . . .

I like to massage a bit of jasmine oil on my lower back and abdomen during menstruation to help relax and relieve cramps. I've also noticed that the aroma of jasmine has helped relieve mental stress. Jasmine is a good oil to use diluted for a sensuous massage, to warm and soften the body and relax the mind.

Lavender Oil

The best lavender oil is obtained from English lavender *(Lavandula vera* or *L. officinalis).* It is much stronger than oil from French lavender or any other species. The flower heads and stalks may both be used in the steam distillation process, though the finest oils come from the flower heads alone. Lavender oil is used commercially for perfume, toilet water, soaps, cosmetics, sachets, and potpourris. A lavender sachet made from the flower and the oil is perfect for tucking inside your bed; every night its clean smell will refresh you for a gentle sleep and pleasant dreams.

Lavender has a long history in herbal tradition. It was used by the Romans to scent their baths, hence its name from the Latin *lavare,* to wash. I remember associating the aroma of lavender with smelling salts, used for fainting spells or feelings of weakness, and have a vague childhood memory of my great aunt carrying these in her purse. In somewhat the same vein a cloth soaked in lavender water can be applied to the forehead. The aroma is very refreshing to the senses and can certainly help revive dampened or depressed spirits.

John Parkinson wrote:

> Lavender is almost wholly spent with us, for to perfume linnen, apparell, gloves and leather and the dryed flowers to comfort and dry up the moisture of a cold braine.

> This is usually put among other hot herbs, either into bathes, ointment or other things that are used for cold causes . . . [It is of] especiall good use for all griefes and paines of the head and brain.

Culpeper adds:

> Two spoonfuls of the distilled water of the flowers help them that have lost their voice, the tremblings and passions of the heart, and fainting and swoonings, applied to the temples or nostrils, to be smelt unto . . . It strengthens the stomach, and frees the liver and spleen from obstructions, provokes womens' courses. . . .

The oil has been found in many studies to be antiseptic. It was used during World War I to help relieve inflammation from wounds, burns, and dermatitis.[4]

My grandmother had an old-fashioned glass bottle with a stopper that contained a brown liquid she simply called her cure-all. I remember that it smelled strongly of lavender. Anytime I hurt myself she would lovingly dab some of this cure-all on me. It was good for bites, cuts, bruises, and general childhood maladies. I always felt better and, of course, enjoyed Grandma's attention.

Remember, lavender oil is very strong and should be used with caution and moderation.

Rosemary Oil

Rosemary oil is distilled from the flowering tops of the plant. There are some rosemary oils made from the leaves and stems but they are of a lesser quality. The name *Rosmarinus officinalis* comes from the Latin *ros marinus*, which means dew of the sea and refers to its ability to grow well near the coast. Rosemary thrives on the Mediterranean coast where the plants flourish in the dry, sunny weather.

Once I sat looking out on the ocean on a seat that had been carved into a hillside. The back of it was covered with rosemary that had trailed down from above. When I rested against it the fragrance totally enveloped me—a perfect and natural setting for rosemary therapy.

Rosemary oil is very potent and best used for external purposes. Herbal tradition suggests that a few drops of the oil brushed into the hair will condition it and help cure scalp problems. (I love having an aromatic rosemary halo around my hair.)

Many herbalists throughout history have spoken of rosemary's uses as an aid to digestion, in calming the nervous system, and as a stimulant to the circulation. A few drops can be massaged on the head for headache or on other parts of the body where warmth and stimulation are needed. Culpeper wrote of rosemary's ability to relieve flatulence and coughs and aid the memory, the stomach, liver, eyes, and circulation. He wrote:

> The chymical oil drawn from the leaves and flowers, is a sovereign help for all the diseases aforesaid, to touch the temples and nostrils with two or three drops for all diseases of the head and brain spoken of before; also to take one drop, two or three, as the case requires, for the inward diseases; yet it must be done with discretion, for it is very quick and piercing, and therefore but a little must be taken at a time.

Hungary water was a distilled water made with rosemary. Legend records that it was named after a queen of Hungary who was paralyzed. It was said that the stimulating effect of the rosemary preparation rubbed on her limbs enabled her to walk again. Culpeper mentions that it "is made by distilling a pure spirit from the tops of this plant [rosemary]; or in a coarser way, by mixing a few drops of its oil in such a spirit."

Another tradition that has been passed down through the centuries is that rosemary stimulates the memory. It is often sentimentally associated with marriage and love and is simply defined in the Language of Flowers as Remembrance. Shakespeare wrote in *Hamlet*, "There's rosemary, that's for remembrance; pray you love, remember." You might rub a drop or two of rosemary oil on your lover's forehead to be certain you won't be forgotten.

Chamomile Oil

Chamomile oil is a strong shade of blue from the substance azulene, one of its components. This is surprising considering that the flowers are white and daisy-like, with yellow centers. There are several varieties of chamomile, including two common ones, Roman chamomile *(Anthemis nobilis)* and German chamomile *(Matricaria recutita)*. Both have a sweet, refreshing, fruity smell and a slightly bitter taste. Roman chamomile is a perennial herb ten to twelve inches tall. A low-growing variety of this makes a wonderful lawn. It has a strong taste and is often used for medicinal oils, baths, and other external preparations. German chamomile is an annual plant growing up to twenty-four inches that is sweeter and commonly used as an infusion for tea.

Many herbs that are bitter are also known to be tonic and soothing to the system. This is true of chamomile, which reminds me that the seemingly bitter in life sometimes turns out to have a positive effect. Chamomile tea really isn't excessively bitter and is calming to the nervous system. It has often been recommended by traditional herbalists for women during menstruation.

One year I taught a class on my chamomile lawn. After a while I noticed how relaxed my listeners were, some of them actually lying down and dozing. At first I thought my subject matter or presentation must be boring. Then I realized that the chamomile aroma was having its legendary effect.

Culpeper mentions that the ". . . oil made of the flowers . . . is much used against all hard swellings, pains or aches, shrinking of the sinews, cramps or pains in the joints. . . ." A chamomile bath can soothe the mind and body. Use a few drops of the oil or make a strong chamomile tea and strain it into the tub. A massage with diluted chamomile oil would be just right at the end of a tense day.

Again, use chamomile oil and herb with respect. I've experienced my own limits of drinking the tea when I became sick to my stomach after two strong cupfuls. Now I know that half a cup is right for me. Moderation is the best rule to follow when using botanicals. They are given to us as precious gifts that we must learn to handle respectfully and carefully.

OTHER ESSENTIAL OILS

Other essential flower oils include orange flower, thyme, sweet pea, lilac, gardenia, carnation, and ilang-ilang. Many essential oils are derived from different parts of the plant: basil, peppermint, clary sage, lemon balm, and patchouli come from the whole herb; bergamot, black pepper, and juniper from the fruit; cedarwood and sandalwood from the wood; fennel and cardamom from the seeds; eucalyptus from the leaves.[5]

FRESH FLOWER AROMATHERAPY

Fresh flowers may also be used for aromatherapy. For example, there is a sanitarium in southeast Russia that employs a type of aromatherapy in healing certain ailments. Patients are provided with specific flowers, herbs, and plants to inhale as a treatment. The plants are grown isolated from each other in a greenhouse. The patients sit by the plant recommended for them and breathe in its aroma. This was found to be particularly effective in respiratory diseases.[6]

I remember once when I had a cough that I felt much better when I sat under a grove of flowering eucalyptus trees, and inhaled their penetrating aroma. Another time when I was feeling tired and drained, I was drawn to my peppermint geranium plant. Its soft, fuzzy aromatic leaves are perfect for rubbing on my hands and head to renew my energy. I made an oil from the leaves and flowers to use for massage or simply to smell.

When you respond positively to a floral scent it can nurture your whole being. You can benefit from a type of fresh flower aromatherapy in your home or garden by placing pots of particular flowers wherever you want the effect of their aromas. Their perfume can fill an area for as long as you want. Though cut flowers may not have as prolonged an effect as those that are growing, they may be used in a similar way. Put a bouquet of violets or chamomile by your bed when you're feeling stressful or anxious. Use jasmine and rose to raise your spirits; eucalyptus to clear the sinuses, head, and psyche of congestion; rosemary to stimulate the senses; and orange blossoms to calm and relax you.

In earlier times, especially during the sixteenth and seventeenth

centuries, it was the custom to strew aromatic herbs and flowers in the processions of kings and queens and on the floors of homes. Each step would release a wonderful aroma that hid the odors of poor hygiene. Gerard wrote of mint:

> . . . the smell rejoiceth the heart of man, for which cause they strew it in chambers and places of recreation, pleasure and repose, where feasts and banquets are made.

Imagine the beauty of a wedding with lovely young girls wearing flower wreaths in their hair strewing blossoms from brimming baskets. Perhaps this celebration would take place in a fragrant garden to intensify the aromas. Or picture a "dance of flowers" on a floor covered with fragrant blossoms so that each step would scent the room. A friend of mine once romantically welcomed his wife home by lining the walkway to their house with fresh gardenias, even filling the pool with them.

Honeysuckle, jasmine, rosemary, thyme, mint, lavender, hyssop, orange blossom, rose, lemon balm, rose geranium, lilac, and carnation are a few of the flowers and flowering herbs that are ideal for strewing. They are effective alone or combined in a blend of aromas.

Don't forget that fresh flowers can be floated in your bath or used in steams for their beneficial effects (see Chapter 5). You may dry scented flowers for sachets and potpourris (see Chapter 3). These are easy to use for aromatherapy and are especially nice to sleep with for sweet, scented dreams.

BACH FLOWER REMEDIES

The Bach Flower Remedies were developed by Dr. Edward Bach in England during the 1930s. He was one of the earliest "holistic" physicians; he emphasized the importance of intimately understanding the whole person before choosing the treatment for any illness. Dr. Bach found that being "not at ease" in the mind creates a similar "dis-ease" in the body. He was interested in treating the "whole" individual rather than the external symptoms of the disease. Bach left his successful medical practice in London and sought the gentle and safe remedies from the plants of the countryside. This was a major turning point in his life. Leaving the noise and congestion of the city for a nurturing rural environment enabled him to refine his intuitive powers. He spent many hours hiking in the fields of Wales studying flowers and getting to know the local people. His first remedies were developed by gathering dew drops from flowers growing in the full sun. His finely developed senses enabled him to intuit the healing properties of a blossom. The scientist had taken to the field with his body and mind as his most sensitive instruments. The thirty-eight Bach Flower Remedies provide a guide to understanding human nature and the various states of mind that he felt were the true cause of disease. Bach hoped that his remedies would serve as a:

> . . . guide to those who suffer within themselves the real origins of their maladies, so that they may assist themselves in their own healing.[7]

FLOWER ESSENCES AND THE BACH FLOWER REMEDIES[8]

Bach felt that an individual who suffered from emotional and mental strain was especially vulnerable to illness. He found that his remedies or flower essences would help free a person from the negative effects of such feelings as fear, worry, or despair. If these negative emotions are recognized and dissipated early enough, disease may actually be avoided.

Bach's Flower Remedies use the essence of flowers, as do various kinds of aromatherapy. The "essences" in aromatherapy are the concentrated, fragrant essential *oils* from flowers or plants, usually extracted by means of distillation. They are primarily used externally for the specific effect of their scent. The "essences" of the Bach Flower Remedies are made by extracting the subtle oils from the flower into *water* with the sun's warmth or with heat. This is then diluted and preserved with brandy to be taken internally, several times a day a few drops at a time. These water essences are not necessarily aromatic.

Bach found that the pink impatiens flower was helpful to those experiencing impatience or irritability. Taking the remedy can serve as a reminder to be aware of the stressful state and to encourage a more patient and understanding attitude. The essence of the golden mimulus flower was used to allay many of the doubts and fears that often come up in daily life and specifically the fear of sickness or accidents. The mimulus remedy may be used as a catalyst to help you look at the source of your fears and at the same time develop the confidence and courage to face them. For depression and unhappiness Bach used the bright yellow mustard flower. Wild oat was for those who experience uncertainty about their direction in life. Gorse can help overcome hopelessness and despair, crab apple to purify and cleanse, and holly to open the heart to compassion and love. You can use Bach's remedies to help you begin to see what attitude or feeling you might be experiencing that is causing an imbalance. Then, each time you take it you can affirm a more positive state of mind.

THE FLOWER ESSENCE SOCIETY AND MAKING FLOWER ESSENCES

Most of the species of wild flowers used to make the Bach Flower Remedies grow only in England, where the Dr. Edward Bach Centre prepares the remedies. The Flower Essence Society in California, which exists independently of the Bach Centre, has developed flower essences from flowers growing in the United States that can be used in similar ways. For example, the essence of the vibrant, orange nasturtium is employed to counteract a lack of vitality; wild purple iris for feelings of frustration and inadequacy; clear blue borage to cure discouragement;

fuzzy purple and white star tulip to help develop the emotional and intuitive self.

The sun method of making the flower essences used by Bach is quite simple and lovely. First, find an undisturbed place where there is an abundance of the desired flowers growing. A clear glass bowl and pure water are all the equipment you need. The bowl is placed in the midst of the flowers, which are carefully picked. (First pick a single leaf without touching the stalk. Then, using that leaf like a "potholder," pick the flower by the stalk without letting your hand touch the stalk or the flower head.) Bach felt that touching the flowers would detract from the purity of the essence. The surface of the water should be totally covered with floating blossoms. The bowl is left in the sun for three hours and then the flowers are carefully removed.

Bach Flower Remedies and essences from the Flower Essence Society are available by mail (see Appendix of Sources, page 271) and are sent prepared in what are called "stock bottles." Two drops of this diluted mixture are then put into brandy or pure water in a one-ounce dropper bottle; this is the "dosage bottle." Bach recommended that four drops be taken four times a day. Although the flower essences will not harm you, they should be used with care. It's a good idea to label your dosage bottle with the name of the flower essence, the date when you bottled it, and a thought about the healthful state that you want to obtain.

SIPPING DEWDROPS

This introduction to water-extracted flower essences is meant to stimulate your interest in learning more about them (see the Appendix of Sources and Bibliography). One of the simplest and most delicious ways to experience both the aroma and the essence of a flower is to drink the dew from a rose, jasmine, honeysuckle, or other fragrant edible blossom in your garden early in the morning. Delight in sipping the tiny drops of pure aromatic essence!

7
VISUALIZATIONS
WITH
FLOWERS

Imagine a meadow of wild flowers, vibrant with tones of yellow and pink. Notice how abundantly they are growing, some of them almost two feet tall, others hugging the ground in a dense carpet. The air is scented with the subtle and gentle fragrances of early spring. The sun lights the flowers so that they glow with intense color. You lie down in the midst of them and feel the warm earth against your back.

The ability to actually "see" this scene with your "mind's eye" as you read it is the basis of the technique of visualization. It is something that often happens automatically when you read a book or listen to someone describe an event or scene.

You have seen how flower scents used in aromatherapy can promote emotional and physical well-being; fragrances may also be beneficial and inspiring by evoking floral imagery in your mind. A visualization is the deliberate creation of such imagery to be seen by your mind's eye; indeed flowers can be the basis for the loveliest of visions. You can bring them into your inner world with the help of your imagination.

The fantasy world that is so real to a child can again become a fertile realm in which to enact your flower visualizations. By relaxing the body and directing the mind, you can set the stage for your intuitive and creative self to become expressive. You can go anywhere, do anything, experience everything with your mind's eye. What you envision will often have a real and positive influence on your daily life. You can enjoy the lovely blossoms of your "inner garden" any time of the year, and that private place of flower images can take on all of the shapes, colors, and scents that your fertile mind can create.

FLOWERS IN VISUALIZATIONS

I've always appreciated flowers for their graceful forms and colorful beauty. Blossoms also remind me of many pleasant things—sweet fragrances, spring, success, romance, and celebrations. When I'm in my garden or making flower preparations I often feel calm and at ease. For these reasons I like to use flowers in visualizations. Their images help me to release tension and experience deep relaxation.

The shape of a flower makes it especially well-suited for visualizing. Many common flowers, such as the daisy, calendula, gazania, and rose, have a mandala-like form—a round, symmetrical design with a center from which all parts appear to emanate. This arrangement naturally draws you toward its center, just as you metaphorically go within your own center when visualizing. The Tibetan Buddhists use the mandala as an art form and a tool for meditation. It helps focus the mind, which can then become quiet, allowing daily cares to fall away and a sense of peace to prevail. A flower can be used like a mandala; concentrating on the form, color, petals, stamens, and pistils can put you in a meditative frame of mind.

DEEP RELAXATION AND VISUALIZATION TECHNIQUES

Sit or lie down in a quiet, comfortable place where you won't be disturbed; uncross your legs and arms and relax fully. Close your eyes and look within. Notice what you "see," hear, and feel. Take a deep breath from your lower abdomen and imagine the air that you take in traveling from the top of your head to your toes and back again. Do this several times noting where you are tense or tight; then relax that place as you breathe. If you are holding your shoulders, take a deep breath and let them go. Introduce the word *re-lax* into each breath. On the inhalation draw the *re* into your body and on the exhalation let the *lax* go out with all the tension. Visit, with your inner vision, each part of the body. Relax your toes, feet, calves, knees, thighs, pelvic area, abdomen, solar plexus, spine, chest, back, shoulders, arms, hands, fingers, neck, jaw, tongue, eyes, and forehead. Notice how much better your body begins to feel as all the tightness leaves it.

This relaxation technique will help to relieve stress, still the mind, and focus all your attention within. At this point an image or suggestion may be presented, such as your favorite flower. If you have trouble seeing it clearly, carefully examine a blossom in detail; observe its color, shape, number of petals and its texture. Then close your eyes and see it in your mind's eye. This simple exercise will prepare you for the flower visualizations I'll describe a little further on. These may be practiced alone or with someone else directing you. Or you may want to record them on a cassette tape and play them back so that you can use them to guide yourself.

When following the visualizations be sure to allow yourself to clearly "see" each image before you go onto the next one. If you are leading other people, allow periods of silence long enough for them to formulate their visions. Don't be limited by the content I have presented for these visualizations; use them as guides to inspire you when creating your own.

After you have completed one visualization go on to another or rest and open your eyes when you feel ready. If you are experiencing them with friends, it can be very interesting to share your visualizations when you are finished. Allow your imagination to flower.

BLOSSOMING FLOWER VISUALIZATION

In your mind's eye picture a flower, such as a poppy, rose, or peony, both in bud and in blossom. If you have the flower with you, it will help to study it before beginning. Then close your eyes and take a deep breath that begins in your abdomen, fills your chest, rises to the top of your head, and then is exhaled down to the tips of your toes. Notice the details of the bud with your inner vision. Begin to watch it open into full flower as you breathe in. Imagine the petals unfolding as the flower opens and see the sun bathe it in warm light. As you breathe out, visualize it, once again, as a bud. Inhale and exhale in the rhythm of this slowly opening and closing blossom.

Then envision yourself right in the center of the flower. As you breathe in experience yourself blossoming, your arms are spread wide and you feel calm and radiant. When you breathe out the flower closes and all traces of stress and tightness leave your body. Enjoy the image of your flowering self and notice how you and the flower continue to grow more bright and beautiful. With each breath you feel increasingly expanded and relaxed.

AROMA-COLOR BREATHING VISUALIZATION

Choose a flower that you like or one that expresses your mood of the moment. Examine it. For example, if you choose a carnation, take a deep breath of the sweet, spicy aroma and let it fill your lungs. Then clearly observe the rosy-pink color of the flower and how each petal is slightly shaded with different tones of pink. Close your eyes and move the scent and the color with your breath throughout your body to any tight or tense area. Expand this spot with your inhalation and thoroughly relax it as you exhale. Feel your body being invigorated and restored with each breath.

Different colors have specific effects on the mind and body. Green, for instance, is said to be rejuvenating and revitalizing. It is the color of spring, when new plant life emerges in a symphony of rebirth. Red, orange, and yellow are stimulating and energizing. Blues and violets are cooler and more restful colors. Their presence helps to calm and quiet the nervous system.

If you're feeling anxious and nervous purple stocks, petunias, or violets should have a soothing effect as you breathe in their color and scent. If you're feeling tired or low in energy visualize the orange marigold, red sage, or yellow daffodil. As you absorb their color and aroma you can "watch" them move through your body. If you have trouble visualizing this, practice looking at the flower, smell it, and then close your eyes to picture the essence of its color and scent.

THE MAGIC GARDEN

Visualize your perfect dream garden, a place you've visited, seen in a picture, or created with your imagination. Perhaps it is an expansive area of lush green grasses with rose arbors, purple clouds of lilacs, flowering pink crab apple trees, fragrant plum blossoms, and ponds with banks of brilliant wild flowers. In one area there might be a thick, round lawn of flowering chamomile. Make your garden as simple or as complex as you like.

After you have clearly visualized this environment, put yourself in it. You are walking around smelling the flowers and gathering a bouquet. Then you decide to rest on the inviting chamomile lawn. As you sit on it, notice the fruity aroma and breathe it in deeply. Chamomile, known for its ability to soothe the nervous system, will help you relax. Let your whole body sink into the yielding perfume and softness of the lawn.

Then picture yourself feeling vibrantly refreshed and energetic; watch yourself run, swim, or dance—full of vitality. You can bring others into your vision to share your experience.

I practice this visualization often, playing it out in a variety of imaginary gardens with my family and friends.

SENSUAL VISUALIZATION

Envision yourself lying by a waterfall and pool in the tropics where it's luxuriously warm and the grass is very soft. Ginger and gardenia blossoms sway gently in the light breeze perfuming the air about you. Birds are gliding through the branches of the flowering trees like colorful messengers of love. Everywhere you look there is the thick, lush green of ferns and vines. One of these plants drops its blossoms on the pond and they float in the swirling water like miniature boats. You leisurely bathe and swim, feeling the cool water caress and massage you as it rushes along. You stand by the waterfall and let it shower over your body in prismed drops.

Cleansed and refreshed, you lie on the fragrant grasses, letting the music of the waterfall and the sun's penetrating warmth lull you into deep and dreamy relaxation. Picture the type of flower that best embodies your sensuality—perhaps a rose, lily, gardenia, or hibiscus. Imagine it large enough to cover your entire body. Enjoy your sensual self as it blossoms in this luscious environment.

WATCH A FLOWER GROW

Picture yourself preparing a planter box or large clay pot for planting. In your mind's eye place a layer of pebbles on the bottom and then fill it up with rich, light soil. Take a few seeds of a flower you have always wanted to grow, such as calendula, cosmos, poppy, forget-me-not, or pansy. Put the seeds on top of the filled pot and sprinkle a light layer of soil over them. Water the seeds gently.

Then sit back and let your imagination re-create the natural phenomenon of growth, step-by-step, like a time-lapse film. Watch the seeds begin to sprout with their green bits of life pushing through the earth. The stems grow tall and strong with many rippled leaves. Tiny buds form, nestled among the foliage. You see them swell, grow round and full. One petal unfolds from the protecting calyx, then another, until the blossom opens in all its radiance.

Watch as the plant becomes covered with blossoms. Bees arrive searching for nectar among the stamens and leave with pollen on their legs. The pistil opens above the withered stamens and receives the pollen the bees bring to it. Then watch how the flowers begin to wilt; the petals dry and drop off. The ovary starts to swell with the ripening seeds. When the seed pods are all brown they split apart and the mature seeds scatter to the soil. Picture these new seeds sprouting and growing into new flowering plants. When you feel ready, open your eyes.

This visualization can impart a sense of detachment and understanding of the cycle of life, death, and rebirth. A flower blooms and creates seed in the perfection of its destiny; it is completing its purpose. Watching a flower grow within your imagination might also renew your appreciation of the beauty and wonder of nature.

INNER GARDEN

Form a mental picture of your most ideal and secret garden, a haven that no one else will visit, a totally secure and serene place where you can enjoy the intimacy of your own company. It might be a remote area away from the main part of a large garden. The path to it is so hidden by overgrown bushes that most people would never notice it. The path opens into a small, natural meadow surrounded by large, old trees. They seem to stand like guards, protecting your privacy. A stream runs along one side of it and the music of the rushing brook entrances you. The meadow is full of daffodils in bloom, a wave of golden light. Crocus, iris, and wild strawberries grow along the edge of the meadow. Trilliums bloom in their quiet majesty under the shade of the branches.

You stretch out in the grass surrounded by daffodils and are caressed by their pollen-rich scent, the aroma of spring and warmth. You luxuriate in the calm of your inner garden, totally at ease.

Whenever you feel the need, you can just close your eyes and return to the peacefulness of the setting you have visualized. It might change with your mood or it might be the same place reflecting different seasons. Allow your imagination to take flight in your fantasy garden. Since you are not restricted by the limitations of the everyday world, it can be as extravagant and fantastic as you like, filled with all the plants and flowers you can imagine, in any climate you want. This is the perfect garden of your dreams!

LOVER'S FLOWER FANTASY

Sit opposite your lover or lie next to each other holding hands; make sure you are comfortable. Select an aromatic flower that appeals to both of you, such as a gardenia, lily, rose, iris, or jasmine. It's best to actually have the flower with you. Smell it, touch it, and take it in with all your senses.

Close your eyes, leaving the flower between you, and begin to breathe in the aroma. Inhale or exhale at the same time as your lover. Visualize the flower and the aroma massaging your lover's body. Then picture the flower expanding and filling your inner vision. Let it envelop both of you totally so that with each breath the flower becomes larger and more a part of you. Continue breathing together as you visualize the flower growing beyond your bodies and surrounding you both.

Imagine yourself entwining and completely merging with the flower and your lover. After a while, open your eyes and see in your lover the beautiful flower you have been visualizing.

NATURE SPIRIT VISUALIZATION

Put yourself in an exquisite old-fashioned garden, one that has been loved and tended for many years. Perhaps it is surrounded by a huge evergreen hedge that gives you complete privacy. There are many gently curving paths with stepping-stones to follow. It's springtime and there are huge bushes of rhododendrons, azaleas, and camellias in full bloom, all dressed in bright pinks, apricots, and whites. The garden also has beds of succulent plants and herbs, a birdbath, and wind chimes singing gently in the light breeze. Many benches are tastefully tucked into sheltered areas. Old rosebushes are covered with swelling buds; a few are blooming. There are colorful beds planted with hundreds of bulbs: daffodils and painted tulips, hyacinths and crocus, iris and anemone. Some of them are in full bloom, others are proudly sending their leaves into the sunshine. Enjoy the sounds of the bees and the fragrant warmth of the day. Walk around the garden and observe it in detail. Find a comfortable place to sit, under an arbor of wisteria or clematis. Then bring into your garden an imaginary "nature spirit" whose company you would enjoy. See what it looks like, how it's dressed, and what it does. Is it very tiny, hopping from flower to flower? Does it resemble yourself or anyone you know?

Introduce yourself to the nature spirit and tell it why you have brought it into your garden. Welcome the spirit and ask it anything you'd like to know about the flowers. Listen carefully to its answers. If you can't think of any questions, ask it to tell you a story. If you listen closely, you may discover that the spirit's voice is the embodiment of the nature spirit within you.

SPACE JOURNEY WITH A FLOWER GUIDE

Choose a flower that you are particularly drawn to; hold it in your hands, smell, and enjoy it. Then visualize it guiding you on a journey outside of your body. Ride on the flower as if it were a rocket or one of the lovely, fluffy clouds you see in the sky. Float above where you are sitting and look down at yourself holding the flower. Then, in your mind's eye, keep moving farther away—above your house, your town, your state, your country, the earth, the sun and its planets until you are traveling with the flower out in space. At each stage of your journey watch how small places become and how quickly you leave them behind.

While you are hovering in space, look around you and observe the vastness of the universe. Notice how you feel and what it's like to be so far away from your ordinary surroundings. The concerns or worries of daily life seem insignificant in the immensity of this setting. Then slowly begin your reentry back through space, past the outer planets of our solar system to earth, all the way to your house and to yourself sitting there with the flower that has just been your guide.

Whenever you feel the desire to detach yourself from the limitations and frustrations of everyday life you can close your eyes, choose a flower, and imagine it guiding you on a journey into space.

RELAXING FLOWER JOURNEYS

Meadow of Wild Flowers

Picture yourself overlooking the sea in a gentle meadow of wild flowers. The day is clear and bright with a fairly strong breeze. You can hear the waves breaking in the distance. Lie down in the tall grasses so that you are totally hidden. Watch the wind rushing over the tops of the grass without touching you. Breathe in the smell of the sea and the aroma of the moist, sun-warmed earth. There are so many wild flowers their colors seem to melt together in a soft haze of mauves and golds. Feel the rich, nourishing earth against you and all your tension to drain out of you.

Water Lily

Imagine yourself near a beautiful lake. The water is very clear and there is nothing in sight but trees, water lilies, and cloud-puffed sky. You swim and enjoy the feeling of the cool, supporting water. The constantly changing reflections of clouds paint the surface of the lake. Wild seeds sail through the air like tiny parachutes and land on the water.

As you swim by a family of fragrant water lilies, you think of how nice it would be to float around on one of them. Instantly you are small enough to crawl onto a bright green lily leaf. The flower seems extremely large and its aroma very strong. The pink blossom has become a huge magical sailing ship. Take a tour of the lily and then lie down and relax among its petal-sails. Leave all your cares behind as you travel in your water-lily boat.

Snapdragon

Picture yourself as a tiny bee and buzz around a snapdragon flower. The bright pink and orange-yellow colors attract you and you land on a bottom petal. It opens up and you go inside. Rest a while in the flower and notice how protected you feel. Enjoy the fragrant darkness, the rich aroma of pollen and nectar. You are completely safe and relaxed in your flower home. Use your imagination to shrink and transform yourself into other insects, or hummingbirds, as you visit the flowers.

CREATING FLOWER VISUALIZATIONS

These flower visualizations are just a few of the ones that I most enjoy. Choose your favorite flowers and let them inspire you with their forms, fragrances, colors, symbolic meanings, or uses to create your own visions. Imagine them in dream gardens created to enhance the mood or effect you desire. The quiet realms within you can flower with visualizations that help to promote your health and well-being.

> Flower in the crannied wall,
> I pluck you out of the crannies;—
> I hold you here, root and all, in my hand,
> Little flower—but if I could understand
> What you are, root and all, and all in all,
> I should know what God and man is.
> —ALFRED LORD TENNYSON,
> *FLOWER IN THE CRANNIED WALL*

8
FLOWER FAIRIES
AND
NATURE SPIRITS

Most of us have an image of fairies from the books that we read when we were children. One of my favorite tales was filled with wonderful pictures of fairies dancing happily among the flowers in dresses of prismed gauze and iridescent wings as light as spider webs. They were riding on rainbows, swinging from daisies, jumping between hollyhocks, sliding down strawberries, and playing hide-and-seek in daffodils. Their home was a joyful garden filled with celebration and merriment.

I've often walked into a fully blossoming garden and experienced a strong feeling that held me still for a few minutes with all my senses alert. The flowers seemed to glow and the garden was alive with a quiet hum. Perhaps it is this powerful "presence" that has been symbolized by flower fairies or nature spirits. For me they represent the life force inherent in the flowering world.

I remember one full-moon spring night when I walked into the garden and felt attracted by the strawberry patch. The white blossoms were shining like tiny stars. There was an unusual stillness. I stood for quite a while feeling and absorbing the vitality of the blossoms. When I walked away I felt exhilarated. Later, that summer, my strawberries were exceptionally large and delicious.

My husband and I once walked to a eucalyptus grove that grows on both sides of a shallow ravine. It is the home of many large and lush ferns. We sat down on the ground among the dried eucalyptus leaves, enjoying their refreshing aroma. We both experienced a sense of serenity and heightened awareness that I have come to associate with the true spirit of nature. I lay back and very quickly became deeply relaxed. This brief rest among the fragrant leaves was so revitalizing that I was moved to thank the trees and the "spirits." I left the grove feeling as nurtured and cared for as a gardener's favorite flower.

I have always known people with the proverbial "green thumb." Whatever they want to grow seems to flourish. Through their love of plants and flowers these individuals are working in harmony with nature. Over the years I have realized that every plant I really loved and cared for thrived. When a true communion exists between gardener and nature, plants grow strong and healthy.

The book *The Secret Life of Plants* by Peter Tompkins and Christopher Bird brought to light the possibility and reality that plants can and do respond with a consciousness or "spirit" of their own. Many experiments were made, including testing a dracaena plant with a lie detector and monitoring how it reacted to human actions and thoughts, even unspoken ones. Results showed that plants registered a strong reaction on the detector to threats of harm or negative thoughts. It was also shown that plants responded well to caring attention and positive stimuli. The work of Tompkins and Bird helped encourage many of us to talk to our plants.

The Secret Life of Plants and other books similar to it contributed to the spread of the belief that a consciousness exists in all living things. Your garden can take on a new meaning when you begin to see it as not only alive but also responsive to your care. Try spending some time quietly sitting with flowering, healthy plants in a pleasant environment and see how they respond to you and what you experience. Don't be surprised if you feel as though you have just made some new friends!

A BRIEF HISTORY OF FAIRIES AND NATURE SPIRITS

> When I touch that flower, I am touching infinity. It existed long before there were human beings on this earth and will continue to exist for millions of years to come. Through the flower, I talk to the Infinite, which is only a silent force. This is not a physical contact. It is not the earthquake, wind or fire. It is in the invisible world. It is that still small voice that calls up the fairies.[1]
> —GEORGE WASHINGTON CARVER

Throughout history there have been references to some sort of fairy world existing as a link between humans and nature. These beings have sometimes been associated with fear and evil, but most often with celebration, help, and support. The more recent flower fairy experiences have been in connection with nature and the plant world. In the Celtic tradition of Britain the world of the fairies was important. Shepherds, farmers, and others living close to nature were especially inclined to carry on the belief in these spirits who, they felt, inhabited the earth with them. Celtic folk custom still suggests leaving a bit of food and water or tossing a crumb over your shoulder for the little people.

These were not the fairies I first read about when I was younger, with their lovely gowns, wands, and glittering wings. Those were the ones that were popular in nineteenth-century literature and art. The Celtic fairies were a race of very beautiful, small, invisible people, dressed in the finest clothes, who were much like humans except for their diminutive size. They had their kings and queens and lived in the "hollow hills." Their world was filled with adventures and stories just like the gods and goddesses of ancient Greece and Rome. They were also reputed to make fine crafts in gold and silver. Many legends exist in literature and country folk stories that recount the exploits of the fairies and their interaction with humans.

The Elizabethan view of fairies is expressed in Shakespeare's *A Midsummer Night's Dream*, where Titania and Oberon, queen and king of the fairies, bless the humans and their house and their offspring:

> Hand in hand, with fairy grace,
> Will we sing, and bless this place.
>
> Now, until the break of day,
> Through this house each fairy stray.
> To the best bride-bed will we,
> Which by us shall blessèd be;
> And the issue there create
> Ever shall be fortunate.

Fairies were known to like their privacy and to sometimes be mean to anyone who pried too far into their affairs. There is a story about Robert Kirk, author of *The Secret Commonwealth of Elves, Fauns and Fairies*

in 1691, who spent much time in reputed fairy havens to learn more about his subject. When he died, Kirk was found in one of these supposed fairy places. It was suggested that the fairies took his soul as prisoner, though some thought he died a natural death.

There were many names and forms for fairies. The Irish called them the sidhe, the good people or good neighbors, in hopes that they would act in a friendly way. There were also pixies and elves in England who were often mischievous. Brownies would come in the night to help around the house. Fairies were known as the sylphs to the ancient Celts. In Scandinavia some of the fairies cared for the flowers and are the closest to the lovely winged creatures portrayed in nineteenth and twentieth century books of fairy tales. Whatever their source or activity, fairies have been a part of the human imagination and psyche for hundreds of years.

THOSE WHO DO SEE FLOWER FAIRIES AND NATURE SPIRITS

Since earliest times history has recorded stories about those who possess what is called the "sight." Their visions into invisible realms led them to be called mystics or clairvoyants by those who sympathized with them and witches or sorcerers by those who feared them. This clear seeing is usually considered a special gift, though some may consider it to be simply an overactive imagination.

Some people have recounted seeing flower fairies and nature spirits as a part of their daily reality. Often, it is the innocence of childhood that first inspires this ability. These spirits are sometimes described as a form of radiant light that may take on whatever shape the observers picture in their minds. For example, the daughter of Linnaeus, the renowned botanist and classifier of plants, was said to have often told a story about a startling discovery she had made as a young girl. On a sultry summer night in 1762 she perceived unusual flashes of light sparkling out of some nasturtium flowers in her garden. Goethe, who also wrote on botany, observed similar luminous flashes around Oriental poppies. It apparently became fashionable at the time for serious naturalists and everyday gardeners alike to see such mysterious emanations of light from flowers.

THE COTTINGLEY PHOTOGRAPHS

Two cousins, Elsie Wright and Frances Griffiths, played together in the glen behind Elsie's home in Cottingley, England. It was a wooded area with a stream and waterfall. At home the two girls would often talk of playing with the fairies in the forest. Their parents thought they were simply voicing their childish fantasies.

One day in the summer of 1917, when Elsie was thirteen and Frances was ten, Elsie's father let her borrow his camera so that she could photograph the fairies he had heard so much about. When he developed the plate he was amazed to see a picture of Frances and a whole troupe of fairies with butterfly-like wings dancing in front of her. Some people pointed out that the fairies were dressed in fashionable clothing and hair styles of the day. It was suggested that this happened because the fairies took on the images or thought forms of the girls. Another photograph was taken that same year of Elsie with a gnome-like creature with wings and dressed in tights. Elsie's father put the photographs aside as preposterous, not knowing how the girls could have faked them and also not believing in the fairies or the nature spirits.

Three years later Elsie's mother attended a lecture by a member of the Theosophical Society of England, Edward Gardner. He described nature spirits on earth, called "elementals," and the fairies that are a variety of them. This reminded Mrs. Wright of the girls' photographs; she told Gardner all about them and he became very interested. Sir Arthur Conan Doyle, of Sherlock Holmes fame, who met Gardner through mutual friends, was also fascinated by the photos.

Gardner and Doyle had the original plates subjected to intensive tests, some of which "proved" them to be authentic. But others said they could have been faked by a complex process in a photography studio. The Wrights' simple story and life-style, however, defied the possibility of sophisticated fakery. The photos were published in an article about fairies written by Doyle for the *Strand* magazine. They created quite a stir among the public.

The girls were given cameras and took three more photographs of their fairyland. One is of Frances with a fairy flying in the air by her head and another is of a fairy offering a flower to Elsie. The last photograph is of a cocoon-like shape that was said by clairvoyants who saw the photos, to be a "magnetic bath" that the fairies used during rainy or cloudy weather to energize themselves.

The reactions to all of the photos were mixed. Many people responded with utter disbelief and suggested that the little figures were nothing more than pieces of cut-out cardboard the girls had designed. Doyle and Gardner both wrote books that present the story of the girls and elaborate on the powerful impact the reality of fairies could have in the world.[2] Doyle wrote:

> These little folk who appear to be our neighbors, with only some small difference of vibration to separate us, will become familiar. The thought of them, even when unseen, will add a charm to every brook and valley and give romantic interest to every country walk.[3]

GEOFFREY HODSON
AND DORA VAN GELDER

Very few people have clearly recorded their ability to see flower fairies and nature spirits. Both Geoffrey Hodson and Dora van Gelder are clairvoyants who have written books published by The Theosophical Society about their experiences.

Hodson describes in detail what fairies, brownies, elves, gnomes, and other spirits are like from his personal observation. He poetically relates how a particular nature spirit or "builder" is drawn to the seed of a plant as it begins to grow. The plant thrives with the help of these "tiny etheric creatures."

When the flower-stem and flower are to be built, a new set of builders arrives on the scene. . . . as soon as coloration is to begin, the fairies proper appear and implant their special rate of vibration, changing the white and green into the particular colour corresponding to the note which called them and by which they work.[4]

Hodson continues to explain that these fairies stay close to the flower and enjoy the admiration of people; like an artist having a painting admired. They are anxious that no harm come to the flower and continue to care for a blossom even when it is cut for an arrangement. As the flowers open there is an ecstatic release of "fragrant sound":

> When the completely flowered condition is reached the full chord is sounding forth, and, could we but hear it, our gardens would have an additional joy. We do not, however, hear that chord, though it may be that, in some cases, we contact it as a scent. We may smell the sound![5]

Dora van Gelder observed fairies in her childhood and continued to do so as an adult. To her it was as natural as watching bees or butterflies. She describes that dawn is the time that the fairies begin their work in the garden, caring for the plants and flowers. Each one has its special flower to tend and they do so with a fervor of love and happiness. Van Gelder describes their "hearts" as radiating "golden light" and beating in rhythm with the plants they are tending. Their bodies are not solid like material objects, but rather "finer matter, more subtle than the rarest gas." Their work is to support, tend, and energize the plants and flowers that thrive from their presence. As she wrote:

> Love for flowers and a conscious invitation to the fairies to help is a way to come to know them, and perhaps even to see them. It is love of living things which is the great bridge between the two kingdoms.[6]

> The fairies are happy to work side by side with men, to cooperate in making a spot of loveliness for mutual enjoyment, and if only more human beings knew how eager the fairy kingdom is to help, gardens would be still more like fragments of heaven here on earth than they are now to most of us.[7]

THE FINDHORN GARDENS

Peter and Eileen Caddy moved to the Caravan Park on the windswept dunes of Findhorn Bay in Morayshire, England, in 1962. Peter, a former Royal Air Force Squadron leader, had pursued a spiritual path in Tibet and later married Eileen, a clairvoyant. With them was Dorothy Maclean, also a sensitive. They spent a cold, first winter in Findhorn, trusting that they had been guided to this inhospitable environment for a purpose.

Peter spent his first months at Findhorn studying organic gardening techniques from books, and in the spring of 1963, as a totally inexperienced gardener, he began to make compost to enrich the poor, sandy soil. All the necessary ingredients were provided just when they were needed by friendly neighbors. Eileen received "guidance" that they were to plant vegetables and fruits. Soon they discovered that Dorothy was in contact with the devas, the individual spirits of the plants. When they were confronted with a specific gardening problem, Dorothy would simply ask the deva of that particular plant what to do and received an immediate answer. The "Landscape Angel" was their name for the spirit who spoke for the entire area and the rest of the devas. From this being they learned the importance of nourishing the soil and plants with love and organic substances rather than with chemicals. Peter describes the devas and nature spirits:

> The Devas are Angelic Beings. . . . There is one of these for every species of the plant kingdom. . . . The Nature Spirits, or Elementals, are concerned with using energy to build the form. . . . In effect the Devas provide the blueprint and energy and the Nature Spirits carry out the actual work.[8]

The results of this cooperative effort between devas, nature spirits, and people were impressive. Peter described growing astonishingly healthy and vibrant foods, such as forty-pound cabbages! All of the plants at Findhorn flourished in a way that surprised everyone involved.

Another important contributor to Findhorn was Robert Ogilvie Crombie, or "Roc," who was gifted with the ability to actually see the spirit world. It was he who brought to Findhorn an awareness of the presence of the nature spirit the ancient Greeks called Pan. Pan was said to be a leader of the nature world and helped to vitalize the garden. One of Pan's messages was that it was important for humans to work with and respect the nature spirits. This was tested one day at Findhorn when Peter directed some flowering gorse to be cut out of the way of the fruit trees. Roc arrived to find the nature spirits very upset and ready to leave the garden. Their homes in the flowers had been destroyed and they felt that humans were insensitive to their needs. Pan instructed Roc that there should always be a "wild area" in the garden for the nature spirits to have as their home and that this area must be left untouched.

Many people visited the garden over the years, and the flowers, trees, fruits, and vegetables continued to be remarkably healthy and vibrant. Findhorn attracted more and more attention among people from around the world seeking gardening knowledge as well as spiritual guidance. The approach to gardening used at Findhorn was based on an attentiveness to each plant and a receptivity to the nature spirits and devas. Peter Caddy wrote about the Findhorn garden experience:

> It is one which would seem to prove, beyond doubt, that man, working in proper harmony with the devas and nature spirits and in absolute obedience to the Will of God, can bring down even to the most barren plot of this earth, clear and tangible evidence of His Kingdom.[9]

FAVORITE FAIRY FLOWERS

FLOWER FAIRIES OF THE GARDEN

Flower fairies of the garden
Prancing 'bout the favored lands,
Late, late at night
Beneath the summer's moon.
Singing songs of cheer
While tending to the flowers,
Their tapered figures vanish
At the first glimpse of light.
One fairy left behind
Hides among the flowers
Watching the children
Who have come to play.

—EVA POMERANTZ

Literature, tradition, and myth of earlier times describe the most magical and specially chosen flowers of the fairies. Cowslips, forget-me-nots, bluebells, broom, ragwort, tulips, wood sorrel, and periwinkle were all flowers noted as being favored by fairies and, therefore, were to be treated with great care. Saint-John's-wort, yarrow, and mugwort protected people against fairy spells and could be hung in doorways to keep out mischievous fairies. Four other important flowers in fairy lore are foxglove, primrose, wild thyme, and pansy (or Johnny-jump-up).

Foxglove

Foxglove, with a long, tall flower stalk that rises from a rosette of leaves, thrives in the woods by streams where fairies love to play. The flowers are bell-shaped, one half to two inches long, in pink and white with darker pink spots inside. In the wild they grow three to four feet tall; the cultivated variety in my garden has grown to ten feet. A friend of mine who didn't know these were special fairy flowers dug up some foxglove from a lush wooded area of ferns and forget-me-nots. She told me she saw fairies out of the corner of her eye and hopes they might now be living in her garden where she transplanted the flowers.

Foxglove has been called fairy gloves, fairy fingers, folk's glove, and fairy caps. Perhaps the fairies delight in wearing these flowers on their fingers when they "dress up" or on their heads for elegant hats. However, since fairies are usually quite small, they may enjoy most of all playing in the flowers and swinging from blossom to blossom in fairy-like abandon.

Primrose

The primrose blooms early in the year and is among the first of the flowers to greet the spring sun. The flowers grow in clusters on stalks about five to six inches tall, rising above a rosette of oblong leaves. In the wild they are usually yellow; cultivated primroses are also white, purple, blue, pink, and red.

Shakespeare's *A Midsummer Night's Dream* is filled with the playfulness of fairies caring for flowers as well as for lovers. In it is a reference to beds of primrose for both fairies and humans to enjoy:

> And in the wood where often you and I
> Upon faint primrose beds were wont to lie.

There is an old legend from Cornwall, England, that tells of a little girl who was playing and gathering primroses one day when she sat down next to a fairy hill. All the fairies came out to frolic with her and enjoy one of their favorite flowers. Many people heard the girl's story and one man, who was interested in fairy secrets, tried to find the fairies at the same place. He disappeared, never to be seen again!

Primrose flowers are edible and eating them has been thought to be a sure way to see the fairies.

Wild Thyme

Wherever it is growing wild thyme scents the summer air; its pure fragrance is especially refreshing on a hot day. A member of the mint family, it grows from six to twelve inches tall, with purplish flowers circling round the tops of the stems.

Fairies love to dance on thyme flowers. In *A Midsummer Night's Dream*, Oberon, king of the fairies, speaks of the favorite resting place of Titania, queen of the fairies:

> I know a bank where the wild thyme blows,
> Where oxlips and the nodding violet grows,
> Quite overcanopied with luscious woodbine,
> With sweet musk roses, and with eglantine.
> There sleeps Titania sometime of the night,
> Lulled in these flowers with dances and delight.

What an elegant and fragrant bed for the fairy queen, while all her fairy subjects dance in "moonlight revels" on Midsummer Eve. There must be an intoxicating fragrance on the nights when all the little fairy feet step lightly on the wild thyme; the gentle scent of fairy magic.

Pansy or Johnny-jump-up

This is one of my favorite fairy flowers, its bright, small, purple, yellow, and white face looks as if it's smiling. It "jumps up" all over my garden from the many seeds it naturally spreads. This flower has numerous names—heart's ease, love-in-idleness, Johnny jumper. As a pansy, its name comes from the French *pensée*, meaning thought; Shakespeare refers to it in *Hamlet* ". . . and there is pansy, that's for thought."

In *A Midsummer Night's Dream* Oberon describes how Cupid's arrow of love

> . . . fell upon a little western flower,
> Before milk-white, now purple with love's wounds,
> And maidens call it love-in-idleness.

This same little pansy Oberon uses to put a spell on Titania. He says:

Fetch me that flow'r, the herb I showed thee once:
The juice of it on sleeping eyelids laid
Will make a man or woman madly dote
Upon the next live creature that it sees.

The innocent looking little Johnny-jump-up can become a potent
tool for fairy spells.

HOW TO SEE FAIRIES

Traditionally, it is said that the best times to see fairies are on
Midsummer Eve, May Day, and Halloween. On full-moon nights the
fairies are also visible dancing and celebrating in fairy rings. These rings
are thought to be magical and capable of entrapping the human who
stumbles into one. Groups of mushrooms growing in a circular form are
called fairy rings and often look like little dancing fairies.

The following recipe is offered as an aid to seeing fairies. The
ingredients might be difficult to find; but the air of ritual inherent in the
recipe suggests an attitude that might facilitate contact with the fairies
and nature spirits.

TO ENABLE ONE TO SEE THE FAIRIES

A pint of sallet oyle and put it into a vial glasse; and first wash it
with rose-water and marygolde water; the flowers to be gathered
towards the east. Wash it till the oyle becomes white, then put
into the glasse, and then put thereto the budds of hollyhocke,
the flowers of marygolde, the flowers or toppes of wild thyme the
budds of young hazle, and the thyme must be gathered near the
side of a hill where fairies use to be; and take the grasse of a fairy
throne; then all these put into the oyle in the glasse and sette it to
dissolve three dayes in the sunne and then keep it for thy use.[10]

—Receipt dated 1600,
Ashmolean Museum, Oxford

The real and simple magic of fairy lore is that any flower you truly
love can become a favorite fairy flower.

NOTES ON THE TEXT

CHAPTER 2

1. This technique is based on my studies of Alan Chadwick's Bio-Dynamic Intensive Methods and modified by my own years of gardening experience.

CHAPTER 4

1. Platt, Sir Hugh, *Delights for Ladies*, 1594; Smith, E., *The Compleat Housewife*, 1736; W.M. (Cook to Queen Henrietta Maria), *The Queens Closet Opened*, 1655, mentioned in Rohde, Eleanour Sinclair, *A Garden of Herbs* (New York: Dover, 1969, 1936), pp. 244–262, pp. 295–299.
2. Caldecott, Moyra, *Adventures by Leaf Light* (La Jolla, California: Green Tiger Press, 1978), p. 6.

CHAPTER 6

1. Tisserand, Robert B., *The Art of Aromatherapy* (New York: Inner Traditions, 1977), pp. 41–43.
2. *Ibid.*, p. 43.
3. Grieve, Mrs. M., *A Modern Herbal* (New York: Dover, 1971, 1931), p. 686.
4. *Ibid.*, p. 472.
5. Tisserand, *Aromatherapy*, pp. 176–289.
6. Jensen, Dr. Bernard, "Russian Fragrance Therapy," *The Herbalist* 4 (September, 1979):14–15.
7. Bach, Dr. Edward, *Heal Thyself* (Saffron Walden, England: C.W. Daniel Co., Ltd., 1974, 1931), p. 5.
8. Bach, Dr. Edward, *The Twelve Healers and Other Remedies* (Saffron Walden, England: C.W. Daniel Co., Ltd., 1975, 1933), pp. 9–23.

CHAPTER 8

1. Tompkins, Peter, and Christopher Bird, *The Secret Life of Plants* (New York: Avon, 1973, 1974), p. 156.
2. Doyle, Arthur Conan, *The Coming of The Fairies* (New York: Samuel Weiser, 1972); Gardner, Edward L., *Fairies, The Cottingley Photographs and Their Sequel* (London: The Theosophical Publishing House, Ltd., 1966, 1945).
3. Doyle, *Coming of the Fairies*, pp. 57–58.
4. Hodson, Geoffrey, *Fairies at Work and at Play* (London: The Theosophical Publishing House, Ltd., 1976, 1925), p. 19.
5. *Ibid.*
6. Van Gelder, Dora, *The Real World of Fairies* (Wheaton, Illinois: The Theosophical Publishing House, 1977), p. 14.
7. *Ibid.*, p. 61.
8. Caddy, Peter, *et al.*, *The Findhorn Garden*, Parts 1–4 (Forres, Moray, Scotland: The Findhorn Trust), p. 9.
9. *Ibid.*, p. 23.
10. Rohde, Eleanour Sinclair, *A Garden of Herbs* (New York: Dover, 1969, 1936), p. 171.

APPENDIX OF SOURCES

GARDEN CATALOGS

Mail-order sources for flowers and herb seeds, live plants, and often, a variety of tools and gardening information are listed below. Write for their catalogs. Of course, you will also find varieties of flowers and herbs that grow well in your area at local nurseries or garden supply centers.

Abundant Life Seed Foundation
P.O. Box 772
Port Townsend, Washington 98368
Untreated and organically grown seeds of herbs, wild flowers, and vegetables.

Applewood Seed Company
P.O. Box 4000
Golden, Colorado 80401
Seeds for wild flowers, everlastings, herbs, flowering house plants, and sprouts.

Burpee Seed Company
Warminster, Pennsylvania 18974
or
Clinton, Iowa 52732
or
Riverside, California 92502
A complete selection, including seeds for everlasting flowers, bulbs, and garden supplies.

Cook's Geranium Nursery
712 N. Grand
Highway 14 North
Lyons, Kansas 67554
Fine geraniums, many scented varieties.

Dutch Gardens
P.O. Box 168
Montvale, New Jersey 07645
Dutch flowering bulbs; colorful catalog.

Fox Hill Farm
444 W. Michigan Avenue, Box 7
Parma, Michigan 49269
Scented geraniums and herb plants.

Greer Gardens
1280 Goodpasture Island Road
Eugene, Oregon 97401
Rhododendron and azalea specialists.

Hastings
434 Marietta Street, N.W.
P.O. Box 4274
Atlanta, Georgia 30302
Seeds and plants for the southern gardener.

Hemlock Hill Herb Farm
Hemlock Hill Road
Litchfield, Connecticut 06759
Herb plants.

Hilltop Herb Farm
Cleveland, Texas 77327
Herbs, scented geraniums.

Jackson & Perkins Company
201 Rose Lane
Medford, Oregon 97501
Flower seeds and lovely rose catalog.

Rod McLellan Company
"Acres of Orchids"
1450 El Camino Real
South San Francisco, California 94080
Quality orchid growers; plants shipped.

Midwest Wildflowers
Box 64
Rockton, Illinois 61072
Wild flower seeds; informative catalog.

The Naturalists
P.O. Box 435
Yorktown Heights, New York 10598
Wild flower seeds for the eastern
gardener.

Nichols Garden Nursery
1190 North Pacific Highway
Albany, Oregon 97321
Herb seeds and plants, flower
seeds, and a fascinating catalog of
unusual items, including saffron
crocus bulbs, everlasting flower
seeds, and flower drying kits.

George Park Seed Company, Inc.
Highway 254 N.
Greenwood, South Carolina 29647
Complete selection of flower seeds,
plants, bulbs, wild flowers, herbs,
and gardening supplies.

Clyde Robin Seed Company
P.O. Box 2855
Castro Valley, California 94546
Wild flower seed mixtures for every
region of the country.

Roses of Yesterday and Today
802 Brown's Valley Road
Watsonville, California 95076
Wonderful selection of unusual,
old-fashioned and new roses.

Schreiner's Gardens
3625 Quinaby Road, N.E.
Salem, Oregon 97303
An iris lover's dream; exquisite full-
color catalog.

Smith & Hawken Tool Company
68 Homer Dept. R 22
Palo Alto, California 94301
Fine quality English tools.

Spring Hill Nurseries
Catalog Reservation Center
P.O. Box 1758
Peoria, Illinois 61656
Perennials, annuals, ornamentals.

Swan Island Dahlias
Box 800
Canby, Oregon 97013

A catalog full of dahlias.

Taylor's Herb Gardens, Inc.
1535 Lone Oak Road
Vista, California 92083
Good variety of herb plants and
seeds.

Thon's Garden Mums
4811 Oak Street
Crystal Lake, Illinois 60014
A complete collection of mums for
every garden.

Tropicals Unlimited
595 Ulukaku Street
Kailua, Hawaii 96734
Tropical plants and seeds.

K. Vanbourgondien & Sons, Inc.
245 Farmingdale Road, Route 109
Babylon, New York 11702
Bulbs and other flowers.

Wayside Gardens
Hodges, South Carolina 29695
Flowering plants, seeds, bulbs, and
garden accessories. Quality, colorful
catalog.

Well-Sweep Herb Farm
317 Mt. Bethel Road
Port Murray, New Jersey 07865
Herb seeds and plants, perennials,
and scented geraniums.

White Flower Farm
Route 63
Litchfield, Connecticut 06759
Bulbs, flowers, and some tools in
spring and fall catalogs. Three
editions of garden "Notes. Very
Informative."

Gilbert H. Wild & Son
677 Joplin Street
Sarcoxie, Missouri 64862
Peonies, iris, and day lilies.

Wilson Brothers Floral Company, Inc.
Roachdale, Indiana 46172
Flowering house plants, scented
geraniums, tropical plants, and
African violets.

DRIED FLOWERS AND HERBS, ESSENTIAL OILS

There are specialty shops and many natural-food stores that sell dried flowers and herbs, as well as essential oils. Use these for potpourris, sachets, baths, steams, aromatherapy, teas, and in other forms of flower craft, alchemy, or when cooking. Below are some well-known mail-order sources for these items.

Aphrodisia
28 Carmine Street
New York, New York 10014

Complete line of dried flowers and herbs, essential oils, fixatives for potpourris, and an informative catalog.

Caswell-Massey Company
320 W. 13th Street (Catalog)
New York, New York 10014
518 Lexington Avenue (Store)
New York, New York 10017

Basic potpourri needs and many other herbal goods.

Country Herbs
Box 357
Stockbridge, Massachusetts 01262

Potpourri ingredients as well as herb plants.

Indiana Botanic Gardens
P.O. Box 5
Hammond, Indiana 46325

Fascinating catalog of herbal lore and products—dried flowers and herbs, essential oils, prepared potpourri, and sachets.

Nature's Herb Company
281 Ellis Street
San Francisco, California 94102

Quality dried flowers and herbs, essential oils, and potpourri ingredients.

Nichols Garden Nursery
1190 N. Pacific Highway
Albany, Oregon 97321

Dried scented flowers and herbs, fixatives, essential oils, potpourri recipes and books, and much more.

Penn Herb Company, Ltd.
603 North 2nd Street
Philadelphia, Pennsylvania 19123

A catalog full of dried botanicals, essential oils, herb seeds, books, and herbal products.

Kiehl Pharmacy
109 Third Avenue
New York, New York 10003

Although no mail-order service is provided from this establishment, it carries the finest, pure essential oils, dried flowers and herbs, and their own creations. Worth a visit when in New York City.

NATURAL DYEING

Many plants and seeds of flowers used for natural dyeing may be obtained from the suggested garden catalogs above or from your local nursery. Mordants and other dyeing materials can be found in weaving or yarn stores. Below are several mail-order places that offer dye plants and one that provides all the necessary supplies.

Flintridge
Route 1, Box 187
Sister Bay, Wisconsin 54234
Dye plants, herb seeds, dried herbs,
and essential oils.

J.L. Hudson Seedsman
A World Seed Service
P.O. Box 1058
Redwood City, California 94069
Dye plant seeds as well as one of
the world's largest selections of
seeds.

Snug Valley Herb Farm
Box 394 R.D. #3
Kutztown, Pennsylvania 19530
Vegetable dyes, mordants,
chemicals, natural fibers, and
spinning and weaving supplies.

Straw Into Gold
5533 College Avenue
Oakland, California 94618
Complete dyeing supplies,
including mordants and plants.

BACH FLOWER REMEDIES AND THE FLOWER ESSENCE SOCIETY

Bach Flower Remedies

The Dr. Edward Bach Healing
Centre
Mount Vernon, Sotwell,
Wallingford, Oxon. OX10 OPZ
England
Supplies the thirty-eight Bach
Flower Remedies, all the literature,
and "The Bach Remedy News
Letter."

C.W. Daniel Company, Ltd.
1 Church Path
Saffron Walden
Essex
CB10 1JP
England
Prints the books on the Bach
Remedies; you can order directly
from them.

Flower Essence Society

The Flower Essence Society
P.O. Box 459
Nevada City, California 95959
Provides their flower essences, a
newsletter, and communication
network.

BIBLIOGRAPHY

The following list includes sources that I have used in research and some of my favorite flower books. Most of the books are in my personal library. They can help guide you in expanding your knowledge and appreciation of flowers.

Abehsera, Michel. *The Healing Clay.* New York: Swan House, 1977.

Adrosko, Rita J. *Natural Dyes and Home Dyeing.* New York: Dover, 1971.

Anderson, Frank J. *An Illustrated Treasury of Cultivated Flowers.* New York: Abbeville Press, 1979.

——. *An Illustrated Treasury of Redouté Roses.* New York: Abbeville Press, 1979.

——. *An Illustrated Treasury of Orchids.* New York: Abbeville Press, 1979.

Angier, Bradford. *Field Guide to Edible Wild Plants.* Harrisburg, Pennsylvania: Stackpole Books, 1974.

Bach, Dr. Edward. *Heal Thyself.* Saffron Walden, England: C.W. Daniel Co., Ltd., 1974 (1931).

——. *The Twelve Healers and Other Remedies.* Saffron Walden, England: C.W. Daniel Co., Ltd., 1975 (1933).

Barker, Cicely M. *Flower Fairies of the Spring* (Flower Fairy Series). London: Blackie & Son, Ltd.

Bianchini, Francesco, and Corbetta, Francesco. *Health Plants of the World.* New York: Newsweek Books, 1977.

Briggs, Katherine Mary. *The Fairies in English Tradition and Literature.* Chicago: University of Chicago Press, 1967.

——. *The Vanishing People.* New York: Pantheon, 1978.

Bryan, John E., and Castle, Coralie. *The Edible Ornamental Garden.* San Francisco: 101 Productions, 1974.

Burnett, Frances Hodgson. *The Secret Garden.* New York: Lippincott, 1938.

Busch, Phyllis S., and Dowden, Anne Ophelia. *Wildflowers and The Stories Behind Their Names.* New York: Scribner, 1977.

Caddy, Peter, *et al. The Findhorn Garden,* Parts 1–4. Forres, Moray, Scotland: The Findhorn Trust.

Caldecott, Moyra. *Adventures by Leaf Light.* La Jolla, California: Green Tiger Press, 1978.

Chancellor, Philip M. *Handbook of The Bach Flower Remedies.* Saffron Walden, England: C.W. Daniel Co., Ltd., 1971.

Christopher, Dr. John R. *School of Natural Healing.* Provo, Utah: BiWorld, 1976.

Condon, Geneal. *The Complete Book of Flower Preservation.* Englewood Cliffs, New Jersey: Prentice-Hall, 1977.

Crockett, James Underwood. *Crockett's Flower Garden.* Boston, Toronto: Little, Brown, 1981.

Crowhurst, Adrienne. *The Flower Cookbook.* New York: Lancer Books, 1973.

Culpeper, Nicholas. *Culpeper's Complete Herbal.* London: W. Foulsham & Co., Ltd., 1652.

Cuthbertson, Tom. *Alan Chadwick's Enchanted Garden*. New York: Dutton, 1978.

Dowden, Anne Ophelia. *Look at a Flower*. New York: Thomas Y. Crowell, 1963.

———. *The Blossom on the Bough*. New York: Thomas Y. Crowell, 1975.

Doyle, Arthur Conan. *The Coming of the Fairies*. New York: Samuel Weiser, 1972.

Earle, Alice Mors. *Old Time Gardens*. New York: Macmillan, 1921.

Evans, Jane. *The Benefits of the Bach Flower Remedies*. Saffron Walden, England: C.W. Daniel Co., Ltd., 1974.

Evans-Wentz, W. Y. *Fairy Faith in Celtic Places*. Atlantic Highlands, New Jersey: Humanities Press, 1973.

The Findhorn Community. *The Findhorn Garden*. New York: Harper & Row, 1975.

Floyd, Harriet. *Plant It Now, Dry It Later*. New York: McGraw Hill, 1973.

Foster, Catherine Osgood. *Organic Flower Gardening*. Emmaus, Pennsylvania: Rodale Press, 1975.

Froud, Brian, and Lee, Alan. *Faeries*. New York: Abrams, 1978.

Gardner, Edward L. *Fairies, The Cottingley Photographs and Their Sequel*. London: The Theosophical Publishing House, 1966 (1945).

Gawain, Shakti. *Creative Visualization*. Mill Valley, California: Whatever Publishing, 1978.

Genders, Roy. *Perfume through the Ages*. New York: Putnam, 1972.

———. *Growing Herbs as Aromatics*. New Canaan, Connecticut: Keats Publishing, 1977.

Gerard, John. *The Herbal or General History of Plants*. New York: Dover, 1975 (1597, 1633).

Gibbons, Euell. *Stalking the Healthful Herbs*. New York: David McKay, 1966.

Grae, Ida. *Nature's Colors: Dyes from Plants*. New York: Macmillan, 1974.

Greenaway, Kate. *Language of Flowers*. New York: Avenel Books, 1884.

Grieve, Mrs. M. *A Modern Herbal*. New York: Dover, 1971 (1931).

Hawken, Paul. *The Magic of Findhorn*. New York: Bantam, 1975.

Hedrick, U.P., ed. *Sturtevant's Edible Plants of the World*. New York: Dover, 1972 (1919).

Hodson, Geoffrey. *Fairies at Work and at Play*. London: The Theosophical Publishing House, Ltd., 1976 (1925).

Holden, Edith. *The Country Diary of An Edwardian Lady*. New York: Holt, Rinehart and Winston, 1977 (1906).

Hylton, William H., ed. *The Rodale Herb Book*. Emmaus, Pennsylvania: Rodale Press, 1974.

James, Wilma Roberts. *Know Your Poisonous Plants*. Healdsburg, California: Naturegraph Publishers, 1973.

Jeavons, John. *How to Grow More Vegetables*. Berkeley, California: Ten Speed Press, 1979.

Jensen, Dr. Bernard. "Russian Fragrance Therapy," *The Herbalist* 4 (September 1979):14–15.

Kaufman, William Irving. *Perfume*. New York: Dutton, 1974.

Kerr, Jessica, and Dowden, Anne Ophelia. *Shakespeare's Flowers*. New York: Thomas Y. Crowell, 1969.

King, Ronald. *Botanical Illustration*. New York: Clarkson N. Potter, 1978.

Kingsbury, John. *Poisonous Plants of the United States and Canada*. Englewood Cliffs, New Jersey: Prentice-Hall, 1964.

Kloss, Jethro. *Back to Eden.* Coalmont, Tennessee: Longview Publishing House, 1969 (1939).

Lautié, Raymond, and Passebecq, André. *Aromatherapy.* Wellingborough, Northamptonshire, England: Thorsons Publishers, 1979.

Lewis, Walter H., and Elvin-Lewis, Memory P.F. *Medical Botany.* New York: John Wiley & Sons, 1977.

Lust, John. *The Herb Book.* New York: Bantam, 1974.

MacNicol, Mary. *Flower Cookery.* New York: Fleet Press, 1967.

Marsh, Jean. *The Illuminated Language of Flowers.* New York: Holt, Rinehart and Winston, 1978.

Menzies, Robert. *The Herbal Dinner.* Millbrae, California: Celestial Arts, 1977.

———. *The Star Herbal.* Millbrae, California: Celestial Arts, 1981.

Mességué, Maurice. *Of Men and Plants.* New York: Bantam, 1974.

———. *Health Secrets of Plants and Herbs.* New York: Morrow, 1979.

Meyer, Joseph E., and Meyer, Clarence. *The Herbalist.* Glenwood, Illinois: Meyerbooks, 1960 (1918).

The Mother. *Flowers and Their Messages.* Auroville, India: Auropress Publications, 1973.

Muenscher, Walter Conrad. *Poisonous Plants of the United States.* New York: Macmillan, 1975 (1939).

Niehaus, Theodore F., and Ripper, Charles L. *A Field Guide to Pacific States Wildflowers.* Boston: Houghton Mifflin, 1976.

O'Keeffe, Georgia. *Georgia O'Keeffe.* New York: Viking Press, 1976.

Organic Gardening Magazine Staff. *The Encyclopedia of Organic Gardening.* Emmaus, Pennsylvania: Rodale Press, 1978.

Otis, Denise, and Maia, Ronaldo. *Decorating with Flowers.* New York: Abrams, 1978.

Parkinson, John. *Herball.* 1640.

Penn, Irving. *Flowers.* New York: Harmony Books, 1980.

Perry, Frances, ed. *Complete Guide to Plants & Flowers.* New York: Simon & Schuster, 1974.

Peterson, Roger Tory, and McKenny, Margaret. *A Field Guide to Wildflowers of Northeastern and North Central North America.* Boston: Houghton Mifflin, 1968.

Philbrook, Helen, and Gregg, Richard. *Companion Plants and How to Use Them.* Old Greenwich, Connecticut: Devin-Adair, 1966.

Pizzetti, Ippolito, and Cocker, Henry. *Flowers, A Guide For Your Garden.* New York: Abrams, 1968.

Powell, Claire. *The Meaning of Flowers.* Boulder, Colorado: Shambala, 1979.

Rickett, Harold William. *Wild Flowers of the United States* (Six Volumes). New York: McGraw Hill, 1966–70.

Robertson, Laurel. *Laurel's Kitchen.* New York: Bantam, 1978.

Rohde, Eleanour Sinclair. *The Old English Herbals.* New York: Dover, 1971 (1922).

———. *A Garden of Herbs.* New York: Dover, 1969 (1936).

———. *Rose Recipes from Olden Times.* New York: Dover, 1973 (1939).

Rose, Jeanne. *Herbs & Things.* New York: Grosset & Dunlap, 1972.

———. *The Herbal Body Book.* New York: Grosset & Dunlap, 1976.

———. *Kitchen Cosmetics.* San Francisco: Panjandrum/Aris Books, 1978.

————. *Herbal Guide to Inner Health*. New York: Grosset & Dunlap, 1979.

————. *The Herbal: Jeanne Rose's Guide to Living*. New York: Bantam, 1982.

Samuels, Mike, and Samuels, Nancy. *Seeing with The Mind's Eye*. New York: Random House, 1975.

Seymour, John. *The Self-Sufficient Gardener*. New York: Doubleday, 1980.

Shibayama, Abbot Zenkei. *A Flower Does Not Talk*. Tokyo, Japan: Charles E. Tuttle, 1970.

Staff of the L.H. Bailey Hortorium. *Hortus Third*. Cornell University, Ithaca, New York: Macmillan, 1976.

Sunset Gardening Books Series. *Gardening In Containers, Garden Color, How To Grow Bulbs, etc.*, Menlo Park, California: Lane Publishing Co.

Teshigahara, Wafu. *Ikebana: A New Illustrated Guide to Mastery*. Tokyo, New York: Kodansha International, Ltd., 1981.

Tisserand, Robert B. *The Art of Aromatherapy*. New York: Inner Traditions, 1977.

Tompkins, Peter, and Bird, Christopher. *The Secret Life of Plants*. New York: Avon, 1973.

Tozer, Zibby. *The Art of Flower Arranging*. New York: Warner Books, 1981.

Valnet, Dr. Jean. *Aromatherapy*. Saffron Walden, England: C.W. Daniel Co., Ltd.

Van Gelder, Dora. *The Real World of Fairies*. Wheaton, Illinois: The Theosophical Publishing House, 1977.

Weeks, Nora. *The Medical Discoveries of Edward Bach, Physician*. Saffron Walden, England: C.W. Daniel Co., Ltd., 1973.

Weeks, Nora, and Bullen, Victor. *The Bach Flower Remedies, Illustrations and Preparation*. Saffron Walden, England: C.W. Daniel Co., Ltd., 1976 (1964).

Wheeler, F.J. *The Bach Remedies Repertory*. Saffron Walden, England: C.W. Daniel Co., Ltd., 1952.

Wilder, Louise Beebe. *The Fragrant Garden*. New York: Dover, 1974 (1932).

Yepsen, Roger B., Jr., ed. *Organic Plant Protection*. Emmaus, Pennsylvania: Rodale Press, 1976.

INDEX

Acacia (*Acacia* spp.), 65, 95, 110, 113, 115, 122, 135, 185, 187, 190
dye experiment with, 123
Acroclinium (*Helipterum roseum*), 67, 95, 110
African daisy (*Osteospermum fruticosum*), 62, 122
African violet (*Saintpaulia ionantha*), 78
Agar-agar, 136
Ageratum (*Ageratum houstonianum*), 72, 99
Ajuga (*Ajuga reptans*), 81
Alfalfa (*Medicago sativa*), 31, 49
Allium (*Allium* spp.), 75
Almond (*Prunus dulcis* var. *dulcia*), 30, 190
Alyssum (*Alyssum* spp.), 68, 72
Amaryllis (*Hippeastrum* spp.), 75, 78
Anemone (*Anemone coronaria*), 72, 75, 81, 91, 99, 122, 249
Angelica (*Angelica archangelica*), 63, 64, 225
Anise (*Pimpinella anisum*), 64
Anther, 20
Anthurium (*Anthurium andraeanum, A. scherzeranum*), 29, 91
Antiseptic flowers, 186
Antony and Cleopatra (Shakespeare), 224
Apollo, 106
Apple (*Malus* spp.), 29, 30, 65, 113, 115, 135, 173–174
Apple geranium (*Pelargonium odoratissimum*), 92
Apple mint (*Mentha suaveolens*), 92
Arabian jasmine (*J. sambac*), 230
Aroma-color breathing visualization, 246
Aromas, effect of, 228
Aromatherapy, 223–240, 242
Aromatic flower waters, 187–189
Aromatic flowers, 186–187
garden of, 64–65
for potpourris and sachets, 113–114

Aromatics, history of, 223–226
Arranging flowers, 89–93
Arrowroot, 136
Artichoke (*Cynara cardunculus* var. *scolumus*), 92
Aster (*Aster* spp.), 70, 72, 91, 99, 115
Astringent bath, 213
Astringent flowers, 185
Attar of roses, 230
Autumn crocus (*Colchicum autumnale*), 134
Avicenna, 187, 224
Avocado-chamomile mask, 201
Azalea (*Rhododendron* spp.), 72, 78, 81, 99, 102, 249

Baby blue eyes (*Nemophila menziesii*), 70
Baby pillow, 127
Baby's breath (*Gypsophila elegans, G. paniculata*), 67, 72, 91, 92, 102, 110
Bach, Dr. Edward, 236, 237, 238, 240
Bach Flower Remedies, 236–238, 240, 274
Bachelor's button (*Centaurea cyanus*), 72, 78, 91, 99, 103, 114
Balms, 199–200
Basil (*Ocimum basilicum*), 64, 65, 82, 92, 133, 138–139, 235
Basket of roses, 110–111
Baths, 207, 210–214
flower petal, 219
Bay (*Laurus nobilis*), 110
Bean sprouts, 136–137
Beans, 83
Beds, raised, 48–50
Bee balm (*Monarda didyma*), 64, 65, 113, 115, 133, 187
Bees, 23–24
Begonia (*Begonia* spp.), 72, 75, 78, 81
Bells of Ireland (*Moluccella laevis*), 67, 91, 92, 110

Benzoin, gum *(Styrax benzoin)*, 116
    tincture of, 193–194
Bergamot *(Citrus bergamia)*, 92, 115,
    183, 235
Bergenia *(Bergenia* spp.), 81
Bible, 224
Bindweed *(Convolvulus arvensis)*, 102
Bird, Christopher, 255, 256
Bird-of-paradise *(Strelitzia reginae)*,
    72, 81, 91
Bitter orange *(Neroli)*, 115
Black locust *(Robinia pseudoacacia)*, 65
Blackberry *(Rubus* spp.), 30
Black-eyed Susan *(Rudbeckia hirta)*,
    70, 99
Black-eyed Susan vine *(Thunbergia
    alata)*, 75, 78
Blazing star *(Mentzelia lindleyi)*, 70
Bleeding heart *(Dicentra spectabilis)*,
    72, 81
Blooming flower visualization, 245
Blossoms, 84–85
Blue clay, 204
Blue flax *(Linum perenne)*, 70
Bluebell *(Endymion non-scriptus)*, 264
Blue-eyed grass *(Sisyrinchium* spp.),
    70, 92, 102
Bone meal, 60
Books of pressed flowers, 102–103
Borage *(Borago officinalis)*, 82, 114,
    131, 134, 170–171, 183, 185
    for herb tea, 168
Borax, 96, 98
Botticelli, Sandro, 106
Bougainvillea *(Bougainvillea* spp.),
    36, 72, 77, 78, 99, 102, 115
Bract, 29
Bromeliad, 78
Broom *(Cytisus* spp.), 31, 65, 102,
    110, 122, 264
Brownies, 258, 260
Buckwheat, wild, *see* Wild buck-
    wheat
Bud, 53
Bulb, 19
Burbank, Luther, 24
Burdock *(Arctium lappa)*, 34, 58, 186,
    210
Burmese honeysuckle *(Lonicera hil-
    debrandiana)*, 76
Buttercup *(Ranunculus acris, R. re-
    pens)*, 70, 102, 114, 122
Butterflies, 24

Cabbage, 82, 83
Cabbage rose *(Rosa centifolia)*, 165,
    229
Caddy, Eileen, 261, 262
Caddy, Peter, 261–262
Calamus *(Acorus calamus)*, 116
Calceolaria *(Calceolaria* spp.), 78
Calendars, pressed flower, 105
Calendula *(Calendula officinalis)*, 26,
    34, 72, 78, 82, 91, 99, 114, 122,
    134, 145, 163, 166, 183, 186,
    206, 210
    for herb tea, 168
California poppy *(Eschscholzia califor-
    nica)*, 70
Calla *(Zantedeschia* spp.), 29, 75, 78,
    81
Calming flower sauna, 216
Calypso *(Calypso bulbosa)*, 34
Calyx, 20
Camellia *(Camellia* spp.), 72, 81, 91,
    99, 122, 249
Campanula *(Campanula* spp.), 72,
    81
Campion, rose, *see* Rose campion
Canary bird vine *(Tropaeolum per-
    egrinum)*, 75
Candied flowers, 131
Candytuft *(Iberis* spp.), 29, 72
Canna *(Canna* spp.), 75, 78
Canterbury bell *(Campanula medium)*,
    25, 72, 122
Cape primrose *(Streptocarpus
    hybridus)*, 78
Caraway *(Carum carvi)*, 162
Caraway thyme *(Thymus herba-bar-
    ona)*, 140
Cardamom *(Elettaria cardamomum)*,
    235
Cardinal climber *(Ipomoea quamoclit)*,
    75
Cardinal flower *(Lobelia cardinalis)*,
    81, 115
Cardoon *(Cynara cardunculus* var.
    altilis), 95
Cards, pressed flower, 105
Carnation *(Dianthus caryophyllus)*,
    26, 65, 72, 91, 99, 113, 115, 116,
    135, 161–162, 164, 186, 187, 190,
    235
Carnation lip balm, 199
Carnation massage oil, 220
Carob, 136, 174

Carolina jasmine (*Gelsemium semper-virens*), 135
Carpels, 20
Carrots, 82, 83
Carver, George Washington, 256
Cassia oils, 224
Catkin, 29
Catnip (*Nepeta cataria*), 32, 64, 209
Cattail (*Typha latifolia*), 92, 95, 134
Cattleya (*Cattleya* spp.), 79
Cayenne, 137
Ceanothus (*Ceanothus* spp.), 65
Cedarwood (*Juniperus virginiana*), 224, 235
Celosia (*Celosia cristata*), 67, 72, 78, 91, 95, 110
Cesalpino, Andrea, 103
Chamomile, *see* German chamomile
Chamomile oil, 234–235
Chamomile tea, 168, 234
Cherry (*Prunus avium*), 30
Chervil (*Anthriscus cerefolium*), 64
Chickweed (*Stellaria media*), 58, 134, 157, 185
  for garden salad, 151
Chicory (*Cichorium intybus*), 35, 70, 102, 134
  for herb tea, 168
Chilean bellflower (*Lapageria rosea*), 77
Chilean jasmine (*Mandevilla laxa*), 77
Chinese lantern (*Physalis alkekengi*), 67, 95, 110
Chives (*Allium schoenoprasum*), 63, 64, 82, 133
Chrysanthemum (*Chrysanthemum morifolium*), 72, 78, 91, 99, 114, 122, 135, 146–147
Cineraria (*Senecio hybridus*), 66, 72, 78, 81, 102, 122
Citronella (*Cymbopogon nardus*), 115
Clarkia (*Clarkia* spp.), 70, 102
Clary sage oil, 116
Classification of plants, 25–27
Clay pack, 218
Clays, flower, 203–205
Cleansing flowers, 186
Cleavers (*Galium aparine*), 185, 186
Clematis (*Clematis* spp.), 65, 77, 102, 115
Cleome (*Cleome spinosa*), 91
Cleopatra, 224
Climbing hydrangea (*Hydrangea anomala*), 77
Climbing plants, 75–77
Climbing rose, 77
Clivia (*Clivia miniata*), 75, 78, 81
Clove (*Eugenia caryophyllata*), 113, 116, 119, 185, 186, 187
Clove pink (*Dianthus caryophyllus*), 135
Clover, red (*Trifolium pratense*), 31, 134, 185, 186, 206, 210
  for herb tea, 168
Codeine, 41
Colorful flowers for potpourris and sachets, 114–115
Columbine (*Aquilegia* spp.), 70, 81, 91, 99, 115, 185
Columnea (*Columnea "Stavanger"*), 78
Comfrey (*Symphytum officinale*), 49, 64, 183, 185, 206
Companion plants, flowers as, 81–83
Compleat Housewife, The (recipe book), 131
Composite (*Compositae*), 34–35
Compost, 60–61
Congestion steam, 209
Container flower gardens, 71–72
Containers, 52
Coral vine (*Antigonon leptopus*), 77
Coralbells (*Heuchera sanguinea*), 81, 102
Coreopsis (*Coreopsis* spp.), 66, 70, 91, 122
Coriander (*Coriandrum sativum*), 64, 133
Cornelian cherry, *see* Dogwood
Corolla, 20
Corymb, 29
Cosmos (*Cosmos* spp.), 72, 92, 99, 102
Costmary (*Chrysanthemum balsamita*), 113
Cottage pinks (*Dianthus plumarius*), 135
Cottingley photographs, 258–259
Cotton ball oil method for extracting flower oils, 192–193
Cotyledons, 53
Cowslip (*Primula veris*), 131, 132, 135, 185, 264
Crab apple (*Malus* spp., *Malus pumila*), 238

Creeping thyme (*Thymus praecox arcticus*), 264, 265
Cress, garden (*Lepidium sativum*), 64
Crocus (*Crocus* spp.), 75, 78, 122, 248
Crombie, Robert Ogilvie, 262
Cucumber, 83
Cucumber-rose petal facial, 200
Culpeper, Nicholas, 25, 131, 132, 145, 190, 225, 229–234
Cultivated flowers for arrangements, 91–92
Cultivating, 58–59
Cup of gold vine (*Solandra guttata*), 77
Cup-and-saucer vine (*Cobaea scandens*), 77
Cupid, 106
Cupid's dart (*Catananche caerulea*), 95, 110
Cutting flower gardens, 68–69
Cyclamen (*Cyclamen* spp.), 72, 75, 78, 81
Cymbidium (*Cymbidium* spp.), 79, 81
Cyme, 29

Daffodil (*Narcissus pseudonarcissus*), 65, 75, 92, 99, 114, 122
Dahlia (*Dahlia* spp.), 72, 75, 92, 99, 122
dye experiment with, 123–124
Daisy (*Bellis perennis*), 34–35, 70, 92, 99, 102, 114, 122, 135, 185
Damask rose (*Rosa damascena*), 165, 229
Dandelion (*Taraxacum officinale*), 27, 34, 134, 185
for green salad, 151
Daphne (*Daphne odora, D. cneorum*), 65, 72, 81
Daphne (mythological nymph), 106
Day lily (*Hemerocallis* spp.), 81, 99, 135, 176–177
De Materia Medica (Dioscorides), 229
Delights for Ladies (recipe book), 131
Delphinium (*Delphinium* spp.), 92, 99, 102, 114
Desiccants, 96–99
Dewdrops, sipping, 239
Dicotyledons (Dicots), 27
Dill (*Anethum graveolens*), 65, 83, 92, 133, 139–140, 154, 156–157, 158

Dioscorides, 229
Division, 26
Dock (*Rumex crispus, R.* spp.), 58, 92, 95, 110, 122, 185
dye experiment with, 124
for green salad, 151
Dr. Edward Bach Centre, 238
Doctrine of Signatures, The, 25
Dogtooth violet (*Erythronium denscanis*), 75
Dogwood (*Cornus florida, C. mas*), 36–37
Dogwood family (*Cornaceae*), 36–37
Doyle, Sir Arthur Conan, 259
Dracaena (*Dracaena massangeana*), 255
Dried flowers, 94–99
arrangements of, 99
desiccants for, 96–99
mail-order sources of, 273
upside-down method for, 95
Dusty miller (*Centaurea cineraria*), 72, 92
Dutch iris, 75, 78
Dutchman's pipe (*Aristolochia durior*), 77
Dwarf citrus (*Citrus* spp.), 78
Dye flower gardens, 66–67
Dyeing with flowers, 89, 119–125
experiments in, 123–125
flowers for, 122
mail-order sources of plants for, 273–274
steps in, 120–122

Edible flower gardens, 62–64
Edible flowers and flowering herbs, 132–135
Eglantine (*Rosa eglanteria*), 265
Elder flower (*Sambucus canadensis, S. caerulea*), 131, 134, 185, 186, 187, 190, 206, 210
for herb tea, 168
Elder flower water, 189
Elder flower-honey-yogurt facial, 200
Elementals, 259
Elves, 258, 260
Embryo, 53
Emollient flowers, 184–185
Endosperm, 54
Energizer steam, 209
English lavender (*Lavandula vera*), 232

Essence method for extracting
flower oils, 193
Essences, 238–240
Essential oils, 115–116, 229–235
aromatherapy with, 228
mail-order sources of, 273
Eucalyptus *(Eucalyptus globulus)*,
110, 116, 186, 209, 235
Evening primrose *(Oenothera* spp.),
70
Evergreens, 110
Everlasting flower gardens, 67
Exacum *(Exacum affine)*, 78
Exercising in the garden, 47–48
Eyebright *(Euphrasia officinalis)*, 25

Facial masks, 202, 204–205
Facial ritual, flowering, 217–218
Facial steams, 207–210
Facial vinegars, 205
Facials, 200–203, 218
Fairies
descriptions of, 258–262
favorite flowers of, 264–267
history of, 256–258
recipe for seeing, 267
Fairy primrose *(Primula malacoides)*,
71, 72, 264, 265
Farewell-to-spring *(Clarkia amoena)*
(Godetia amoena), 70, 177
Fennel *(Foeniculum vulgare)*, 64, 65,
113, 122, 133, 185, 187, 206, 235
for herb tea, 168
Fertilization, 22, 60
Feverfew *(Chrysanthemum par-
thenium)*, 62, 82, 83, 92
Filament, 20
Findhorn gardens, 261–262
Fireweed *(Epilobium augustifolium)*,
70, 102
Fixatives, 116
Flats, 52, 54
Flies, 24
Flora (goddess of flowers), 106
Florentine iris *(Iris florentina, I. ger-
manica* var. *florentina)*, 38, 116
Florist's "frog," 90
Flower arranging, 89–93
Flower balm oil, 195
Flower clay pack, 218
Flower clays, 203–205
Flower in the Crannied Wall
(Tennyson), 252
Flower Essence Society, 238, 274

Flower Fairies of the Garden
(Pomerantz), 264
Flower feast weekend, 179–180
Flower foods, recipes for, *see*
Recipes for flower foods
Flower oils, 189–193
five methods for extracting,
192–193
herb, 193
recipes for, 194–195
Flower parts, 19–22
Flower press, 100
Flower sauna tea, 215
Flower skin toner, 218
Flowering maple *(Abutilon
hybridum)*, 78, 81
Flowering vines, 75–77
Flowers from the Holy Land, 100
Forget-me-not *(Myosotis sylvatica)*,
70, 78, 81, 92, 102, 114, 264
Forsythia *(Forsythia* spp.), 15, 65, 92
Foxglove *(Digitalis purpurea)*, 70, 81,
264
Fragrant bath, 213
Fragrant flower vinegar, 157
Frangipani *(Plumeria rubra)*, 65, 106,
113, 115, 187, 190
Frankincense, 224, 225
Freesia *(Freesia* spp.), 65, 75, 78, 92,
113
Fresh flower aromatherapy, 235–236
Fritillaria *(Fritillaria* spp.), 75
Fruit trees, 82, 83
Fuchsia *(Fuchsia hybrida)*, 24, 72, 78,
81, 92, 99, 115, 185
Fully flowering facial, 202

Gaillardia *(Gaillardia* spp.), 92, 114
Garden catalogs, mail-order sources
of, 271–272
Garden cress, *see* Cress, garden
Garden flower salve, 197
Garden flowers for pressing, 102
Garden sage *(Salvia officinalis)*,
32–33, 64, 65, 92, 102, 110, 113,
134, 185, 186, 209
for herb tea, 168
Garden thyme *(Thymus vulgaris)*, 32,
65, 92, 113, 134, 140, 185, 186,
187, 209, 235
for herb tea, 169
Gardenia *(Gardenia jasminoides)*, 65,
72, 78, 92, 113, 115, 187, 235
Gardenia-papaya-banana mask, 202

Gardens
    aromatic flowers, 64–65
    container flowers, 71–72
    cutting flowers, 68–69
    dye flowers, 66–67
    edible flowers, 62–64
    everlasting flowers, 67
    flowers for pressing, 102
    indoor flowers, 77–79
    shade flowers, 79–81
    wild flowers, 69–70
Gardner, Edward, 259
Garlands, 105–106
Garlic (*Allium sativum*), 64, 83, 95
Garlic chives (*Allium tuberosum*), 92,
    133, 143
Gattefossé, Rene-Maurice, 225–226
Gazania (*Gazania rigens leucolaena*),
    62, 243
Gentle salve, 197
Gently heated oil method for ex-
    tracting flower oils, 192
Genus, 26
George IV, King, 93
Geranium (*Geranium* spp.,
    Pelargonium spp.), 62, 72, 78,
    83, 92, 102, 122, 135, 160, 185
Gerard, John, 106, 131, 166, 176,
    225, 229, 236
German chamomile (*Matricaria re-
    cutita*), 34, 64, 65, 82, 113, 122,
    133, 185, 186, 187, 206, 209,
    210, 234
Geum (*Geum* spp.), 92, 99
Gillyflower (*Dianthus caryophyllus*),
    131, 132
Ginger (*Zingiber officinale*), 65, 78,
    113, 186, 187, 190
Gladiolus (*Gladiolus* spp.), 75, 92,
    99, 135, 175
Globe amaranth (*Gomphrena globosa*),
    67, 95, 110
Globe thistle (*Echinops exaltus*), 67,
    95, 110
Globeflower (*Trollius* spp.), 81
Glory-of-the-snow (*Chionodoxa* spp.),
    75
Gloxinia (*Sinningia speciosa*), 72, 79,
    81
Gnomes, 260
Godetia, *see* Farewell-to-spring
Goethe, Johann Wolfgang von, 258
Gold fields (*Lasthenia chrysostoma*),
    70

Goldenrod (*Solidago* spp.), 29, 92,
    95, 122, 185, 186
Gorse (*Ulex europaeus*), 239, 262
Grape hyacinth (*Muscari* spp.), 75,
    79
Grapefruit, 115
Green clay, 204
Greenaway, Kate, 94
Griffiths, Frances, 258–259

Hair rinses, 205–207
Halloween, 267
Hamlet (Shakespeare), 233, 266
Hawthorn (*Crataegus* spp.), 134
Head, 29
Headache ritual, flowering, 217
Heather (*Calluna vulgaris*), 92, 95,
    110
Heliotrope (*Heliotropium arborescens*),
    65, 113, 115, 187
Hellebore (*Helleborus* spp.), 81
Hepatica (*Hepatica* spp.), 81
Herb flower oils, 193
Herb potpourri or sachet, flowering,
    117
Herb teas, flower, 167–169
Herbal (Gerard), 106, 166
Herbaria, 89
Herbs
    flowering
        for arrangements, 92
        edible, 132–135
    mail-order sources of, 273
    for potpourris and sachets,
        113–114
    salve, 196
Heroin, 41
Hibiscus (*Hibiscus* spp.), 79, 102,
    115, 122, 134, 171, 185
    for herb tea, 168
Historia Naturalis (Pliny), 229
Hodson, Geoffrey, 260–261
Holly (*Ilex aquifolium*), 110, 238
Hollyhock (*Alcea rosea*), 92, 95, 99,
    102, 115, 122, 135, 141, 170, 185
Homer, 210, 224
Honesty (*Lunaria annua*), 67, 95, 110
Honey guides, 23
Honey-rosemary-rose petal facial,
    202–203
Honeysuckle (*Lonicera* spp., *L.
    japonica*), 77, 99, 113, 115, 135,
    185, 187, 190
Honeysuckle flower water, 189

Hop *(Humulus lupulus)*, 209
Hosta *(Hosta* spp.), 81
Hummingbirds, 24
Hyacinth *(Hyacinthus orientalis)*, 65,
    75, 79, 99, 113, 115, 122
Hydrangea *(Hydrangea macrophylla)*,
    81, 95, 99, 102, 110, 114, 115
Hyssop *(Hyssopus officinalis)*, 64, 92,
    133, 186
    for herb tea, 168

Iceland poppy *(Papaver nudicaule)*,
    41, 62, 72
Ikebana, 90–91
Ilang-ilang *(Cananga odorata)*, 113,
    115, 187, 235
Iliad (Homer), 224
Impatiens *(Impatiens* spp., *I. glan-
    dulifera)*, 72, 79, 81, 238
Indian paintbrush *(Castilleja* spp.),
    36, 70, 92, 102
Indoor flower gardens, 77–79
Inflorescence, 27
Inner garden (visualization), 248
Insect repellent sachet, 118
Insect-pollinated plants, 20–22, 25
Io, 161
Iris *(Iris* spp.), 37–38, 65, 75, 81, 92,
    99, 122
    dye experiment with, 125
Iris (mythological goddess), 37
Iris family *(Iridaceae)*, 37–38
Itch and inflammation bath, 213
Ivy *(Hedera* spp.), 81
Ivy geranium *(Pelargonium peltatum)*,
    72

Jacob's ladder *(Polemonium
    caeruleum)*, 81
Japanese flower arranging, 90–91
Jasmine *(Jasminum* spp., *J. officinale,
    J. sambac)*, 65, 77, 113, 115, 135,
    187, 190, 209
Jasmine oil, 230–231
    for massage, 220
Jesus, 183–184
Johnny-jump-up *(Viola tricolor)*, 72,
    79, 102, 115, 135, 155, 264,
    266–267
Journals of pressed flowers, 102–103
Juniper *(Juniperus communis)*, 235
Juno, 161, 224
Jupiter, 161

Kaffir lily, *see* Clivia
Kalanchoe *(Kalanchoe* spp.), 79
Karnak, Temple of, 38
Kelp, 137
Kenilworth ivy *(Cymbalaria muralis)*,
    81
Kingdom, 26
Kirk, Robert, 257–258

Labdanum *(Cistus ladanifer)*, 116
Ladies' tresses *(Spiranthes* spp.), 32
Lady's slipper *(Paphiopedilum* spp.),
    34, 81
Lamb's ears *(Stachys byzantina)*, 95,
    110
Language of flowers, 93–94
Language of Flowers (Greenaway), 94
Lantana *(Lantana* spp.), 72, 79
Larkspur *(Consolida ambigua)*, 92, 99,
    102, 115
Lavender *(Lavandula* spp., *L. of-
    ficinalis)*, 32, 64, 72, 92, 95, 110,
    113, 116, 134, 168, 185, 186,
    187, 190, 206, 209
Lavender flower water, 189
Lavender oil, 232
Lavender-rose-rosemary potpourri
    or sachet, 117
Leaves, 19
Lecithin, 136
Leis, 106
Lemon balm *(Melissa officinalis)*, 32,
    64, 65, 92, 113, 134, 185, 187,
    190, 235
Lemon blossom *(Citrus limon)*, 113,
    115, 135, 167, 185, 209
Lemon geranium *(Pelargonium
    crispum)*, 92, 135
Lemon thyme *(Thymus citriodorus)*,
    140
Lemon verbena *(Aloysia triphylla)*,
    65, 92, 113, 115, 134, 187
Lemongrass *(Cymbopogon citratus)*,
    115, 171
Licorice *(Glycyrrhiza glabra)*, 31, 145,
    146
Lilac *(Syringa vulgaris)*, 65, 92, 99,
    113, 115, 116, 135, 187, 190, 235
Lily *(Lilium* spp.), 65, 75, 113, 185,
    190
Lily of the Nile *(Agapanthus orien-
    talis, A. africanus)*, 79
Lily of the valley *(Convallaria ma-
    jalis)*, 65, 75, 81, 99, 113, 115

Lime *(Citrus aurantiifolia)*, 113, 115
Linaria *(Linaria maroccana)*, 70, 72, 92
Linden *(Tilia europaea)*, 113, 209
Linnaeus, 26, 258
Lip balm, carnation, 199
Lipstick plant *(Aeschynanthus radi-cans)*, 79
Lobelia *(Lobelia erinus)*, 62, 72, 102, 115, 122
Lotions, 197–199
Lotus *(Nelumbo lutea, N. nucifera)*, 65, 113, 115, 187
Love pillow, 127
Love-in-a-mist *(Nigella damascena)*, 67, 79, 95, 99
Love-in-idleness *(Viola tricolor)*, 266
Lover's flower fantasy (visualiza-tion), 249
Lupine *(Lupinus spp.)*, 31, 70, 122
    dye experiment with, 124–125

MacLean, Dorothy, 261, 262
Magic garden visualization, 246
Magnolia *(Magnolia spp.)*, 65, 99, 113, 115
Mallow *(Malva spp.)* *(Althaea officinalis)*, 70, 102, 115, 134, 185
    for green salad, 151
Mandala, 243–244
Manure, 60
Marguerite *(Chrysanthemum frutescens)*, 66, 72, 92, 122
Marigold *(Tagetes spp.)*, 72, 79, 83, 92, 99, 102, 114, 122
Mark Antony, 224
Massage oil, jasmine or carnation, 220
May Day, 267
May Day baskets, 92–93
Meadow rue *(Thalictrum spp.)*, 81
Meadow of wild flowers (visualiza-tion), 251
Melilot *(Melilotus officinalis)*, 185, 187
Melon, 83
Metamorphoses (Ovid), 105
Mexican flame vine *(Senecio con-fusus)*, 77
Midsummer Eve, 267
Midsummer Night's Dream, A (Shakespeare), 257, 265, 266
Mignonette *(Reseda odorata)*, 65, 81, 113

Mild floral flowers, edible, 135
Mild herbs, edible, 134
Millet, 137
Mimosa *(Acacia baileyana)*, 115
Mimulus, *see* Monkey flower
Miner's lettuce *(Montia perfoliata)*, 185
    for green salad, 151
Mint *(Mentha spp.)*, 64, 65, 83, 185, 186, 209
    See also Apple mint; Orange mint
Mint family *(Labiatae)*, 32–33
Mint water, 189
Miso, 136, 137
Mock orange *(Philadelphus spp.)*, 15, 65
Money plant, *see* Honesty
Monkey flower *(Mimulus spp., M. cardinalis, M. guttatus)*, 29, 81, 238
Monkshood *(Aconitum napellus)*, 81
Monocotyledons (Monocots), 27
Montbretia *(Crocosmia crocosmiiflora)*, 75
Moonflower *(Ipomoea alba)*, 65, 77
Mordants, 120, 121
Morning glory *(Ipomoea tricolor)*, 77, 122
Morpheus, 41
Morphine, 41
Moth and insect repellent sachet, 118
Mother-of-thyme, *see* Creeping thyme
Moths, 24
Mugwort *(Artemisia douglasiana, A. vulgaris)*, 92, 122, 264
Mulching, 58
Mullein *(Verbascum thapsus)*, 70, 92, 95, 114, 122, 134, 183, 185, 194, 206
Mustard *(Brassica spp.)* *(Sinapis arvensis)*, 19–22, 83, 92, 102, 134, 142–143, 151, 186, 238
Myrrh, 116, 224, 225

Narcissus *(Narcissus spp.)*, 65, 75, 79, 81, 92, 113, 115
Nasturtium *(Tropaeolum majus)*, 38–39, 65, 72, 79, 83, 92, 114, 115, 134, 138, 141–142, 165–166, 173, 185, 186
    as natural food, 131

Natural-food stores, 273
Nature spirits
  descriptions of, 258–262
  history of, 256–258
  visualization, 249
Nemesia *(Nemesia strumosa)*, 72
Nettle *(Urtica dioica)*, 206
New York Botanical Garden, 103
Nicotiana *(Nicotiana sanderae, N. syl-
  vestris)*, 62, 65, 72, 79, 81, 92,
  113
Night-blooming jasmine *(Cestrum
  nocturnum)*, 1, 65
Nightshade family *(Solanaceae)*,
  39–41
Nosegay, 94
Nutmeg geranium *(Pelargonium fra-
  grans)*, 92
Nutritional yeast, 136

Oak *(Quercus* spp.), 25
Oakmoss *(Evernia prunastri)*, 116
Oberon, 257, 265, 266
Odyssey (Homer), 224
Oil method for extracting flower
  oils, 192
Oils
  essential, 115–116, 229–235
    aromatherapy with, 228
    mail-order sources of, 273
  flower, 189–193
    five methods for extracting,
      192–193
    recipes for, 194–195
  herb flower, 193
  super flower skin, 194, 218
Onions, 82, 95
Opium, 41
Opium poppy *(Papaver somniferum)*,
  41, 135
Orange, *see* Bitter orange; Sweet
  orange
Orange flower water, 189
Orange mint *(Mentha piperita* var.
  citrata), 32, 92, 113
Orchid, *see* Cattleya; Cymbidium;
  Phalaenopsis
Orchid family *(Orchidaceae)*, 33–34,
  92, 99
Orchid flower vine *(Stigmaphyllon
  ciliatum)*, 77
Order, 26

Oregano *(Origanum vulgare)*, 64, 134,
  143
Organic gardening, 48
Oriental poppy *(Papaver orientale)*, 41
Orrisroot *(Iris florentina, I. germanica
  var. florentina)*, 116, 119
Ovary, 20
Ovid, 105
Oxlips *(Primula elatior)*, 265

Pain-relieving drugs, 41
Painted daisy *(Chrysanthemum coc-
  cineum)*, 92
Pampas grass *(Cortaderia selloana)*, 95
Pan, 262
Panicle, 29
Pansy *(Viola wittrockiana)*, 72, 79, 92,
  99, 102, 114, 115, 122, 135, 178,
  185, 264, 266–267
Parkinson, John, 229, 232
Parsley *(Petroselinum crispum)*, 29,
  64, 201
Passionflower *(Passiflora* spp., *P.
  manicata* hybrid, *P. caerulea)*, 77,
  79, 134
  for herb tea, 168
Patchouli *(Pogostemon patchouli)*, 235
Pea family *(Leguminosae)*, 31–32
Peach *(Prunus persica)*, 30
Pear *(Pyrus communis)*, 30
Pearly everlasting *(Anaphalis mar-
  garitacea)*, 92, 95
Peat pots, 54
Pennyroyal *(Mentha pulegium)*, 95,
  110, 113, 116, 193
Penstemon *(Penstemon* spp.), 70,
  102, 122
Peony *(Paeonia* spp.), 92, 99, 135
Peppermint *(Mentha piperita)*, 32, 92,
  113, 116, 204, 235
Peppermint geranium *(Pelargonium
  tomentosum)*, 92, 135
Perfume, 223–224, 226–227
Perianth, 20
Periwinkle *(Vinca* spp.), 81, 185, 264
Persian violet, *see* Exacum
Petunia *(Petunia hybrida)*, 24, 39–41,
  65, 72, 79, 83, 92, 122, 135
Phalaenopsis *(Phalaenopsis* spp.), 79
Phlox *(Phlox* spp.), 72, 92, 102
Pictures, pressed flower, 104–105
Pikake *(Jasminium sambac)*, 106
Pillows, 89, 127–128

Pincushion flower (*Scabiosa* spp.),
    92, 122
Pink (*Dianthus caryophyllus, D.
    plumarius*), 65, 102
Pistillate flowers, 25
Pistils, 20
Pixies, 258
Plant parts, 19–22
Plantain (*Plantago major, P. lan-
    ceolata*), 29, 58, 92, 151, 185
Planter boxes, 52
Plants
    classification of, 25–27
    climbing, 75–77
    companion, flowers as, 81–83
Plastic pots, 54
Pliny, 229
Plum (*Prunus domestica*), 30, 135
Plumeria, *see* Frangipani
Poinsettia (*Euphorbia pulcherrima*),
    36, 79
Pollen baskets, 24
Pollen as natural food, 132
Pollination, 22–25
Pomanders, 89, 119
Pomerantz, Eva, 264
Poppy, *see* Iceland poppy; Opium
    poppy; Oriental poppy; Shirley
    poppy
Poppy family (*Papaveraceae*), 41, 92,
    102, 114, 115, 135
Poppy seed heads, 95
Pore-cleansing steam, 209–210
Portulaca (*Portulaca grandiflora*), 62,
    72
Pot marigolds, *see* Calendula
Potato vine (*Solanum jasminoides*), 77
Potpourris, 89, 112–118
    recipes for, 116–118
Pots, 52
    peat, 54
Powders, 207
Pressed flower calendars, 105
Pressed flower cards, 105
Pressed flower craft, 102–105
Pressed flower pictures, 104–105
Pressed flowers, 100–102
"Primavera" (Botticelli), 106
Primrose (*Primula vulgaris*), 71, 72,
    81, 102, 114, 115, 135, 185, 264,
    265
Protea (*Protea* spp.), 92, 95
Provence rose (*Rosa gallica*), 229

Pruning, 59
Pure rose potpourri or sachet, 117
Purslane (*Portulaca oleracea* var.
    sativa), 58
Puschkinia (*Puschkinia scilloides*), 75
Pyracantha (*Pyracantha* spp.), 110
Pyrethrum (*Chrysanthemum cin-
    erariifolium*), 82, 83

Quaking grass (*Briza maxima*), 70, 95
Queen Anne's lace (*Daucus carota*),
    29, 70, 92, 95
Queen's Closet Opened, The (recipe
    book), 131

Raceme, 29
Ragweed (*Ambrosia* spp.), 25, 34
Ragwort (*Senecio pauperculus*), 264
Raised beds, 48–50
Ranunculus (*Ranunculus asiaticus*),
    75, 79, 92
Raspberry, 30
Recipes for flower foods, 138–181
    appetizers, soups and sandwiches,
        138–142
        basil mushroom puffs, 138–139
        flowered vegetable dip, 139
        fruit blossom strawberry soup,
            141
        hollyhock sandwiches, 141
        nasturtium leaf sandwiches,
            141–142
        stuffed nasturtiums, 138
        summer cool cucumber soup
            with dill flowers, 139–140
        thyme flower soup, 140
    breads and spreads, 161–166
        aromatic blossom butter,
            164–165
        calendula petal mixture, 166
        carnation spice muffins,
            161–162
        curried nasturtium spread,
            165–166
        Elizabeth's herb flower bread,
            162
        Roberta's golden pumpkin-
            calendula bread, 163
        rose petal jam, 165
        sprouted wheat herb flower
            bread, 163–164
        tofu waffles with carnation
            sauce, 164

desserts, 172–178
  apple petal crisp, 173–174
  blossom berry pie, 177–178
  Cindra Joy's pansy parfait, 178
  flower nut torte, 172–173
  frozen gladiolus dessert, 175
  Martin's flowered fruit whip,
    175–176
  Mia's blueberry day lilies,
    176–177
  Perissa's carob silk pie, 174
  rose treats, 176
  sweet nasturtiums, 173
dressings and sauces, 157–161
  carnation sauce, 159–160
  chickweed dressing, 157
  date nut dressing, 160
  dreamy herb flower dressing,
    158
  frozen flower vinegar, 159
  rose geranium syrup, 160
  violet honey, 161
drinks, 167–172
  blossoming summer smoothie,
    171
  flower herb tea, 167–169
  flower ice cubes, 172
  flower nectar sun and moon
    tea, 169
  hibiscus tropical fruit tea, 171
  hollyhock punch, 170
  lemon blossom lemonade, 167
  strawberry borage cooler,
    170–171
  woodruff juice, 169
flower entrees, 142–148
  calendula quiche, 145
  chrysanthemum vegetables,
    146–147
  curried fruit flower, 148
  hearty rice, bean and flower
    casserole, 143–144
  Onica's vegetable casserole with
    savory blossoms, 145–146
  saucy grains with mustard
    flowers, 142–143
  spicy flower tostadas, 144
  squash blossom feast, 147–148
flower feast weekend, 179–180
salads and vegetables, 148–157
  artichokes with lemon sauce
    and lemony flowers, 155
  chive flower salad bowl, 153

flowered fruit salad, 154–155
flowering circle salad, 150–151
Greek flower salad, 149
herb garden potato salad, 149
herbed bean salad, 152–153
marinated vegetable mix with
  herbs and herb flowers, 156
Mother's dill pickles, 156–157
nutty cucumber salad with dill
  flowers, 154
tabouleh onion flower salad,
  152
wild spring-green salad,
  151–152
Recipes for flower oil, 194–195
Recipes for potpourris and sachets,
  116–118
Red clay, 204
Red clover, see Clover, red
Relaxation technique, 244
Relaxing bath, 212–213
Relaxing flower journeys (visualiza-
  tions), 251
Rhizome, 19
Rhodanthe (Helipterum manglesii),
  67, 95, 110
Rhododendron (Rhododendron spp.),
  81, 249
Rice, 137
Roman chamomile (Chamaemelum
  nobile), 65, 234
Roots, 19
Rose, see Cabbage rose; Damask
  rose; Provence rose; Wild rose
Rose beads, 110, 111
Rose campion (Lychnis coronaria), 62,
  92
Rose clay, 204
Rose facial vinegar, 111
Rose family (Rosaceae), 30, 65, 72,
  82, 83, 92, 99, 110, 113, 115,
  131, 135, 185, 186, 187, 190
  basket of, 110–111
  for herb tea, 168
Rose geranium (Pelargonium gra-
  veolens), 92, 115, 135, 160, 185
Rose geranium-almond mask, 201
Rose hip, 30
Rose jam, 111
Rose oil, 229–230
Rose potpourri or sachet, pure, 117
Rose treats, 111
Rose water, 111

Rose-chamomile-lavender lotion, 198
Rose-lavender flower lotion, 198
Rose-rosemary honey facial, 218
Rosemary *(Rosmarinus officinalis)*, 32, 64, 65, 83, 92, 110, 113, 116, 122, 134, 185, 186, 187, 190, 206, 209
   for herb tea, 168
Rosemary honey facial, 111
Rosemary oil, 233
Rosemary water, 189
Rudbeckia *(Rudbeckia hirta "Gloriosa Daisy")*, 66, 92, 114, 122
   dye experiment with, 125
Rue *(Ruta graveolens)*, 83, 92

Sachets, 89, 112–118
   recipes for, 116–118
Safflower *(Carthamus tinctorius)*, 92, 95, 110, 134
Saffron crocus *(Crocus sativus)*, 134
Sage, *see* Garden sage; Scarlet sage
Sagebrush *(Artemisia californica)*, 90
St. John's bread, 136, 174
Saint-John's-wort *(Hypericum perforatum)*, 70, 92, 102, 122, 185, 193, 264
Salad burnet *(Poterium sanguisorba)*, 134
Salad dressing facial, 201–202
Salpiglossis *(Salpiglossis sinuata)*, 72, 79, 92
Salves, 195–197
   basic recipe for, 195–196
Sand, 96, 98
Sandalwood *(Santalum album)*, 235
Santolina *(Santolina chamaecyparissus)*, 92, 110
Saunas, 207, 214–216
Savory herbs, edible, 133–134
Scabiosa *(Scabiosa* spp.), 66
Scarlet pimpernel *(Anagallis arvensis)*, 102
Scarlet runner bean *(Phaseolus coccineus)*, 77
Scarlet sage *(Salvia splendens)*, 72
Scented geranium, 64, 65, 72, 79, 110, 113, 187, 190
   See also Apple geranium; Lemon geranium; Nutmeg geranium; Peppermint geranium; Rose geranium

Schizanthus *(Schizanthus pinnatus)*, 72, 79, 81, 102
Scilla *(Scilla* spp.), 81
Scotch broom *(Cytisus scoparius)*, 92, 95
Sea holly *(Eryngium amethystinum)*, 95, 110
Seaweed, water-soluble, 60–61
Secret Commonwealth of Elves, Fauns and Fairies, The (Kirk), 257
Secret Life of Plants, The (Tompkins and Bird), 255
Seedling trays, 54
Seeds, 53–55
Self-heal *(Prunella vulgaris)*, 90
Self-pollinators, 25
Sensual flower ritual, 219–220
Sensual visualization, 247
Sepals, 20
Shade flower gardens, 79–81
Shakespeare, William, 224, 233, 257, 265, 266
Shasta daisy *(Chrysanthemum maximum, C. superbum)*, 92
Sheep sorrel *(Rumex acetosella)*, 58, 92
   for green salad, 152
Shell ginger *(Alpinia zerumbet)*, 81
Shirley poppy *(Papaver rhoeas)*, 41
Shooting star *(Dodecatheon* spp.), 81
Siberian squill *(Scilla siberica)*, 75
Siberian wallflower *(Erysimum hieraciifolium)*, 70
Sidhe, the, 258
Silica gel, 96, 98
Silique, 22
Silver-lace vine *(Polygonum aubertii)*, 77
Silver thyme *(Thymus vulgaris "Argenteus")*, 140
Simples, 184
Sinus flower sauna, 215
Skin oil, super flower, 218
Skin toner, flower, 218
Skin-softening bath, 214
Skunk cabbage *(Symplocarpus foetidus)*, 24
Sleep pillow, soothing, 128
Snapdragon *(Antirrhinum majus)*, 66, 72, 92, 99, 115, 122
   visualization, 252
Snowdrop *(Galanthus* spp.), 75
Soil, 48–49

Solitary flower, 27
Song of Solomon, 224
Soothing sleep pillow, 128
Sore muscle bath, 212
Sorrel, *see* Sheep sorrel
Soy sauce, 136, 137
Space journey with a flower guide
    (visualization), 250
Spacing, 55–57
Spadix, 29
Spanish broom *(Sparitum junceum)*,
    65
Spanish jasmine *(Jasminum gran-
    diflorum)*, 230
Sparaxis *(Sparaxis tricolor)*, 75
Spathe, 29
Spearmint *(Mentha spicata)*, 31, 92,
    113, 116
Specialty shops, 273
Species, 26
Species Plantarum (Linnaeus), 26
Spike, 29
Spring bulbs, 72–75
Spring snowflake *(Leucojum vernum)*,
    75
Spring wild flower herb salve, 196
Sprouts, 136–137
Squash, 82, 83
Squash blossom *(Cucurbita* spp.),
    135, 147–148
Stalk, 53
Stamens, 20
Staminate flowers, 24
Star everlasting, *see* Starflower
Star jasmine *(Trachelospermum jas-
    minoides)*, 65, 81
Star tulip *(Calochortus tolmiei)*, 90,
    238
Starflower *(Scabiosa stellata)*, 67, 95,
    110
Statice *(Limonium* spp.), 67, 92, 95,
    110
Steams, flower, 207, 217–218
Stem, 19
Stigma, 20
Stimulating flower sauna, 216
Stimulating flowers, 186
Stimulating pillow, 128
Stock *(Matthiola incana)*, 65, 72, 92,
    99, 113, 122
Strand (magazine), 259
Strawberry *(Fragaria ananassa)*, 30,
    82, 141, 170–171, 177–178

Strawflower *(Helichrysum brac-
    teatum)*, 67, 92, 95, 110
Style, 20
Subclass, 26
Subdivision, 26
Sun cup *(Camissonia* spp.), 102
Sunflower *(Helianthus annuus)*, 34,
    83, 95, 135
Super flower skin oil, 194, 218
Sweet alyssum *(Lobularia maritima)*,
    55, 65, 72, 102
Sweet garden potpourri or sachet,
    118
Sweet marjoram *(Origanum major-
    ana)*, 64, 92, 113, 134, 143
Sweet orange *(Citrus sinensis)*, 65,
    113, 115, 135, 185, 187, 190, 235
    for herb tea, 168
Sweet pea *(Lathyrus odoratus)*, 31–32,
    65, 77, 92, 99, 113, 187, 190, 235
Sweet scent flower sauna, 216
Sweet William *(Dianthus barbatus)*,
    29, 65, 72, 92, 113, 115
Sweet woodruff *(Galium odoratum)*,
    63, 113, 134, 169, 187
    for green salad, 152
Sweetly floral flowers, edible,
    134–135
Sylphs, 258

Tahini, 136
Tangerine *(Citrus reticulata)*, 115
Tansy *(Tanacetum vulgare)*, 83, 92,
    95, 114, 186
Tarragon *(Artemisia dracunculus)*, 143
Teas
    flower herb, 167–169
    flower nectar sun or moon, 169
    flower sauna, 215
    moonlight flower, 219–220
Teasel *(Dipsacus* spp.), 70, 95
Tennyson, Alfred Lord, 252
Theosophical Society of England,
    259, 260
Thistle *(Cirsium* spp.), 34, 92, 95,
    135
Thyme, *see* Caraway thyme; Creep-
    ing thyme or Mother-of-thyme;
    Garden thyme; Lemon thyme;
    Silver thyme; Woolly thyme
Tidytips *(Layia platyglossa)*, 70
Tiger lily *(Lilium lancifolium, L.
    tigrinum)*, 114

Tigridia *(Tigridia pavonia)*, 16, 75
Tincture of benzoin, 193–194
Titania, 257, 265, 266
Tofu, 136
Tomato, 82, 83
Tompkins, Peter, 255, 256
Toners, flower skin, 218
Toning flowers, 185
Tools, 49
Transplanting, 55–57
Trillium *(Trillium* spp.), 27, 81, 248
Tropaeolum family *(Tropaeolaceae)*,
    38–39
Tropical garden potpourri or sachet,
    118
Trumpet vine *(Campsis* spp.), 77
Tuber, 19
Tuberose *(Polianthes tuberosa)*, 65,
    106, 113, 187
Tulip *(Tulipa* spp.), 79, 92, 99, 135,
    264
Tutankhamen, 183
Tuzzy-muzzy, 93–94

Umbel, 29
Upside-down method of drying
    flowers, 95

Valnet, Dr. Jean, 225, 226
Van Gelder, Dora, 260, 261
Varieties, 26
Verbena *(Verbena* spp.), 72
Vetch *(Vicia* spp.), 31
Victoria, Queen, 93
Vinegars
    facial, 205
    fragrant flower, 157
Vines, flowering, 75–77
Viola *(Viola cornuta)*, 72, 79, 81, 92,
    102, 114, 115, 122, 135, 185
Violet *(Viola odorata)*, 42–43, 65, 70,
    92, 95, 102, 113, 115, 131, 135,
    161, 185, 187, 190, 265
Violet family *(Violaceae)*, 42–43
Visualization technique, 244
Visualizations with flowers, 243–252
Vitamin B, 136
Vitamin C, 30, 39, 131, 151
Vitamin E, 136, 198, 201
Von Linné, Carl, *see* Linnaeus

Wallflower *(Cherianthus cheiri)*, 65,
    72, 92, 113, 187

Warming balm, 199–200
Watch a flower grow (visualization),
    247–248
Water lily *(Nymphaea* spp.), 65
    visualization, 251–252
Water method for extracting flower
    oils, 192
Watercress *(Nasturtium officinale)*, 64
Watering, 57
Water-soluble seaweed, 60–61
Weeding, 58–59
White clay, 204
White pyrethrum *(Chrysanthemum
    cinerariifolium)*, 82
Wild buckwheat *(Eriogonum* spp.),
    95, 110, 137
Wild flower gardens, 69–70
Wild flowers
    for arrangements, 92
    for pressing, 102
Wild ginger *(Asarum* spp.), 81
Wild iris *(Iris douglasiana)*, 38
Wild oat *(Bromus ramosus)*, 238
Wild onion *(Allium triquetrum)*, 92
    for green salad, 152
Wild radish *(Raphanus raphanistrum)*,
    83, 102
    for green salad, 152
Wild rose *(Rosa californica, R. ca-
    nina)*, 30, 92, 102, 165
Wild strawberry *(Fragaria chiloensis,
    F. vesca)*, 248
Wild thyme, *see* Creeping thyme
Willow *(Salix* spp.), 29
Wind pollination, 24–25
Wind-pollinated flowers, 20, 25
Winged everlasting *(Ammobium
    alatum)*, 67, 95
Winter aconite *(Eranthis hyemalis)*,
    75
Wintergreen *(Gaultheria procumbens)*,
    116
Wisteria *(Wisteria* spp.), 77
Wood aconite, 75
Wood hyacinth *(Endymion* spp.), 75
Wood sorrel *(Oxalis* spp.), 81, 102,
    264
Woodbine *(Lonicera periclymenum)*,
    265
Woodruff, sweet, *see* Sweet wood-
    ruff
Woolly thyme *(Thymus
    pseudolanuginosus)*, 140

Wormwood *(Artemisia absinthium)*, 34, 92
Wreaths, 108–110
Wright, Elsie, 258–259

Xeranthemum *(Xeranthemum annuum)*, 67, 95

Yarrow *(Achillea millefolium, A. m.*

var. *rubrum, A. filipendulina)*, 26, 34, 67, 70, 83, 92, 95, 110, 113, 122, 134, 185, 186, 264
for herb tea, 169
Yeast, nutritional, 136
Yellow clay, 204
Yucca *(Yucca* spp.), 134, 187

Zinnia *(Zinnia* spp.), 47, 72, 92, 95